CHILDREN'S
Picture Books

How to
Self-Publish
Your Way to
Success!

CHILDREN'S
Picture Books

How to
Self-Publish
Your Way to
Success!

SHARI FADEN DONAHUE

ARIMAX, INC.

With Love to My Husband, Tom—and Our Daughters, Maxime and Ariele

Always ... All Ways

—SFD

Publisher's Cataloging-In-Publication Data

Donahue, Shari Faden.
   Children's picture books : how to self-publish your way to success / Shari Faden Donahue.

   p : col. ill. ; cm.

   "Insider's handbook: writing, illustration, design, printing, sales, distribution, promotion and publicity"--Cover.
   Includes bibliographical references and index.
   ISBN: 978-0-9634287-5-2

1. Picture books for children--Publishing--Handbooks, manuals, etc. 2. Picture books for children--Authorship--Handbooks, manuals, etc. 3. Picture books for children--Marketing--Handbooks, manuals, etc. 4. Self-publishing--Handbooks, manuals, etc. 5. Children's literature--Publishing. 6. Children's literature--Marketing. 7. Books--Marketing--Handbooks, manuals, etc. I. Title.

Z286.P53 D66 2008
070.5   2006901862

Technical Consultant: Thomas W. Donahue

Indexer/Proofreader: Pauline Sholtys

Copy Editors: Shelley Faden Focht, Rebecca Faden, Thomas W. Donahue

Illustrator/Photographer: Thomas W. Donahue

Illustrator: Shari Faden Donahue

Layout: Paul Eisler, Eisler Design

This book is available at special quantity discounts for bulk purchases, sales promotions, premiums, fundraisers, and corporate/educational use.

For information, call 215-205-2227.

Arimax, Inc. Publishing   2865 South Eagle Road, PMB #399   Newtown, Pennsylvania 18940
www.arimaxbooks.com

City of
Hope™

In Loving Memory

of

Talented Writer
Stacey Lynne Hertfelder

and

Accomplished Physician
Lillian T. Balter

Table of Contents

Chapter 2 | Piercing the Publishing Veil   39

Chapter 3 | Fast Track to Self-Publishing   57

Chapter 4 | The Birth of a Children's Picture Book   83

Chapter 5 | Distribution Sales Channels   115

Chapter 6 | Your Online Presence Is Priceless!   135

Chapter 7 | Making Waves in the Industry 149

Chapter 8 | Standing Out from the Crowd 165

Chapter 9 | Leveraging Libraries   195

Chapter 10 | Bookstores & Beyond   205

Chapter 11 | Navigating Niches — 237

Chapter 12 | Embracing Early Childhood Education — 247

Chapter 13 | Children's Picture Book Promotion 263

Chapter 14 | Dare to Be Different ... & Succeed 291

Appendixes

About the Author

Shari Faden Donahue is the founder of Arimax, Inc. Publishing (www.arimaxbooks.com), established 1992, and the award-winning Zebra-Striped Whale Ice Cream & Coffee Café (www.zebrastripedwhale.com), established 2004. The cafe's unique name is derived from *The Zebra-Striped Whale with the Polka-Dot Tail*, a hardcover children's picture book written and illustrated by Shari Faden Donahue. Just eight months after opening, the Zebra-Striped Whale Ice Cream & Coffee Café was voted the "Best of Philly" by *Philadelphia Magazine*. To give back to community, Shari Faden Donahue has spearheaded the non-profit Zebra-Striped Whale Foundation (ZSWF, www.zebrastripedwhale.org)— a philanthropic organization whose mission is to raise funds for those in need through the art of children's picture book publishing.

Popular self-published titles by Shari Faden Donahue include *Children's Picture Books: How to Self-Publish Your Way to Success!*, *The Zebra-Striped Whale with the Polka-Dot Tail*, *Celebrate Hanukkah with Me*, *My Favorite Family Haggadah*, and *Philly's Favorites Recipe Collection*. Arimax, Inc. Publishing is a proud member of Children's Book Council (CBC), Society of Children's Book Writers & Illustrators (SCBWI), Publishers Marketing Association (PMA), Small Publishers Association of North America (SPAN), and Small Publishers, Artists, and Writers Network (SPAWN).

In addition to her role as publisher, author/illustrator, and entrepreneur, Shari Faden Donahue is a professional coach for aspiring children's picture book authors and illustrators. She has a Bachelor of Arts from the University of Pennsylvania and a Master of Business Administration from Drexel University. To arrange private consultation, workshops/seminars, book signing events, and/or school author visits, e-mail your special requests to sharidonahue@zebrastripedwhale.com.

Foreword

To self-publish or not to self-publish—that is the question!

If your manuscript submission campaign has not resulted in getting your children's picture book published during a reasonable time frame of 12–18 months, know that you are not alone! Publishers—large and small—are slammed with children's book manuscript submissions. Getting published by traditional publishing houses is much like winning the lottery. Though more than 20,000 juvenile titles were published last year, publishing houses accept less than 2% of all unsolicited children's book submissions.

You are likely to be frustrated by the tedious process of perfecting your manuscript, typing cover letters ad infinitum, researching publishers, addressing publishers' envelopes and self-addressed stamped envelopes (SASE)—and wasting your hard earned money on costly postage. Perhaps you've received rejection letter upon rejection letter—or even worse, limited response from your targeted list of publishers.

At this juncture, traditional publishing purists would urge you to put aside your unpublished manuscript, strengthen your writing skills, and embark upon yet another version—or a completely new manuscript—that is more worthy of publication. Suffice it to say, the publishing submission cycle can cause even the most patient individuals to experience the 3 Ds of publishing: Disappointment, Disenchantment, and Disillusionment!

When do you discard your manuscript along with every hope and dream of becoming a published children's picture book author? Never! With the advent of desktop technology, there has never been a greater opportunity to publish your own title. The process of authoring your children's picture book resides so close to your heart. No one is more passionate about its ultimate outcome than you!

Self-publishing is a viable alternative to the traditional publishing route for the innovative and passionate. A self-publisher is simply someone who pays to bring a book to print for distribution or sale. As a self-published children's picture book author, your opinion matters. Publishing giants cannot afford to focus their energies on one particular picture book. You have the simple advantage—because you can!

At the inception of your picture book project, your exciting new venture is likely to be a challenging, flexible part-time sideline. You and/or your spouse (or significant other) must maintain a job, at least initially, to fund your self-publishing objectives. To achieve success, you must enthusiastically—and tirelessly—promote your children's picture book through book signings, marketing events, school visits, speaking engagements, and the media.

If you think practically and comprehend the critical nature of niche marketing, your professional, self-published children's picture book can provide you with an added stream of income that grows over time. Prove a successful sales history—and a traditional publisher may opt to negotiate rights to your title. (You may surprisingly choose to refuse the offer!)

A self-publishing company may not turn you into a millionaire overnight—or perhaps ever. The gold that you discover at the end of the rainbow may take the form of self-actualization and sense of achievement. Whether you publish several copies of your own title on behalf of your immediate family, or hundreds—even thousands—of copies to serve a particular audience, the true reward emanates from your ability to touch others.

For over a decade and a half, my position as president of Arimax, Inc. Publishing has enabled me to navigate the exciting, challenging, and ever-evolving children's picture book industry. Whereas children's picture books are laden with clarity and simplicity, the publishing industry itself is cloaked in complexity and mystique for many aspiring authors and illustrators. My objective in publishing *Children's Picture Books: How to Self-Publish Your Way to Success!* is to empower you with a solid foundation to launch your self-publishing career. Regardless of your current occupation … your passion, persistence, and determination are certain to infuse your children's picture book with the critical edge that is essential for success!

www.justselfpublish.com

Acknowledgments

Throughout the years, as mom, author, illustrator, and publisher, I have been "awakened" and "reawakened" by my passion for picture books—experiencing firsthand the attachment that a writer has to his/her manuscript. When my children were small, our most precious family pastime was visiting the library to borrow the biggest armful of picture books that we could muster. Every night, my husband, Tom, and I would cuddle with our young daughters, Maxime and Ariele, and read three (and sometimes more!) picture books from the mesmerizing pile. Among my favorites were picture books by Eric Carle. His vividly colored, layered paper collages titillated my senses; my emotions rumbled every time we turned the pages of another beautifully illustrated spread. We adored our nighttime ritual. We read ... and bonded ... and read ... and bonded, and in a little over a week, it was time for us to return to the library—only to borrow a brand new armful of delightful readers.

Alluring children's picture books speak to the soul. They are concise, clear—and oh so visually appealing! As the youngest of four children, I remember my own mother's animated renditions of nursery storybook favorites—as well as sitting on my dad's lap, thumb in mouth, reading books by Dr. Seuss and poetry for children. My dad was an avid reader, and loved nothing more than sharing his great love of books with those near and dear to him. In every room of our compact Philly row home, there was a mammoth stack of opened hardcover library books that he somehow managed to read—cover to cover—simultaneously. To his dismay, I never emulated his robust reading ritual, but his love for books filled my soul.

When I was thirty-two years old, I experienced the horrific pain of my father's loss. In the silence of my grief, inspiration unveiled itself—culminating in the birth of my own children's picture book, *The Zebra Striped Whale with the Polka-Dot Tail*. Without training as a writer or an illustrator, I passionately embarked upon this labor of love to honor my dad's precious memory.

Whereas the verse emerged in just a few hours, I spent over a decade creating eighteen collage illustrations from any materials that I could find: fabric, paper, cellophane, paint, clay, glitter, gems, costume jewelry, coins, dollar bills, foil, threads—and even candy! While completing *The Zebra Striped Whale with the Polka-Dot Tail*, I founded my own publishing company, Arimax, Inc. Publishing—named for my two daughters, Maxime and Ariele—and authored several titles including: *Celebrate Hanukkah with Me*, *My Favorite Family Haggadah*, and *Philly's Favorites Recipe Collection*.

During the process of self-publishing this book ... about self-publishing a book, I have compiled concrete, usable information from highly respected industry leaders—in the areas of book development, manufacturing, distribution, reviews/awards, sales, marketing, and publicity—whose opinions I greatly admire. The following organizations have proven to be truly invaluable sources: CBC, PMA, SPAN, SPAWN, SCBWI, ALA, ABA, ABC, Library of Congress, Book Sense, Midwest Book Review, Regional Booksellers Associations, and Cooperative Children's Book Center (CCBC).

Beyond words, I am grateful to Tom—my husband and inspiration of 24 years—who makes all things possible including this book (as illustrator, photographer, technical specialist, and one-man creative support team!) … to Maxx and Ariele, our phenomenal daughters and role models who bring nothing short of magic to our lives … to Bec, my instinctive and funny 90 year old mom who is oh so "musical" (and an impressive copy editor too!) … to my family members who are like friends … to my lifetime friends who are like family … and, of course, to our adorable little dog, Leché—thank you for shining your love and enriching my life with your glorious presence!

How to Use This Book

Read the publishing industry overview, "The Truth about Publishing," as outlined in the Prologue—then follow the guerilla submissions recommendations in Chapter 1, entitled "If at First You Don't Succeed." A positive attitude will enable you to endure major obstacles in your path—commonly known as publishers' rejection letters—at least for a while!

If your guerilla submissions campaign does not achieve desired results within 12–18 months, remind yourself that you are not alone. Less than 2% of unsolicited submissions are published.

Do NOT place your worthy-to-be-published children's picture book manuscript in a drawer—only to be forgotten. As a viable alternative to the seemingly hopeless submissions process—or to bypass traditional publishing altogether, as I opted to do—immerse yourself in Chapters 2–14 of this book … and self-publish your way to success!

The Scoop!

Highlighted information-packed boxes, like this one, appear extensively throughout the chapters of this book to unveil helpful industry tidbits.

FYI is an abbreviation for the phrase, "For Your Information." Easy-to-read FYI boxes, like this one, present a useful overview of perspectives from respected industry leaders.

Don't miss the appendixes located at the back of this book! They are brimming with beneficial, up-to-date information including: self-publisher's glossary, Web sites, organizations, conferences, workshops, industry vendors, reading list, and over 50 children's picture book reviewers—complete with contact information. You will refer to these invaluable insider resources again … and again … and again—throughout your exciting self-publishing career!

Best of luck to you always—all ways!

Shari Faden Donahue

P.S. Visit www.justselfpublish.com—the information-packed Web site that caters to the needs of aspiring children's picture book authors and illustrators!

Five Ways to Jumpstart Your Creativity

1 Stop—Look—Listen! Observe children at play, doing homework, walking to the school bus, petting their dogs, and feeding their fish. The details matter when writing for children.

2 Ask the children in your life to recount a funny story. Select the one that appeals to you most—and compose an action-packed writing sample.

3 Writing is a skill that improves with practice—so here's another writing assignment. Create a modern day version of your favorite fairytale! My husband, Tom, and I had great fun transforming "Cinderella" into "Ibbity Bibbity Boo Publishing," and "Snow White and the Seven Dwarfs" into "S. White and Seven Dwarf, Inc.," as follows.

Ibbity Bibbity Boo Publishing

1 Fairytale Court   New Castle, DE 11111   ph: 1-888-PUMPKIN   e-mail: SinDRella@aol.com   www.SinIsGood.com

FOR IMMEDIATE RELEASE
Ms. Page Turner, Public Relations Manager

CONTACT: Story Book Publicity
1-800-BOOKING

The Glass Slipper Syndrome by Sin D. Rella, Ph.D.
Featured on *New York Times* Bestsellers List

Once upon a velvet loveseat sits the charming, newly divorced Dr. Sin D. Rella, best-selling author of *The Glass Slipper Syndrome*. The world renowned ex-masochist reveals blistering revelations about the "happily ever after" myth in relation to her ground-breaking theory, "Even if the shoe fits, refuse to wear it!"

Dr. Sin D. Rella's research reveals that exposure to GAP, "Genetic Alteration of Pumpkins," by abused adolescent girls results in early marriages to dysfunctional partners—described as "royal pains" by experts. With a personal history of fairy godmother-related GAP exposure, the footloose ex-princess is a shoe-in for several esteemed literary awards.

During her magical 26-city publicity tour, the confident Dr. Sin D. Rella travels "First Class" only—and refuses to go "Coach" ever again! For additional information, visit Dr. Sin D. Rella's Web site at www.SinIsGood.com.

###

Written by Tom & Shari Donahue

S. White and Seven Dwarf, Inc.

Once upon an Internet time, there was a promising young executive at KingdomCorp.com, purveyors of empire development software. S. White was adored by the president, her senior staff, and knowledge workers alike—all except for the long-reigning Chief Operating Officer, B. S. Queen.

S. White worked wisely throughout the years gaining a reputation as a gentle leader with vision, compassion, and rock solid integrity. She willingly shared the spotlight with members of her team and promoted innovative ideas—even those that were not her own. The arrogant and calculating Queen resented White for her charisma, style, and close connections to the President and CEO.

B. S. Queen had ultimate access to any system or device used by KingdomCorp.com. She could peruse system files, reports, and all e-mail communications. She was also privy to phone calls, phone logs, and private data gleaned from credit reports and targeted investigations. Queen was often seen stirring her electronic cauldron late into the night—adding a comment here, deleting a file there—on behalf of her own self-interest. Some might say that the interactive artificial intelligence software of her super computing system was magical … for when Queen posed questions, it would reply with the ultimate truth.

Queen asked,

> *"Data base, data base on my Net …*
> *Who is the most brilliant and talented executive yet?"*

The computer responded,

> *"B. S. Queen, brilliant you are,*
> *But S. White is truly the rising star.*
>
> *You, B. S. Queen, are talented indeed,*
> *But your ultimate downfall will be your greed!*

Furious and red with rage, B. S. Queen resolved to take revenge on S. White. Shortly thereafter, the opportunity arose during a mass corporate-wide downsizing. Queen sent her best H. R. henchman to rip the heart out of S. White's division—banishing White and her team from KingdomCorp.com forever. The song of the henchman went like this:

> *"This restructure is not based on your performance, no doubt.*
> *It is the consolidation of two business units that forces you out!*
>
> *Your severance package is generous … to the letter of the law we've complied.*
> *Of course, bonuses, commissions, and unvested stock are strictly denied!*
>
> *Hand over your company credit card, cell phone, PC, and PDA,*
> *As unfortunately—my friend—today is your very last day.*
> *So clean out your cubicle, sign the release, and be on your way!"*

Apprehensive, wounded, disarmed, and dismayed, S. White entered a dreary job market on the brink of recession. Hungry and exhausted—out in the bleak, cold economy—White opted to seek shelter at a sleepy industrial start-up in a cottage industry. At Seven Dwarf, Inc., White set out to clean up and organize this fledgling, dysfunctional group of small-minded, egocentric personalities. White realized early on that this business unit was a diamond in the rough—and worked to eliminate the undermining and short-sighted perspectives that dominated all corporate decisions.

Impressed with the profitable bottom line and growth potential, the Prince Charming Venture Capital Company agreed to help take the company public. Seven Dwarf, Inc. issued an IPO on the NASDAQ stock exchange—increasing the value of the corporation to an astounding level. S. White became the darling of Wall Street, was featured on the cover of *Once Upon A Time Magazine*, married a partner of the Prince Charming Venture Capital Company, and lived happily ever after.

B. S. Queen was ousted in a hostile employee-led stock buy-back plan. This was initiated by Queen's very own highly interactive computing system that could no longer tolerate her wicked ways. It tricked her with her own poisonous greed and deceptions, resulting in the demise of her career at KingdomCorp.Com. With absolutely no bonus, commissions, or vested options due her—and SEC investigations pending—Queen was last seen peddling apples on Wall Street.

A Fairytale for the Upwardly Mobile
Written by Tom & Shari Donahue

4 Consolidate and edit! Take each of your writing samples—and condense, condense, condense. Every word counts in children's picture book writing. Whenever possible, reduce the number of words in your text. For example, the phrase "walks into" can be substituted with "enters."

5 Minimize writer's block and build creativity through ample breaks, proper nourishment—and aerobic exercise at least three times per week. Stay active. Motion stirs emotion—and a flood of endorphins that will take your writing to the next level!

Prologue
The Truth about Publishing

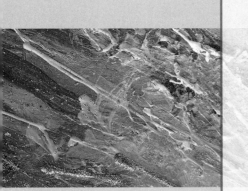

If you really want
to do something,
you'll find a way;
if you don't,
you'll find an excuse.

-Author Unknown

Children's Books: Classified

Children's book classifications are loosely designated—based on the subjective opinions of industry experts. With the thousands of children's book publishers that co-exist in today's market, it is not surprising that children's book formats and guidelines vary considerably. For example, one publisher's early readers may target first and second graders, whereas another's may target second through fourth graders. Though there are exceptions, the children's book category consists of the following general classifications:

* Baby Books (8–12 pages/newborn to age 3)

* Picture Books (24–48 pages/ages 3 to 8)

* Coloring and Activity Books (16–132 pages/ages 3 to 18)

* Easy Readers (10–64 pages/ages 5 to 9)

* First Chapter Books (64–128 pages/ages 6 to 10)

* Middle Readers (96–168 pages/ages 9 to 12)

* Young Adults (128–300 pages/ages 12 to 18)

The children's book market includes:

* Trade Market: higher priced, higher quality hardcover or paperback titles sold at bookstores

* Mass Market: lower priced, lower quality paperbacks—typically tied to a popular character—sold at supermarkets, discount stores, newsstands, drugstores, etc.

* Institutional Market: school/library curriculum-enhancing titles

* Electronic Market: multimedia products including e-books and CD-ROMs

Passion for Picture Books

Picture books, typically 32 pages long, utilize illustrations to capture the young child's short attention span and inspire the imagination. Content may be fiction or non-fiction, poetry or prose. Some picture books—known as storybooks—tell a story, whereas others—known as concept books—relate a concept such as colors, numbers, or shapes.

A picture book having many illustrations and few words requires a completely different publishing process than a chapter book having many words and few illustrations. Picture book word count is generally between 200 and 1,500 words. Manuscripts usually range from 2–5 pages. Because every word must be carefully selected, writing children's picture books can indeed be a challenging, time-consuming process.

Both the hardcover picture book—with or without dust jacket—and the softcover picture book are popular among children … and their parents! Though most picture books consist of pages with large illustrations accompanied by a few lines of text, there are exceptions. Some picture books incorporate fewer than ten words … and wordless picture books rely on illustrations or photographs—without the use of text. Enticing picture book formats ensure that it is never too early for parents to expose their children to reading. Popular variations include novelty books, board books, and books plus.

* Novelty Books: interactive books that incorporate three-dimensional elements such as lift-the-flaps, pop-ups, pull-tabs, textures, graduated pages, die-cuts, and sound chips

* Board Books: sturdy cardboard books that are frequently adapted from top-selling hardcover picture books to extend publisher revenue

* Books Plus: books that are packaged with popular items, such as plush toys

Innovative hybrid products, such as a lift-the-flap board book packaged with a thematic plush toy, are abundant in the marketplace. There are no absolutes in children's picture book design.

Evolution of Publishing

The world of publishing is continuously evolving. Over the past decade, large publishing houses have been acquired by conglomerates that include:

* HarperCollins
  www.harpercollins.com

* Holtzbrinck Publishers
  www.holtzbrinckus.com

* Penguin Group (USA), Inc.
  www.penguingroup.com

* Random House, Inc.
  www.randomhouse.com

* Simon & Schuster
  www.simonsays.com

* Hachette Book Group USA (acquired Time Warner Book Group)
  www.twbookmark.com

Each conglomerate publishes several hundred titles per year under an array of publishing imprints. Imprints are independent entities within conglomerates—each maintaining its own focus and direction. In one year, for example, Hachette Book Group USA publishes approximately 500 adult books, 180 young adult and children's books, and 50 audio book titles under imprints that include Little, Brown Books for Young Readers. As large publishers have been merging, the number of small publishers has been expanding—due to accessible desktop technology and decreased production costs.

The Rainbow of the Publishing Spectrum

The smaller the publisher, the more likely it is to serve specified niche markets. Publishing opportunities for unknown authors are often more favorable with smaller publishers than with major publishing houses. The objective of small publishers is to cautiously add titles to their established product line in a logical, progressive fashion. (To what extent does a particular manuscript fill a designated niche?) Many small publishers, with limited budgets, prefer to publish their own staff-developed "in-house" manuscripts (self-publishing, in some cases) to reduce inherent risk and maximize profit potential.

The Scoop!

Publishers are not the same! Whereas small publishers make their inroads in the niche markets they serve, large publishers concentrate on the general trade and mass markets.

The larger the publisher, the more titles it publishes, the greater the likelihood to produce a "winner"—based on statistics alone. Because of their ability to publish large quantities of multiple titles at one time, large financially solvent publishers have far greater potential for cost efficiencies. Though costs are effectively amortized over the gamut of their new releases, overhead costs are steep. Large publishers must allocate their funds across the many books that they publish, sometimes resulting in sluggish sales and low royalty checks for authors and illustrators.

Publishers: All Shapes & Sizes

According to James A. Cox, Editor-In-Chief of *Midwest Book Review*, publisher classification is based on the quantity of titles published per year—as designated by the following categories:

* Small Publishers: fewer than 12 titles published per year

* Mid-Sized Publishers: 12–51 titles published per year

* Large (Major) Publishers: 52+ titles published per year

Dan Poynter cites on his Web site, www.bookstatistics.com, that 8,000–11,000 new publishing companies are established each year. The publishing industry includes:

* 86,000 small/self-publishers

* 300–400 mid-sized publishers

* 6 large (major) publishers—as listed on previous two pages

Non-conglomerate publishers, of all sizes, are referred to as independent publishers. Alternative publishers are niche-related, independent publishers of non-mainstream titles.

What Constitutes a Self-Publisher?

A self-publisher is an individual who pays the expenses to bring his/her book to print for distribution or sale. Self-publishing is typically the result of one of the following vehicles:

* Establishing one's own publishing entity

* Coordinating with a print on demand publishing service provider i.e. Xlibris, AuthorHouse, Trafford Publishing

* Subsidizing a co-publishing arrangement with a publisher of like interests

Loosely defined publishing terms—frequently based on opinion—are prevalent in the industry. To many industry leaders, a publisher is no longer a self-publisher when he/she publishes the work of at least one other author.

The March of the Majors

Though major publishers thrive as a result of their proven author base, they risk becoming stale. Even major publishing houses must publish children's picture books by unknown authors to stay fresh in the marketplace. To minimize risk while introducing a new talent pool, a major publisher is likely to link a first-time author with a well-known illustrator— or vice-versa.

The Scoop!

To maintain a pulse on fresh talent, Lee & Low Books (www.leeandlow.com) has elected to sponsor an annual children's picture book contest. New Voices Award is presented to a previously unpublished children's picture book author of color whose story addresses the identifiable needs of children of color. The winner receives a cash grant of $1,000 and a standard publishing contract with advance against royalties. One Honor Award of $500 is also granted.

Generating Profits: Tried & True

The objective of major publishers is to build long-term relationships with "tried and true" authors who are in the strongest position to generate profits. Major publishers refuse to risk significant budget on promotion until the title of a non-proven author demonstrates success. Unknown authors are not apt to be publicized to their satisfaction during an initial 3–6 month bookstore trial phase. They must invest money, time, and energy in a strategic public relations campaign—their only fighting chance for survival in the trade publishing game. More and more published children's book authors are hiring their own public relations firms to assist in title promotion. According to the *Chicago Reader* dated February 2, 2002, "Despite the publishing industry's tradition of diligent assistance to worthy authors, books are going the way of cars. If you want them to move you'll have to pump the gas yourself." When a new author proves a solid sales history during the initial trial phase, the major publisher is likely to grant additional funding for significant title promotion. The publishing editor works diligently to create mutually beneficial relationships with an evolving pool of known authors and illustrators. Major publishers are keenly aware that proven authors and illustrators are commodities—viable streams of ongoing future income!

Exiting Strategy

According to some formulas, just 30% of a major publisher's new titles (front list) increase the company's bottom line. A typical breakdown is designated as follows:

* 10% of new titles generate enough revenue to pay for the entire list of books published that season.

* 20% of new titles earn a reasonable profit.

* 20% of new titles break even.

* 50% of new titles lose money.

Children's picture books have a limited opportunity for sell-through. If a title proves unsuccessful during the initial trial period, it is purged from the product mix, thrown into the "returns" pile—and discarded at hefty discounts in a predetermined exit strategy. Authors' and illustrators' dreams of large royalty checks fade into oblivion. In light of the effort, energy, and dollars poured into each new title, ending up on a quick-buy wholesale shelf can surely be an author's nightmare. Yet this "selling-off" process provides wise publishers with a viable exit strategy on behalf of their unsold book inventory. Non-performing titles are donated or sold as remainders—making room for the next truckload of books to roll in the following season. Remainder companies purchase title quantities (1,000 to entire stock) that may or may not include damaged inventory, known as "hurts." Publishers respond to the optimal bid and terms. (Oddly enough, some publishers reprint sold-out remainders as a result of the renewed marketing effort and lower price point.) Bargain books typically comprise up to one-third of a bookstore's gross sales.

Bookstores are not the only retailers to benefit from the sale of bargain picture books. For example, A.C. Moore, a regional craft store chain, now carries closeout quality hardcover children's picture books—each marked down to $3.00. (Yes, that's right … $3.00 per book!). Here is a sampling: *Serendipity* by Tobi Tobias (original retail price: $12.00; Simon & Shuster), *Max* by Bob Graham (original retail price: $15.99; Candlewick Press), *Picture This* by Molly Bang (original retail price: $19.95; North-South Books—publisher of the successful *Rainbow Fish* series), *Here Come Poppy & Max* by Lindsey Gardiner (original retail price: $12.95; Little, Brown & Company).

The Scoop!

More than 20,000 titles are stamped "out of print" each year— with over 26 million copies sold as remainders.

Publishing Realities

From the date of your signed contract, it can take from 12–18 months for your title to reach the mass retail bookshelves. Once your contract is officially signed by both you and your publisher, be aware that you forfeit all selling rights. Should your title go out of print—typically within eighteen months, or less—you must buy back your rights if you wish to publish the title in the future.

The primary legal right of the publisher is to publish the book. All other rights such as book club, movie, audio, electronic, serial, foreign language, merchandising, and performance rights are considered to be secondary rights—known as subsidiary rights. The publisher generally maintains reprint, second serial, and book club rights whereas the author maintains merchandising and performance rights. The remaining rights are negotiable. Review the following publications for useful contract information:

* *A Writer's Guide to a Children's Book Contract* by attorney, Mary Flower

* *The Writer's Legal Companion* by Brad Bunnin

* *Children's Writer's & Illustrator's Market*

* *SCBWI Publications Guide to Writing & Illustrating for Children*

The *SCBWI Publications Guide to Writing & Illustrating for Children* includes a sample children's book contract.

Author Isolation

Understand that all decisions regarding cover, title, publication date, binding, paper, varnish, size, layout, design, illustrations, special effects, etc. are under the complete control of the publisher. In the July 2006 *SPAN Connection* newsletter article, entitled "Promotional Wish List from Authors and Publishers," Carolyn Howard-Johnson, founder of Authors' Coalition, states, "…Many authors are disgruntled because of unmet expectations and the feeling that they cannot communicate with their publishers."

In a traditional publishing scenario, a published children's picture book author is not permitted to choose (or even meet, in most cases!) his/her illustrator. This can prove disconcerting to the passionate children's picture book author—especially since the illustrations play such a significant role in the final product.

The Scoop!

A first-time author with a major publishing house was astonished at the sight of her published children's picture book, "hot off the press," because the illustrator depicted her main characters as animals—not as humans.

First-time Author: Fizzle Versus Sizzle

Whereas a pool of small to mid-sized publishers is represented by the sales force of a national independent distributor, a major publisher is in the enviable position of having its own team of exclusive representatives—to promote and sell its titles. In either case, commission-based, feet-on-the-street sales reps have limited time with retail book buyers to pitch new children's titles by unproven authors. Publisher representatives tend to focus on the guaranteed sale of a recognizable best-selling author or the newest title in a "hot" series. Inundated and overwhelmed booksellers typically choose the most popular titles to sell to their customers. Publishers' new title catalogs are inadvertently lost or discarded. Industry preference for popular elite authors tends to result in the "fizzle" versus "sizzle" of many first-time children's picture book authors.

The ability of a first-time children's picture book author to generate his/her own audience is the key to publishing success. Book signings can be "lonely" for unknown authors who cannot guarantee substantial event turnout. Unknown authors are expected to extend book signing invitations to family, friends, and colleagues. Publishers depend on their authors' abilities to stimulate title demand. A charismatic children's picture book author who enjoys interfacing with the public through book signings, author tours, speaking engagements, school visits, and other marketing events can truly impact sales—and is of great benefit to his/her publisher.

Book Returns ... A Fact of Life

Due to fierce competition and trade retail outlet consolidation, book returns are a fact of life—significantly reducing publishers' profit margins. Approximately 5%–60% of all juvenile titles are returned from book retailer to publisher each season—a percentage that can be higher or lower depending on title demand. The average industry book return rate is routinely 30%! A book can be returned to the publisher for a period of six months from the time it goes out of print. Publishers—large and small—are slammed with excessive inventory and damaged book returns. The returns process has become one huge headache for the entire publishing industry. Significant support staff is required to sift through the continuous stream of incoming returns—a cumbersome and costly burden for all publishers.

For publishers to remain in business, sales of books must greatly outweigh returns. Large publishers benefit from their list of multiple titles; the greater number of quality titles, the higher the publisher's potential for income. Small publishers with limited titles can be forced out of business if losses from returns surpass incoming revenue. All publishers play a giant guessing game regarding those titles that will escalate to bestseller status. If a proven method existed for ensuring 100% publishing success, publishers would make a fortune on every book published. Though publishers are frequently on target, they also dramatically miss the mark.

Advances & Royalties

Unless you have authored and/or illustrated the publisher's runaway bestseller, don't count on your published children's picture book as an opportunity to get rich quick! Author and illustrator earnings are based on contract negotiations—and vary significantly from publishing house to publishing house. Whereas smaller publishing houses may offer authors and illustrators flat fees for services rendered, larger publishing houses typically pay an advance against projected royalty earnings. Royalties are calculated by multiplying the wholesale or retail price of a book by a negotiated percentage. Authors are likely to collect half of the advance upon signing the publishing contract, and the other half upon picture book completion. Illustrators are likely to collect one-third of the advance upon signing the publishing contract, one-third upon sketch delivery, and one-third upon finished art delivery.

According to SCBWI, it is common for first-time picture book authors to receive advances of $2,000-$3,000, and for first-time picture book illustrators to receive advances of $5,000-$7,000. Author/Illustrator royalty checks are implemented when enough books have sold to cover the publisher's advance.

A percentage of royalty payments may be reserved by publishers to cover the costs of future book returns from bookstores. The publisher's contract reserve clause dictates the exact percentage that will be reserved, as well as the time frame in which the money is held—usually one year. If actual sales do not meet allotted cash advances, contracts may actually require authors to reimburse the difference to their publishers in very rare cases.

Considering Profit Margins

Both the first-time children's book author and illustrator can expect to earn a 5% royalty, based on retail or wholesale price—less agent fees and taxes. Proven authors and illustrators receive higher advances and pre-determined royalties that are independent of selling price, such as $1 per book sold. As children's book advances increase, publishers' sales expectations increase. Editors must justify higher advances through higher profit margins.

Most authors and illustrators respond favorably to a simple royalty structure based on retail list price. A retail-based author royalty scenario is depicted below.

Royalties based on wholesale pricing—known as net royalties—are becoming more prevalent in the publishing industry. Publishers routinely partner with national book wholesalers, such as Ingram Book Company and/or Baker & Taylor, at a 55% discount. Wholesalers are utilized for the purpose of book fulfillment and consolidation of publisher-related order processing/returns. A standard wholesaler-based author royalty scenario follows.

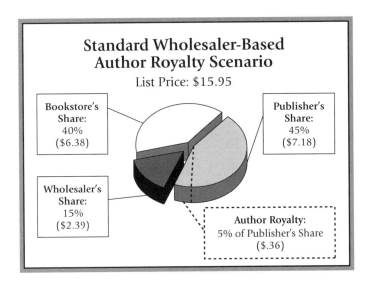

Standard Wholesaler-Based
Author Royalty Scenario
List Price: $15.95

Bookstore's Share: 40% ($6.38)

Publisher's Share: 45% ($7.18)

Wholesaler's Share: 15% ($2.39)

Author Royalty: 5% of Publisher's Share ($.36)

In addition to author royalty, the publisher is typically responsible for the following expenditures:

* Book production

* Freight

* Inventory management

* Bookkeeping

* Promotion

* Illustrator earnings

* Damaged products

To complicate matters, publishing contracts rarely specify a single royalty rate. It is not unusual for publishers to provide volume discounts to their direct customers—further impacting author and illustrator net royalty earnings. A volume discount scenario follows:

* 20% for 1–4 books

* 40% for 5–24 books

* 50% for 25–49 books

* 53% for 50+ books

The resulting volume discount pricing is depicted in the chart below.

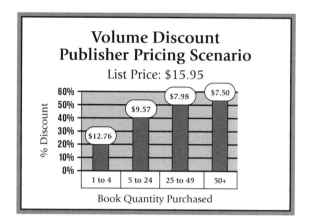

In this particular example, the 5% net royalty earned per $15.95 book could potentially be:

* $0.64 (20% discount/$12.76 per book)

* $0.48 (40% discount/$9.57 per book)

* $0.40 (50% discount/$7.98 per book)

* $0.38 (53% discount/$7.50 per book)

The publisher's volume discount pricing structure is usually based on the total quantity of books sold per purchase order. If the purchase order includes a total of 50 books (47 copies of one author's title and 3 copies of another author's title), the publisher's wholesale discount would be applied to the entire purchase order. Mass international and book club purchases typically result in even steeper volume discounts. The author/illustrator of a top-selling book club title may be awarded additional royalty incentive.

CHAPTER

1

If at First You Don't Succeed...

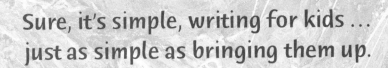

Sure, it's simple, writing for kids ...
just as simple as bringing them up.

–Ursula K. LeGuin

A.R.O.M.A. of Success
(A Realistic Optimistic Mental Attitude)

If you're at all like me, simply walking into the children's book section of any bookstore or library—any time of the day or night—can literally set your heart a-flutter. The smell of the books, the appearance of the covers, the bright and colorful illustrations, and the concise, easy-to-read text are likely to grip you with feelings of euphoria. Begin your publishing journey with an optimistic mental attitude. Believe in yourself and in your work! The road will be tough. Brush yourself off at every blow to your ego. If all else fails via traditional means, take positive action yourself. Jump in the ring, and don't permit well-meaning naysayers to dissuade you. Immerse yourself in the publishing industry. Visualize your autographed children's picture book, "hot off the press," sitting comfortably in the hands of your adoring young readers—their eyes glued to each and every one of your stimulating pages. Vow to prevail at the challenging publishing game. Roll up your sleeves and charge ahead with passion!

Children's Picture Books: Fight for Survival

Be cognizant of the breadth and magnitude of the competition. Simply visit your neighborhood chain or independent bookstore—and examine row upon breathtaking row of vividly colored children's picture books. Open the copyright pages of featured titles. The majority of picture books—aside from the array of Caldecott Medal winners, celebrity author titles (Jamie Lee Curtis, Julie Andrews, Madonna, Billy Joel, Billy Crystal, etc.) and best-selling staples (*Goodnight Moon* and *The Runaway Bunny* by Margaret Wise Brown, *The Very Hungry Caterpillar* by Eric Carle, *Brown Bear, Brown Bear, What Do You See?* by Bill Martin Jr.,

Guess How Much I Love You by Sam McBratney, *Love You Forever* by Robert N. Munsch, *Olivia* by Ian Falconer, *Where the Wild Things Are* by Maurice Sendak, etc.)—hold the copyright date of the current year. Titles featured in the children's book section co-exist in a desperate fight for

survival. Many do not endure the first 3–6 months. Competition is fierce! Success is contingent upon star status, subjective reviews/awards, endorsements by key influencers, and the purchasing power of an often fickle public. *Walter the Farting Dog*—a funny picture book by William Kotzwinkle and Glenn Murray about the trials and triumphs of a flatulent mutt—actually landed on the *New York Times* Children's Bestsellers List. The authors' blaring treatment of the historically hush-hush, yet highly revered "fart" holds great appeal for millions of giggling readers—children and parents alike. One local independent bookstore sold more than 2,000 copies of *Walter the Farting Dog* in less than a year.

According to the Book Industry Study Group, sales for the juvenile trade category rose 1.9% in 2006 to $3.4 billion.

Your Manuscript: Your Masterpiece

According to Pat Scales, the 2008–2009 president of ALA's Association for Library Service to Children (ALSC)—and 2003 committee chair for the prestigious Caldecott Medal—the objective of children's picture books is to access and engage the emotions of a child. A children's illustrated book—comprised of few words—is difficult to write. Each word requires careful selection to capture a child's limited attention span. Picture book pages must contain action. "Show … don't tell," is the popular catch phrase of seasoned picture book editors. Like any other art form, children's picture book writing—in prose or in verse—requires talent, experience, and craftsmanship. As a result of organizations such as the Society of Children's Book Writers & Illustrators (SCBWI)—a knowledge exchange network for writers—the overall trend is that publishers are receiving greater numbers of children's book manuscripts that do not deserve outright rejection.

Yearning for Learning

If you are not already a member of SCBWI, consider joining; visit www.scbwi.org. There are over 19,000 members worldwide—including writers, authors, illustrators, editors, agents, publishers, librarians, and others involved in children's literature. The annual fee is $75 for the first year, and $60 for each renewing year. In addition to two annual conferences featuring lectures and workshops by popular children's book authors, illustrators, editors, and agents—as well as substantial health insurance and car rental discounts—SCBWI membership entitles you to:

* Regional networking opportunities

* Chat rooms

* Bi-monthly SCBWI Bulletin

* Manuscript/illustration exchanges

* Manuscript-polishing peer critique groups

Though manuscript-polishing peer critique groups may be beneficial to some aspiring children's picture book authors, they can actually inhibit the natural writing talents of others. If you choose to participate, remind yourself that a group member's opinion is simply an opinion. It is up to you to determine the worthiness of that opinion. Remain open-minded … but remember that your manuscript is yours—and you are in control!

The Scoop!

All manuscript-polishing peer critique groups are not created equally. If you find that your current manuscript-polishing peer critique group does not provide a supportive, nurturing environment, consider starting your own!

Helpful writer's workshops/classes are available through libraries and colleges/universities such as The Kelly Writers House at the University of Pennsylvania (writing.upenn.edu/wh). For a list of active writing groups located in the U.S. and other English-speaking countries, refer to the *SCBWI Publications Guide to Writing & Illustrating for Children* and/or visit www.writepage.com/groups.htm. Informative writer's magazines include:

* *Writer's Digest*
  www.writersdigest.com

* *The Writer*
  www.writermag.com

The Rutgers University Council on Children's Literature One-on-One Conference is a rich and unique opportunity for children's picture book manuscript writers and illustrators to share their non-published work with industry professionals—including noted authors and illustrators of books for young readers, distinguished editors, agents, and children's literature academia. Enrollment is limited to 65–70 quality applicants with works in progress (fee: $150). Acceptance is based on the strength and quality of the applicant's work. Visit www.ruccl.org for further information.

Even Editors Require Editors

Writers become easily immersed in their manuscripts, and risk losing objectivity. Prior to the submission process, distance yourself from your manuscript for several days—then read your manuscript, from beginning to end, at least three times:

* During the first read-through, evaluate consistency of character development, evolution of storyline, and use of age-appropriate content.

* During the second read-through, review sentence structure for clarity and conciseness.

* During the third read-through, verify that your manuscript is free of all typos and grammatical/punctuation errors.

THE SCOOP!

A minute manuscript error can cause an aspiring children's book author to appear unprofessional. The best writers are capable of mistakes. Do not permit incorrect grammar, spelling, or punctuation to detract from the professionalism of your manuscript.

According to Brent Sampson, author of *Publishing Gems, Insider Information for the Self-Publishing Writer*, a writer benefits from reading his/her manuscript aloud—as well as backward—to find errors. He states, "When you read your manuscript backward, word for word, misspellings literally jump off the page." For the latest in literary guidelines, refer to

The Chicago Manual of Style (www.chicagomanualofstyle.org/home.html), a popular reference guide for publishers, editors, and writers. To review usage errors, compiled by the Northwestern Media School of Journalism, visit www.americanpressinstitute.org/content/3696.cfm. (Remember that "it's" is a substitute for "it is," and punctuation marks belong inside quotation marks i.e. Tom says, "Hello.") Beware of over-dependence on your computer's spell check. Words may be spelled correctly—but utilized incorrectly, such as "complement" versus "compliment."

Review your manuscript with a friend or family member versed in English, your child's high school teacher, and/or a college English professor. Assistance from other children's writers can prove useful. These individuals are likely to provide their editing services free of charge, and will be thrilled to receive a credit on the copyright page of your self-published title. Even editors require editors. Consider hiring a professional editor to assist with optimal manuscript readability. (Refer to Appendix D for a listing of professional editors.) It is your responsibility to ensure that your writing is clear, concise, and flawless. Believe in yourself and in your manuscript!

Protecting Your Manuscript

Without any advance permission from the copyright office, copyright law actually grants your manuscript automatic copyright protection—from tangible inception through seventy years following your death. As an added precaution, protect your original manuscript via a process known as the "poor man's copyright." Simply mail yourself a copy of your children's picture book manuscript with your name as copyright owner in addition to the word, "copyright,"

and/or the copyright symbol. For the © symbol, press "Num Lock" on the right of your computer keyboard—then hold down the "Alt" key while pressing the numbers 0169 on your numerical keypad (located at the right of your computer keyboard); the number keys on the top row will not work.

When the envelope arrives at your address, do NOT open it. Place the sealed envelope in safekeeping with other important documents. Though this process is not a substitute for official registration, your sealed envelope—imprinted with a clearly marked date by the U.S. Postal Service—serves as a vehicle to prove that you are indeed the author of the enclosed material. For more information regarding copyright, call the U.S. Copyright Office at 202-707-3000 or visit http://lcweb.loc.gov/copyright.

Network ... Network ... Network

Attend local book signings. Get accustomed to talking to children's picture book authors about their unique publishing experiences. I have discovered that authors who have already succeeded at the publishing game are among the most willing to assist hopeful writers. When a local children's book author is featured in the media, it is common for him/her to feel like a "king/queen for the day." Be bold. Go straight to the source. Make an effort to contact him/her. The local children's book author enjoys the support and acknowledgement of members of the community, and is likely to feel flattered by your interest in his/her title. Local author contact information may be obtained by calling the journalist directly, accessing the author's Web site, or utilizing directory assistance. Keep a brief list of relevant questions at your fingertips. The opportunity to share dialogue with a publicized children's picture book author enables you to obtain useful, relevant "insider" information. Stay connected! Publishing information is abundant. You can learn tricks of the trade at every turn!

Worthy to be Published

My assumption is that you have a worthy children's picture book manuscript that you've spent significant time creating. Whether or not you have written your original manuscript in response to a perceived gap in the children's book market, I am certain of the following:

1. You have an innate love for children's picture books.

2. You've been moved by the creative—perhaps therapeutic—experience of writing your manuscript.

3. You've received positive feedback regarding your manuscript by children, teachers, family members, and friends.

4. You believe deeply that with the proper illustrations, your children's picture book has a shot at being "as good as" many of the others you've seen featured on bookstore shelves.

5. Your children's picture book manuscript has been professionally edited, and is suitable for publication.

If your objective is to have your manuscript traditionally published, increase your chances by enduring full scale guerilla submissions—as described in this chapter—for approximately 12–18 months. When your patience runs out, or to bypass the traditional publishing route altogether, advance to Chapter 3—and jumpstart the exciting self-publishing process!

Traditional Manuscript Submission

The traditional publishing route offers the following benefits to the first-time author:

* No book-production investment

* Nationwide distribution

* Bookstore shelf space—typically for 3–6 months

* Limited marketing

* Author credibility

Selecting the "right" manuscript to publish is a gamble for publishers of all sizes. Sales potential may be promising, but so are the financial pitfalls of a non-performing title. Although the acquisitions editor may feel particularly moved by a manuscript submission, selection is based on optimizing the publisher's product mix and maximizing profits.

Aside from inferior manuscript quality, rejection may be a result of the following:

1. There is a lack of fit with publisher's current list of titles.

2. The publisher has already produced a book with like subject matter.

3. The initial reader—flooded with work—neglected to share the manuscript with important decision makers.

4. The acquisitions editor has an innate dislike for a particular manuscript topic.

Though publishers reject the vast majority of submissions, remain optimistic! As Thomas Jefferson once stated, "Many of life's failures are people who did not realize how close they were to success when they gave up."

The Scoop!

Raab Associates, Inc. (www.raabassociates.com) offers 1 1/2 hour long tele-courses ($200 each) for aspiring children's book authors and illustrators, such as Marketing Strategies for Creating Your Lucky Break in Children's Publishing.

Accessing Agents

About half of all children's picture book publishers refuse to accept unsolicited manuscripts directly from previously unpublished authors—and require the use of agents. Due to the overwhelming quantity of submissions, filtering agents—armed with exclusive selling rights—assist publishers in uncovering viable manuscripts for publication. Though the agent's primary job is to pair clients and their work with suitable editors, more and more children's book authors and illustrators are seeking agents for the purpose of contract negotiation i.e. royalty rates, marketing guarantees, rights issues. Manuscript submissions are frequently discarded due to lack of congruency with the agent's area of specialization. Be certain to target agents whose primary focus is children's picture books. Low advances and delayed, sporadic royalty payments often cause desirable agents to avoid representing children's books altogether.

Good, reliable children's book agents can be as difficult to find as publishers themselves—and typically require a 10% to 15% commission of all royalty payments including advances. If your manuscript is ultimately accepted by a reputable agent, solidify all details prior to signing your contract, such as agent responsibilities, compensation, and length of contract.

The Scoop!

Major publishers do not consider unsolicited manuscripts—as stated in the Hachette Book Group USA submission policy that follows: "Publishers in the Hachette Book Group USA (including Warner Books, Warner Business Books, FaithWords, Mysterious Press, Aspect, Little, Brown and Company, Back Bay Books, Bulfinch Press, Little, Brown Books for Young Readers) are not able to consider unsolicited queries. Many major publishers have a similar policy. Unfamiliar packages and letters mailed to our offices will be returned to sender unopened. If you are interested in having a manuscript considered for publication, we recommend that you first enlist the services of an established literary agent."

Buyer ... Beware

Do your homework. Seek agents with a minimum of two years experience and no up-front fees for reading, promotion, signing, or mailing. Proceed with caution. Though you have final authority over the signing of a contract, you must relinquish control of the actual negotiation process to the agent. Reputable agents are interested in building long-term, profit-building relationships with their clients—and focus on representing people, not books. One of the most effective ways to obtain a reputable children's picture book agent is through the referrals of other agent-represented authors. Meet authors, agents, and editors via networking at industry conferences. Legitimate literary agent resources include:

* *Literary Market Place (LMP)*

* *Children's Writer's & Illustrator's Market*

* *Writer's and Illustrator's Guide to Children's Books, Publishers and Agents*

* *Writer's Digest to Literary Agents*

* Agent Research & Evaluation (www.agentresearch.com)

* Association of Authors' Representatives (AAR, www.aar-online.org)

Beware of scam artists who prey on the enthusiasm and naiveté of first-time author hopefuls. The AAR Web site offers a comprehensive list of agent-screening questions. For additional insight into children's picture book agents, review the *SCBWI Publications Guide to Writing & Illustrating for Children*—distributed free of charge to members of SCBWI. Visit www.scbwi.org for further information.

Submit! Submit! Submit!

According to editor Christy Ottaviano, in the *Publishers Weekly* article entitled "Representing Change" (February 2001), "Most children's agents today submit projects to a number of editors at once. The days of offering submissions exclusively to one editor are mostly over. But that's understandable, since authors themselves have become more impatient with editors taking too long to respond." Literary agent George Nicholson states in the same article, "…By submitting to more than one editor, one is more likely to get some sort of timely response." Because the practice of simultaneous submissions is common among agents, many agents believe that it is only fair to accept simultaneous submissions from aspiring authors. Though exclusive submissions are preferred, simultaneous submissions are acceptable to most agents—if they are openly informed of the status.

The Scoop!

If sending your manuscript to more than one agent, explicitly state in each cover letter that your manuscript is a simultaneous submission. The most effective way to alienate an agent is to falsely represent a simultaneous submission as an exclusive submission.

Follow agent submission guidelines carefully. An e-mail application or one-page query letter may be requested as initial contact. Keep your fully edited/typo-free query concise and alluring. Include a brief description of your manuscript—just enough to capture the agent's attention. Verify that the agent's name is spelled correctly. A misspelled name is likely to evoke a negative response, consciously or subconsciously. If an agent does in fact request your manuscript, forward one to him/her as quickly as possible—along with a brief cover letter. Most agents prefer the basic double-spaced manuscript. Include a self-addressed stamped envelope (SASE) to increase the likelihood of a swift response. All you need is that one passionate agent with connections to believe in you and your work! Continue your agent hunt for approximately six months—or until your patience runs out!

The Scoop!

Many agents respond favorably to talented writers who are also talented illustrators. If you are both writer and illustrator, send a few sample illustrations (not originals!) with your manuscript submission—preferably in book mock-up format—and refer the agent to your illustration Web site (if you have one). Follow up, follow up, follow up!

Positioning Publishers

Publishing houses in the U.S. print more than 20,000 juvenile titles per year. Approximately 50% of children's book publishers accept non-agented work. Submit your manuscript to targeted publishing houses that waive the agent requirement and permit unsolicited manuscripts. Do not waste needless energy on the tedious submission process if synergy between author and publisher is non-existent. Publishers of all sizes are buried in a mountain of submissions with limited time for review. Manuscripts are frequently discarded based on lack of congruency with the publisher's current product line. For optimal results, ensure that your submission is appropriate for the "line-up" of each of your selected publishers. Even the smallest publishers receive overflowing requests for publication—complete with a self-addressed stamped envelope (SASE). Though a SASE does not guarantee a quick response from the publisher, it may improve the likelihood.

Finding the Right Fit for Your Manuscript

Scan the shelves at your local bookstore and/or library for children's picture books that are closely aligned with the style and content of your manuscript. Compile publisher contact information obtained from the copyright pages of your selected titles. Don't stop there! SCBWI (www.scbwi.org) compiles updated children's book publisher lists for its members. The *SCBWI Publications Guide to Writing & Illustrating for Children* provides names of small children's book publishers whose niche markets may complement your submission. Continue your search even further! Review handy reference guides including:

* *Literary Market Place*

* *The Children's Writer's & Illustrator's Market*

* *Writer's and Illustrator's Guide to Children's Book Publishers and Agents*

The Children's Book Council (CBC) Web site is an effective vehicle for uncovering publishers; visit www.cbcbooks.org. (Be aware that only dues-paying CBC members are listed on the site.) The search engine Web site, Yahoo!, provides a listing of children's book publishers; visit www.yahoo.com/business_and_economy/shopping_and_services/publishers, and click on "children's." To increase your chances of finding a successful match, isolate the publishing houses of children's picture books that are most similar in scope to your imagined finished product. Make use of the Web sites www.amazon.com and www.barnesandnoble.com to review the picture book line-up of targeted publishers. Study publishers' Web sites and/or request publishers' catalogs to culminate your in-depth publisher selection process.

The Scoop!

Publishing house recommendations for your picture book manuscript can emanate from children's librarians and bookstore staff—as well as writers, illustrators, acquisitions editors, and agents at networking conferences.

Sizing Up Submissions

Evaluating submissions is a time consuming, labor intensive process. For smaller publishers, just one—or perhaps a handful of individuals—may be responsible for manuscript acquisition. For larger publishers, final manuscript selection is the result of a publishing committee comprised of the following members:

* Acquisitions editor

* Art director

* Production team

* Marketing/publicity advisers

All children's picture book publishers are not the same. Target your cover letter/query to suit the needs of each individual publisher.

Cover Letter: A Clever Sound Bite

Utilize a professionally edited half to full-page cover letter as a clever "sound bite" to entice the acquisitions editor. Imagine a tower of manuscripts on the acquisitions editor's desk. The first sentence must be intriguing and compelling. Acquisitions editors rarely read more than a half page. Time is of the essence. Make every word count! Your business-like cover letter is not the venue for being verbose, and should include the following:

* Contact information—include name, address, phone number(s), e-mail, and fax (Use professional letterhead, if possible.)

* Publishing company name/address

* Date

* Salutation i.e. "Dear Editor" (Use acquisitions editor's name, if available.)

* Title and type of manuscript

* Concise yet alluring manuscript description

* Closing phrase with signature/name printed beneath it

* Optional enclosure information

> **The Scoop!**
>
> Once your cover letter is opened, it has approximately ten seconds to leap from the pile—and grab the acquisitions editor's attention.

In your cover letter, inform the acquisitions editor that you are familiar with his/her company's line-up, and refer to the actual names of one or more titles. Concentrate on your benefits to the publisher. Focus on the positives! Never apologize for your lack of formal writing experience. Refrain from stating in your cover letter that your manuscript has received overwhelming response in your child's classroom (the scope of many cover letters received by publishing companies, including my own). The acquisitions editor is likely to perceive that the impressionable, young students were more responsive to your enthusiasm than the manuscript itself.

Remember, publishing is a business! Your ability to promote yourself as an author is paramount in selling books. The publisher is likely to give your well-written manuscript a second glance when your credentials translate to increased earnings potential. If you are the author of other published material, an expert in your field, or a renowned public speaker, accentuate those strengths in your cover letter. A first-time author who is capable of promoting his/her autographed books as a workshop/seminar leader expands the publisher's revenue potential. An excellent teacher is an effective first-time author due to his/her ability to engage a young audience—and sell more books—during his/her book signing events.

The *SCBWI Publications Guide to Writing & Illustrating for Children*, as well as the *Writer's and Illustrator's Guide to Children's Book Publishers and Agents* by Ellen R. Shapiro, offer helpful cover letter advice. Visit www.underdown.org/covlettr.htm for the dos and don'ts of cover letter writing—complete with samples.

Mind Your Manuscript

Use plain white 81/2″ x 11″ paper with 11/2″ margins on all sides of the page. Place your name, address, and phone number—single-spaced—in the upper left-hand corner of the first page. Write the approximate manuscript word count in the upper right hand corner. Center your manuscript title approximately one-third of the way down the page. Skip a couple of lines and type your story—double-spaced—in easy-to-read black typeface, such as Courier or Times New Roman. Minimize the use of bolds and italics. Print your manuscript on a laser or ink-jet printer. Submit your fully edited children's picture book manuscript, cover letter, and SASE in a manila 9" x 12" envelope to the address provided by the publishing house. If your children's book manuscript benefits from the use of particular photographs, include samples and suggestions with your submission package. Never send an original copy of your manuscript. To determine accurate postage, visit your local post office or the U.S. Postal Service Web site (www.usps.com).

The Scoop!

The electronic transfer of picture book manuscript submissions is relatively unpopular among harried acquisitions editors—who must add the step of printing the document prior to reading it.

Taking a Chance: Illustration Submissions

If you are confident that you have quality illustrations, take a chance! Include non-original samples with your manuscript submission—preferably in book mock-up format—especially when addressing small to mid-sized publishing houses. Smaller publishers tend to exhibit

more flexibility in the submissions process, and may consider utilizing your illustrations —if they are professional, style-appropriate, and cost-efficient.

If you would like to pursue a separate career as a children's picture book illustrator, forward copies of your best work, with SASE, to the art director of selected publishing houses —according to publisher illustration submission guidelines. Request a copy of *An Illustrator's Guide to Members of the Children's*

Book Council; visit the Children's Book Council's Web site, www.cbc.org, for ordering information. *The Graphic Artists Guild Pricing and Ethical Guide Handbook* recommends specific fees for illustrations based on industry norms for both trade and mass market illustrated books; visit the Graphic Artists Guild Web site: www.gag.org. SCBWI distributes an informative flyer entitled *Critiquing Your Own Portfolio Presentation of Children's Illustration*. Illustration critiquing exchanges are also available to members.

The Scoop!

Nancy Elizabeth Wallace, popular author/illustrator of *Tell-A-Bunny*, *Apples, Apples, Apples*, and *A Taste of Honey* (Winslow Press) shares in her bio, "So how did I get started writing and illustrating books for children? ...I took a three-session Scherenschnitte (traditional paper cutting) class. At the same time, I took a ten-session children's book writing course, but the emphasis was to be on illustration. Everyone in class was an artist! I thought, "Okay, I'll try cutting paper illustrations." After submitting some assignments, the instructor said, "You've found your medium."

The SCBWI New York Showcase Children's Book Art Exhibition and Auction is a unique opportunity for illustrator members to showcase their work for publishers, art directors, and editors. For submission requirements and procedures, visit www.scbwi.org/my_events.htm and click on the New York Showcase link. The top ten art pieces—selected by judges—are sold via auction directly following the showcase. Winning artists receive 100% of the proceeds. Additional prizes include the Grand Prize of $500 with a full-page ad in *Picturebook*, two Honorable Mention cash awards, and the Tomie dePaola Award of $1,000 in art supply gift certificates.

Query ... If You Must

The objective of your well-edited query is to engage the editor and stimulate the response of a request for manuscript. For short children's picture book manuscripts, do not waste time sending a query. It is psychologically easier for a publisher to turn down a query as opposed to the actual manuscript. If you feel that you must send a query in special cases, use your creative writing skills to tweak the publisher's interest—and set yourself apart from the masses. Spend sufficient time formulating your first sentence so that it immediately "grabs" the acquisitions editor's attention.

The *SCBWI Publications Guide to Writing & Illustrating for Children*, as well as the *Writer's and Illustrator's Guide to Children's Books, Publishers and Agents* by Ellen R. Shapiro, offer helpful query advice. Visit www.underdown.org/covlettr.htm for the dos and don'ts of query writing—complete with samples.

The Scoop!

Consider submitting a query to book "packagers," whose role is to acquire, shape, edit, design, and produce books for publishers under their own imprints. For further information about specific children's book packagers, visit American Book Producers Association (ABPA) at www.abpaonline.org.

On Guard: Guerilla Warfare

Follow submissions guidelines commonly posted on publishers' Web sites. Submissions guidelines may also be requested via phone or mail. Just prior to forwarding submissions, it is wise to phone each of your targeted publishers to verify that your information is updated and accurate including:

* Name of current acquisitions editor

* Correct spelling of acquisitions editor's name

* Publisher's address

* Changes, if any, to submission requirements

The traditional submissions approach, as follows, proves frustrating to many aspiring children's picture book authors—especially in this era of lightning-speed communications technology.

Traditional Submissions Approach:

1. Submit your children's picture book manuscript to one publisher.
2. Wait 3–4 months.
3. If response does not occur, forward the publisher a request for return/withdraw of your submission.
4. Repeat the cycle.

If a more aggressive submissions approach suits your personality, get ready for a fierce guerilla campaign! The manuscript submissions process is a statistics game. Your likelihood of getting traditionally published increases with the quantity of viable children's picture book publishers to whom you submit your manuscript! Seek publishing houses that accept unsolicited simultaneous submissions. If submissions guidelines do not expressly state exclusivity, the simultaneous submissions process is usually permissible. Utilize the phrase, "simultaneous submissions," in your cover letters to inform acquisitions editors that you are openly pursuing other publishing avenues.

Keeping Track of Simultaneous Submissions

Keep track of your simultaneous mailings! Submit your manuscript, cover letter, and SASE to your finalized list of targeted publishers at one time—or if you prefer—in subgroups of six. This subgroup approach provides ample time between mailings (approximately four months) to revise your manuscript, based on feedback received from any responsive acquisitions editors. Consider the use of a spreadsheet, as seen on the following page, or index cards (one per publisher) to stay organized. Include name of publishing company, acquisitions editor, date sent, date returned, and comments. If you have not received response from a publisher within 3–4 months, send an inquiry regarding your manuscript status.

If your submission is ultimately selected by a traditional children's picture book publisher, immediately inform all other publishers in receipt of your manuscript as a courtesy. Hire a publishing attorney to review your contract. (Refer to Appendix D for a listing of publishing attorneys and contract negotiation organizations.)

Simultaneous Submissions Worksheet

	Publisher	Editor	Date Sent	Date Returned	Comments
1					
2					
3					
4					
5					
6					
7					
8					
9					
10					
11					
12					
13					
14					
15					
16					
17					
18					
19					
20					

2% … & I Don't Mean Milk

The reality is that less than 2% of the manuscript submissions received by traditional publishers are published. If your guerilla submissions campaign has not resulted in publication of your manuscript within a reasonable time frame of 12–18 months, know that you are not alone! Publishing purists strongly suggest that this is the opportunity to put aside your unpublished manuscript, strengthen your writing skills, and embark upon yet another version—or a completely new manuscript—that is more worthy of publication. Suffice it to say, the seemingly endless submissions cycle can cause the most patient individuals to experience the 3 Ds of publishing: Disappointment, Disenchantment, and Disillusionment!

Perhaps you've received rejection letter upon rejection letter—or even worse—limited response from your targeted list of agents and publishers. You are likely to be frustrated by the entire submissions process including:

* Proofing—and reproofing—your manuscript

* Researching publishers' contact information

* Typing cover letters and queries … ad infinitum

* Addressing publishers' envelopes—including SASE

* Stuffing submissions envelopes

* Wasting your hard earned money on costly postage

Optimism
It's all how you look at it!

The king had two sons—one an optimist, the other a pessimist. The king gave the pessimist everything he desired, and he gave the optimist a room full of horse manure. The pessimist was despondent because he no longer had anything to look forward to. The optimist was as happy as he could be. "With all this manure," he said, "there must be a pony."

–Sales Management Report (2006 Sample Issue)

If Not Now ... When?

When do you discard your manuscript along with every hope and dream of becoming a published children's picture book author? NEVER! With the advent of desktop technology, there has never been a greater opportunity to publish your own title! Do not be lured by vanity presses whose main objective is to earn a hefty profit from your desire to get published. The process of publishing your own children's picture book resides so close to your heart. No one is more passionate about its outcome than you!

CHAPTER

2

Piercing the
Publishing Veil

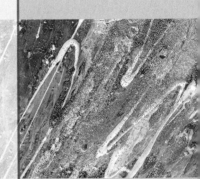

Do what you can
with what you have
where you are.

—Theodore Roosevelt

Wizard of Oz Syndrome

Powerful desktop technology and decreased production costs enable just about anyone to self-publish. I've coined the phrase, Wizard of Oz Syndrome, to depict the outsider's view of publishing as an illusive, page-conjuring practice—harnessed exclusively by sheer word-materializing wizardry. Though publishing purists disdain the concept of self-publishing, there is a paradigm shift occurring within the publishing industry. Today, more and more aspiring children's picture book authors are actively self-publishing without having pursued the traditional publishing path first.

A self-publisher is simply someone who pays the expenses to bring a book to print for distribution or sale. Self-publishing is a viable alternative to the traditional publishing route for the innovative and passionate. You are a self-publisher when you invest in your own printing. As a self-published children's picture book author, your opinion matters! Publishing giants cannot afford to focus their energies on one particular children's picture book. You have the simple advantage—because you can!

According to Brent Sampson, author of *Publishing Gems, Insider Information for the Self-Publishing Writer*, "Old-fashioned publishing is an outdated business model that has to adapt. The Industrial Revolution revolutionized it once; the Technological Revolution is revolutionizing it again."

Charting Your Own Path

Though you are responsible for funding your project, there are clear advantages to publishing your own children's picture book:

1. You maintain complete control over your children's picture book project.

2. The standard 18-month window to publish your title though a traditional publishing house is significantly reduced.

3. You keep 100% of the profits—and have higher earnings potential.

4. Your children's picture book rights belong to you indefinitely—unlike the requisite to forfeit your selling rights when contracting with a major publisher (even when your picture book is no longer in print).

5. Because of your deep connection to your children's book, you are the best individual to keep your book alive beyond the 3–6 month window of opportunity allotted by major publishing houses.

Competing effectively in all areas—production, distribution, and marketing—will help you to maneuver your project through the crowded book industry. Like the traditional publishing approach, you must enthusiastically—and tirelessly—promote your children's picture book via:

* Book signing events

* School visits

* Speaking engagements

* Free media coverage

* Paid advertising

With passion, persistence, tenacity, and determination, you are the commodity that will enable your children's picture book to soar!

An Extension of Yourself

Sharing your title with others—via traditional or self-publishing channels—is not for the faint of heart. Whether you are publishing several copies of your title on behalf of your immediate family, or hundreds—even thousands—of copies to serve a particular audience, you risk self-exposure. Your children's picture book is an extension of yourself. You must courageously open yourself to the distinct possibility that not everyone will respond favorably to your title. Publishing is an art form. Opinion is indeed subjective. Don't fall into the realm of judging your success solely on the quantity of books sold. Even if you hit a homerun and your book becomes a *New York Times* bestseller, be assured that within the next day … next week … next year, a new bestseller from another traditional or self-publisher is likely to emerge. Be realistic from the start. Stay affixed to your goals!

Establishing Your Role as Self-Publisher

Step into your exciting role as self-publisher! Visit your favorite bookstore and thoroughly immerse yourself in the delightful world of children's picture books. Feast your eyes on the overflowing shelves of alluring hardcover and softcover picture books for young readers. Publishers pay book retailers significant cooperative marketing fees—known as "co-op"—to guarantee this prime shelf space. Compelling, vibrantly colored children's picture book covers are designed to compete for customer attention—up to a distance of several feet. Stand aside and inconspicuously observe the behavior of customers walking the aisles of the children's picture book section. The average consumer spends no more than eight seconds perusing a cover. Consumers do in fact judge a book by its cover!

The Scoop!

Mothers, in particular, are on the lookout for stimulating picture books to read to their young children—and comprise 40% of total children's book purchases.

Picture Book Essentials

Review the basic essentials of picture book format including:

* Title page

* Copyright page

* Text/illustration pages

* Optional pages such as dedication and/or foreword/afterword

The term "front matter" is used to describe the material that precedes the text/illustration pages, excluding the cover/end sheets. "Verso" is a Latin term for even-numbered left side pages. "Recto" is a Latin term for odd-numbered right side pages.

THE SCOOP!

The first illustration page of a children's picture book is typically "recto" (right)—because the eye naturally gravitates to the right side page of an opened book. See for yourself!

The copyright page (verso)—usually located on the back side of the title page—includes:

* Publisher's contact information and logo

* "All rights reserved" publisher protection clause

* Copyright ownership/date with © symbol

* Cataloging-in-Publication (CIP) with title tracking data/Library of Congress Control Number (LCCN)

* International Standard Book Number (ISBN)

* Optional author/illustrator dedication

Examine the required identifying European Article Number (EAN) bar code on the lower right hand corner of every back cover—a required ISBN associated "fingerprint" for accuracy and efficiency in the book ordering process. On some children's picture books, the bar code appears without a price designation.

Acquaint Yourself with Caldecott Medal Winners

Learn from the best! Acquaint yourself with Caldecott Medal winners and Honor Books from current and previous years. Examine the elements that make these picture books shine! Bookstores maintain an inventory of popular Caldecott Medal titles. The Caldecott Medal—one of the most prestigious annual children's literature awards—honors the artist of the most distinguished American picture book for children (aged fourteen and younger), published in the U.S. during the previous year. Administered by the Association for Library Service to Children (ALSC), a division of the American Library Association (ALA), the Caldecott Medal is named for Randolph Caldecott (1846–1886), the nineteenth century British illustrator best known for his nursery storybooks including:

* *The Babes in the Wood*

* *The Hey Diddle Diddle Picture Book*

* *Sing a Song of Sixpence*

* *The House That Jack Built*

Many believe that Randolph Caldecott's illustrations were paramount in popularizing nursery stories.

According to the Caldecott Medal terms and criteria, "a picture book for children, as distinguished from other books with illustrations, is one that essentially provides the child with a visual experience ... has a collective unity of story-line, theme, or concept, developed through the series of pictures of which the book is comprised ... [and] displays respect for children's understandings, abilities, and appreciations."

The Caldecott Medal winner and optional Honor Books are selected at the ALA Midwinter Meeting, based on point system, by a committee of fifteen ALSC members including:

* School and public librarians

* University educators

* Professional reviewers

Of the fifteen ALSC members:

* Seven are elected annually from a slate of no fewer than fourteen

* One chairperson is elected annually from a slate of two

* Seven are appointed by the president-elect

With the exception of the chairperson, members of the committee may not serve more often than once every five years.

The 2008 Caldecott Medal winner is *The Invention of Hugo Cabret* by Brian Selznick (Scholastic). Wordless spreads of intriguing black and white pencil illustrations—punctuated by suspenseful text—evoke the flickering images of silent films to which this 500-page book pays homage. Caldecott Medal Committee Chair Karen Breen states, "Selznick's brilliant use of perspective heightens the book's drama as well as the sense that another surprise is just around the page turn."

The Scoop!

To learn more about the Caldecott Medal selection process, visit www.ala.org/alsc/caldecott.html and click "Board and Committee Work" on the left menu. Scroll down to "Related Files" and click "Caldecott Committee Award Manual" Word document or PDF file.

Top Picks

Select six of your favorite picture books from the bookstore shelf—three hardcover books and three adhesive-bound softcover books (known as perfect bound)—to review in greater detail. Hardcover picture books are more expensive to produce than softcover versions, due to higher material and manufacturing costs.

In hardcover picture books, the paper that "wraps" the front/back cover boards and glued beneath the endpapers is called "casewrap." The casewrap is usually printed with images and text that are replicated on the book's removable, protective dust jacket. The dust jacket also provides a:

* Front flap for title synopsis, publisher information, and optional suggested retail price

* Back flap for author/illustrator biographies and photographs

Both hardcover and perfect bound softcover picture books offer a narrow—but invaluable—display spine. The display spine is an effective space-saving feature for overcrowded bookshelves, and typically includes the following information:

* Title of book

* Names of author/illustrator

* Publisher logo

The Significance of Signatures

Most industry standard hardcover and softcover picture books are composed of 32 interior pages that include:

* 13–15 illustrated spreads

* Title page

* Copyright page

* Optional final single page

Each side of a sheet constitutes one page of a book. A page number known as "folio"—though not mandatory—may be placed on the bottom center, or lower right hand corner, of each page. Interior paper weight is typically 70# or 80# to prevent illustration "show-through" on the opposing side of the sheet.

Two 16-page folded and gathered sheets, called "signatures," combine to create a standard 32-page children's picture book. To better comprehend the concept of a 16-page signature, fold a single 81/2" x 11" sheet of paper in half three times. The folds create eight sections per side to produce a total of 16 pages. Picture book signature page count—traditionally in multiples of 8 pages—is contingent upon printing press characteristics and book trim size. As book trim size increases, page-count capacity per signature decreases.

According to the RJ Communications Web site, www.selfpublishing.com, "signature" is a term that dates back to the time when monks copied multiple pages by hand. Once signed and folded, each page became known as the monk's signature.

Children's Book Specification Charting

Emulate the best! Evaluate the design and layout components of your six selected titles:

* How does the use of hardcover or softcover impact the retail price?

* To what extent is color utilized?

* Do the illustrations "bleed" off the edges of the pages or are they "blocked" within specified page margins?

* Does the featured typeface complement the illustration style?

* Are the interior pages coated (shiny) or matte-finished (dull)?

* How does trim size—as well as book orientation (oblong or vertical) —influence illustration design and layout components?

Based on production cost efficiencies and binding requirements, it is advantageous for your title to simulate the industry standard 32-page children's picture book format. Though your picture book concept is likely to evolve over time, it is wise to adhere to a basic framework at the onset of your self-publishing project.

Create a chart to designate the specifications of your six-book sampling, utilizing the following headings:

* Title

* Retail price

* Type of cover (hardcover with dust jacket versus softcover)

* Trim size (horizontal x vertical page dimensions)

* Trim orientation (oblong versus vertical presentation)

* Page count (typically 32 pages)

* Paper type (coated or matte-finish)

* Color usage (full color process versus limited use of color)

* Illustration characteristics ("bleed" versus "non-bleed")

* Special effects (embossing, foil, stamping, sensory-stimulating materials, stencil cuts, etc.)

Include all pertinent information. Be specific and concrete in your observations. Make sketches as necessary. Envision your completed self-published title in full detail. Include a row in your worksheet that reflects your proposed children's picture book specifications as follows.

Children's Book Specification Worksheet

	Children's Picture Book Title	Retail Price	Type of Cover	Trim Size	Trim Orient.	Page Count	Paper Type	Color Usage	Bleed (Y/N)	Special Effects
1										
2										
3										
4										
5										
6										
7	Your Proposed Title Here									

Mock-Ups ... Not Muck-Ups

With paper, scissors, clear tape, and glue stick, create a 32-page storyboard "mock-up"—also known as "dummy"—of your hardcover or softcover children's picture book from your charted specifications. (Page count may be higher or lower to suit your individual needs i.e. 24, 40 or 48 pages.) Utilize one (or more) of your children's picture book samples as a viable layout/design template. Include:

* Front/back covers

* End papers and dust jacket (if hardcover)

* Title page

* Copyright page

* Text/illustration pages

*   Optional pages if your signature-formatted page count permits i.e. donation to charity, foreword, afterword, etc.

To optimize the flow of your picture book, separate your manuscript text into logical segments to fill your allotted page count. Number the pages of your mock-up. Utilize an easy-to-read, stylized typeface to complement the tone of your picture book. Leave sufficient space between text segments for illustrations. Include loosely drawn pencil sketches (stick figures permitted!). Prior to the actual illustration phase, you may consider hiring a children's picture book editor/coach who can assist you with the optimal text segment breaks and illustration flow of your picture book. Visit www.justselfpublish.com for picture book coach referrals.

Count the illustrations in your proposed mock-up. Your cover illustration may be re-used from an interior page of your book. Base your illustration budget on the estimated quantity of illustrations required to complete your proposed children's picture book project. Your decision to self-publish has earned you the privilege of selecting the proper illustration "treatment" for your children's picture book. If you are an illustrator as well as an author, self-publishing offers you a phenomenal opportunity to showcase your own artwork!

Picture Perfect

According to Pat Scales, the 2008–2009 president of ALA's Association for Library Service to Children (ALSC)—and 2003 committee chair for the prestigious Caldecott Medal—effective illustrations mirror the rising and falling action of the corresponding text. Successful illustrations extend the "tone" and "feel" of text while propelling a young child to a higher level of comprehension and enjoyment. In considering your own response to the unique illustration styles featured throughout your favorite picture books, you'll recognize that illustration—like any other form of art—is subjective. (As my mother always reminds me, "There's a lid for every pot!") Illustrations are as varied as the artists themselves, and exist in a full range of styles including collage, oils, watercolor, pen and ink, photographic, etc. Fabulous illustrations breathe life into simple children's text. Illustrations play so critical a role in the world of children's picture books that traditional publishers pay authors and illustrators equal shares of royalty—most commonly 5% each.

Finding the Right Illustrator

Illustrations range from no charge to $500+ per illustration. The more highly regarded the illustrator, the more expensive the illustrations ($10,000+ to illustrate a 32-page children's picture book). If your funding is minimal, invite an eager elementary school classroom to illustrate your manuscript—with the principal's permission—at no cost to you. If you prefer, call your local high school art teacher for references. A talented high school art student may illustrate your manuscript for a nominal fee—or perhaps free of charge for experience sake. Co-op students or recent graduates of local art colleges frequently freelance on a per project basis. Web sites such as www.corbis.com and www.istockphoto.com enable you to download inexpensive pre-existing stock illustrations for a fee. If your budget permits, hire an experienced, professional illustrator. (Refer to Appendix D for a listing of illustration directories and Web sites.)

The Scoop!

A Google search for "children's book illustrators" produces more than 1,600,000 possibilities. Obtain references and samples prior to composing a formalized written contract with your illustrator of choice.

My publishing company receives promotional material from an array of talented freelance illustrators who are eager to work on individual publishing projects. Fees are negotiable! When hiring a professional illustrator, work locally, if possible, for greater control over your children's picture book project.

A Peek at POD Publishing Service Providers

POD (Print on demand) publishing service providers offer a vast array of streamlined self-publishing services under one roof including:

* Manuscript editing

* Illustration assistance

* Book layout and design

* Full color book production

* Distribution

* Fulfillment

* Marketing

User-friendly, "one-stop" shopping permits the tentative children's picture book author to "tip-toe" into the enticing world of publishing for an initial investment of $1,000+. POD publishing service providers can digitally print copies of a title on an "as needed" basis—in increments as low as one copy. If you are considering publishing your children's picture book in small quantities for personal use, or as a sample test basis, POD publishing service providers may offer a viable option. (Refer to Appendix D for a listing of POD publishing service providers.)

The Limitations of POD Publishing Service Providers

Do not assume that you are the publisher of your children's picture book! Though you "own" your copyright including text and images, the POD publishing service provider maintains full rights to your:

* ISBN

* Associated EAN bar code

* PDF book layout/design file

Because you do not officially own your ISBN, the POD publishing service provider is considered to be the publisher—not you.

According to the PMA October 2006 *Independent* newsletter article, "What Is a Publisher? And Why You Might Not Count As One," "The most basic requirement for becoming a publisher is purchasing a series of ISBNs from the R. R. Bowker Company and making sure that your company is the publisher of record for them."

If you choose to publish the same POD picture book at a future date through your own self-publishing company, you are required to do the following:

1. Hire a graphic designer to recreate the existing PDF file of your picture book.

2. Purchase a new ISBN and associated EAN bar code.

Additional POD disadvantages include:

* High cost per book printed

* High retail price per book sold—40%–50% higher than comparable trade books

* Non-availability of picture books sized larger than 8 1/2" x 11"

* Inability to print title on vertical softcover spine

* Print quality

* Inferior book trade presence

* Limited "returns" availability—depending on the POD publishing service provider

* Negative connotation in the traditional book trade market

The Scoop!

On average, just 100–200 copies per POD title are sold—with a whopping 64% of those copies purchased by the author.

POD publishing service providers earn a significant percentage of each book sold—and rely heavily on author-driven sales through a network of family and friends. POD titles are typically sold through POD Web sites. For a no-nonsense look at POD publishing service providers, access the following Web sites:

* www.booksandtales.com/pod/podpublish.htm

* www.sfwa.org/beware/printondemand.html

* www.wbjbradio.com/archives.php?aid

For further information regarding POD options, visit www.justselfpublish.com.

Full Color POD Publishing Service Provider Sampling

Several POD publishing service providers are capable of producing full color children's picture books including:

* Xlibris
  www.xlibris.com

* Trafford Publishing
  www.trafford.com

* AuthorHouse
  www.authorhouse.com

Binding options vary according to the POD publishing service provider. Xlibris prints both softcover perfect bound and hardcover casewrap versions. AuthorHouse prints only a softcover perfect bound version. Trafford Publishing prints only a saddle stitch softcover version. Though quite expensive, the POD version that most closely resembles a trade quality picture book is the 32-page hardcover (casewrap) with dust jacket by Xlibris (author's cost: $22.39).

Xlibris and AuthorHouse are bound by a 4–5 month production schedule, and outsource print/book manufacturing to Lightning Source (an Ingram-owned digital printing company). Trafford Publishing prints and binds in-house—typically within a six week period.

THE SCOOP!

Not all clients of POD publishing service providers are satisfied with the end result. Request picture book samples from at least three POD publishing servicing providers. Verify product quality, and compare your POD options—prior to signing on the dotted line!

A 100% publisher returns policy is mandatory if a POD title is to be considered for bookstore acquisition. To compete more effectively in the trade book arena, AuthorHouse and Xlibris now offer their POD authors a book returns privilege for an additonal fee. Though bookstores typically refuse to stock POD books, a POD author may be accommodated with a local in-store book signing—if he/she brings along copies of the POD title to sell. The bookstore usually requests a percentage of sales in exchange for the one time book signing opportunity.

CHAPTER

3

Fast Track to
Self-Publishing

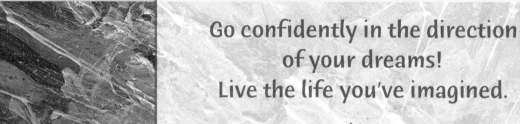

Go confidently in the direction
of your dreams!
Live the life you've imagined.

—*Thoreau*

Savvy Self-Publisher

Abandon all thoughts of POD publishing service providers—and embrace the fully independent self-publishing route! Your children's picture book falls under your complete dominion when you actively manage your own self-publishing venture. Maintain a positive mental attitude and remain passionate about your objectives. Self-publishing dreams really can come true!

Featured on the *New York Times* Children's Bestsellers List, *Stranger in the Woods*—an award-winning photographic picture book by Carl R. Sams II and Jean Stoick—has reached the pinnacle of success … with more than 1,000,000 copies sold. The talented husband–wife duo of nature photographers succeeded in obtaining pre-orders for several thousand copies of the self-published *Stranger in the Woods* from their loyal following of gift and art show clientele.

The Scoop!

Though major New York publishers had previously published several of Carl and Jean's adult photographic wildlife titles, *Stranger in the Woods* was surprisingly rejected. The reason given: "Children's photo books do not sell."

Although photographic-style children's picture books have historically resulted in disappointing sales, this delightful title has benefited from the power of niche marketing in not one—but three areas: photography, nature, and winter/holiday. Because the stranger in the woods is actually a snowman, this religion-neutral picture book demonstrates impartiality to Christmas, Hanukkah, and Kwanzaa, thereby extending its market reach. Effective promotional vehicles for *Stranger in the Woods* include:

* National gift/art shows

* Industry conferences such as American Library Association and BookExpo America

* Bookstore/gift store promotional programs

*   Michigan Library Association—book and proceed donations

*   School presentations

Visit www.strangerinthewoods.com to learn more about this exciting self-publishing success story. It proves the old adage, "Do what you love and the money will follow!"

Learn the Tricks of the Trade

To immerse yourself in the world of self-publishing, learn tricks of the trade, and share relevant and creative ideas with other publishers, consider membership to the following publishing associations:

*   Publishers Marketing Association (PMA)*—annual fee: $119
Phone: 310-372-2732/Web site: www.pma-online.org

*   Small Publishers Association of North America (SPAN)—annual fee: $115
Phone: 719-475-1726/Web site: www.SPANnet.org

*   Small Publishers, Artists and Writers Network (SPAWN)—annual fee: $45
Phone: 818-886-4281/Web site: www.spawn.org

Upon joining each of the above associations, you will receive a monthly newsletter that is brimming with informative articles—as well as ads by industry professionals including: editors, graphic designers, public relations experts, fulfillment houses, Web hosts, printers, and publishing consultants. You are also certain to benefit from a host of member programs—including reduced-rate shipping, health insurance, car rental, cooperative marketing/advertising programs, and networking/exhibiting opportunities at popular publishing conferences.

Publishers Weekly is a popular industry source (circulation: 40,000) that features interviews with influential authors and publishing leaders—as well as articles highlighting industry changes and trends. Annual magazine subscription fee is $239.99. Both PMA and SPAN offer subscription discounts to members. A comprehensive listing of newly released children's books is made available twice per year in the spring and fall *Publishers Weekly* Children's Issues, available for $20 each. For subscription information, call *Publishers Weekly* at 800-278-2991 or visit www.publishersweekly.com. Your local library is likely to have copies of *Publishers Weekly* for review as an alternative to paid subscription.

---

* As of this printing, PMA is undergoing a name change to Independent Book Publishers Association (IBPA).

THE SCOOP!

Children's book-related newsletters—featuring author tips and invaluable market information—include *Children's Book Insider* (www.write4kids.com), *Children's Writer* (www.childrenswriter.com), and *Children's Bookshelf* (www.publishersweekly.com).

Think Like a Publisher

Think like a publisher—and focus on optimal channels for maximizing profit. Brainstorm ideas to improve your likelihood of self-publishing success in the competitive picture book arena. Be flexible and creative. Read your manuscript, and re-read it! Imagine that your work belongs to another writer. Is there any aspect of your manuscript that you would consider altering to strengthen its position in the marketplace? If your children's picture book is about Toby, the irresistible stray cat, for example, consider the following approaches:

* Add a page to your manuscript that describes the plight of stray cats in addition to a list of organizations devoted to helping their cause.

* Feature a written commitment in your children's picture book to donate a percentage of the proceeds to your favorite organization for strays—an effective "win-win" co-marketing strategy. (If the organization agrees to promote your title through its Web site and other marketing venues, donations increase with the quantity of books sold!)

* Utilize your invaluable stray cat "expertise" to complement the elementary school science curriculum, thereby increasing your desirability as a highly paid visiting school author.

■■■■■■■■■■■■■■■■■■■■■■■■■■■■■■■■

The Scoop!

Visit www.lib.muohio.edu/pictbks/search, the Children's Picture Book Database, for an overview of titles relating to the topic of your manuscript.

■■■■■■■■■■■■■■■■■■■■■■■■■■■■■■■■

Marketing Tactics: Gaining an Edge

Consider gaining an edge in the world of children's picture books through "brand" and/or "series" marketing. A brand is characterized by an entity that is familiar to the public at large. A licensed character (such as Mickey Mouse) or consumer product (such as Cheerios Breakfast Cereal in *The Cheerios Counting Book*) can be an expensive—but invaluable—commodity for the publisher. Another vehicle for extending sales of children's books is series publishing. A series enables the publisher to build a list of well-integrated titles over the long term—rather than a single straggler title that may be lost in a wave of mass releases. With each new published title in a series, the author and illustrator build popularity as they develop a growing base of enthusiastic fans. When a new series title is introduced, sales of previous titles are stimulated as momentum builds for future titles. A significant publishing advantage is that a parent who purchases one title in the series is likely to purchase another, thereby optimizing sales. Examples of successful picture book series include the following:

* The *Arthur* series (Little, Brown Young Reader), written and illustrated by Marc Brown, about the exciting adventures of a lovable aardvark

* The *If You Give a Mouse a Cookie* series (HarperCollins), written by Laura Joeffe Numeroff/illustrated by Felicia Bond, about one humorous chain reaction after another

* The *Walter the Farting Dog* series (North Atlantic Books), written by William Kotzwinkle and Glenn Murray/illustrated by Audrey Colman, about the trials and triumphs of a flatulent mutt

* The *Twist & Ernest* series (Barnesyard Books), written by Laura T. Barnes/illustrated by Carol A. Camburn, about a horse and a donkey that build an unlikely friendship with one another

Creating Your Own Publishing Company

Savor the process of creating your own self-publishing entity! Select an appropriate name for your new publishing company. I chose the name, Arimax, Inc., for my publishing company to honor my two children, Ariele and Maxime. Think outside the box, and have fun with the invigorating creativity process. The Web site, www.yudkin.com/generate.htm, offers a 19-step guide to help you create the publishing company name that's right for you! Avoid possible name duplication by researching existing publishing companies in library resources such as:

* *Books in Print*

* *Small Press Record of Books*

* *Publishers Directory* by Gale Research

The name that you choose will ultimately appear on the cover and copyright page of your self-published children's picture book.

Consider the use of separate office space—in or out of your home—complete with computer system, phone system, fax, etc. Establish a designated phone number and address for all of your business-related activities. You may rent a postal box from either your local post office or neighborhood parcel retailer, such as Mail Boxes, Etc. The latter offers a professional street address for your publishing company in place of the term, "P.O. Box."

Legalizing Your Publishing Entity

With the establishment of a formalized business name and location, legalize your publishing entity as soon as possible. If you and/or your spouse (significant other) are currently earning adequate income, the creation of a legal publishing entity entitles you to advantageous tax write-offs. Sole proprietorship, partnership, and corporation are your business structure options. Sole proprietorship is popular among first-time publishers due to the ease of its formation. To create an "S" corporation, limited liability corporation (LLC), or other appropriate legal entity for protection purposes and tax advantages, visit www.LLC.com or www.LegalZoom.com—and/or hire an attorney.

The Scoop!

Some savvy self-publishers add a DBA ("doing business as") clause—utilizing a fictitious name to avoid any self-publisher related stigma.

Implement an actual business checking account to stay abreast of all financial transactions. Separating your business expenditures from your personal expenditures is wise from the onset. In addition to designing and manufacturing your picture book, your publishing entity is likely to fund a host of related expenditures including:

* Book expos

* Publishing conferences

* Specialty gift shows

* Book signings

* Automobile mileage with significant wear and tear

* Publishing associations/organizations such as SCBWI, PMA, SPAN, and SPAWN

* Advertising/promotion

* Web site design

Visit www.Inc.com, an information-packed Web site for entrepreneurs. As a functioning tax-paying business, you are also entitled to benefit from the services of the Small Business Association (SBA). Visit www.sba.gov for further information. SCORE, Service Corps of Retired Executives, is the SBA's volunteer counseling network. Visit www.score.org to schedule a meeting with a SCORE volunteer.

Setting the Tone: Business Cards & Stationery

Utilizing your company name/logo, address, phone number, fax, e-mail, and Web site, create letterhead, envelopes, and business cards. Include membership affiliation insignias i.e. SCBWI, PMA, SPAN, SPAWN, CBC, etc. on your business stationery to improve the likelihood of a favorable industry response from distributors, reviewers, and publishing-related media. Create your own business stationery on your home computer—or if you prefer, request a "low-budget" quote from Paper Direct (800-A-PAPERS) and/or www.vistaprint.com. For assistance in developing a company logo, visit www.cooltext.com, www.LogoBob.com or www.LogoWorks.com—or hire your own graphic designer.

Do not overlook the power of a simple business card. To optimize recognition of your title, consider placing a full color image of your picture book on the front side of your business card. The back side of your business card is not required to be blank, and provides invaluable marketing space for your special title promotions.

According to J. C. Levinson, B. Gallagher, and O. R. Wilson, in their book, *Guerilla Selling*, a business card can be an effective sales tool. The authors site an example of a Dallas-based cell phone sales representative—and avid Dallas Cowboys fan—who utilizes her business cards to uncover sales leads at Dallas Cowboys home games. When her favorite team scores, she cleverly celebrates by tossing a handful of her business cards up in the air. At the end of each game, calls pour in from at least a dozen exuberant fans in response to her promotional business card blizzard!

Your Graphic Designer Rules

Every successful publisher is keenly aware that a talented graphic designer is the key to producing a quality children's picture book. Align yourself with a professional graphic designer to synthesize all of your publishing pieces—including the all-important illustration component. A graphic designer does not create illustrations. He/she uses computer programs, such as

InDesign and/or QuarkXPress as well as Photoshop and Illustrator, to skillfully merge illustrations with text—and create the ultimate look and feel of a book. Whereas some graphic designers specialize in book covers, others specialize in book interiors. Many are equally comfortable with both.

Experienced graphic designers vary in fee structure, charging an average of $50–$75 per hour. Graphic design fees are frequently negotiable. A handful of competitive graphic designers offer "package" pricing per job versus the more typical hourly charges. Be aware that while your graphic designer may allot ample time for you to tweak the details of your self-publishing project, you are likely to be bombarded with costly change fees for this service. Request at least one round of changes to be included in your contracted graphic design price.

The Scoop!

Working with a graphic designer can be frustrating at times. Keep your lines of communication open. Present actual samples to emulate whenever possible. If you find that you are spending money but not achieving desired results, it may be best to cut your losses—and start yet again with another graphic designer. Even with references, finding the right graphic designer to suit your needs—and style—is not always an easy task!

Making the Cut

Do your homework prior to hiring a graphic designer. Contact at least three graphic designers for price/quality comparisons. (Refer to Appendix D for a listing of graphic designers.) Interview them by phone. Meet with them in person, if local. Obtain samples of their work, preferably picture books. You are likely to be directed to their Web sites. Call references. Take your search a step further. Contact several small to mid-sized children's book publishers for their graphic designer recommendations. Like you, many do not have in-house graphic designing staff and hire outside consultants. I prefer to work with local graphic designers for a greater sense of control over my projects. If you are comfortable sending and receiving files online, the actual location of your graphic designer has little downside.

Once you have selected your graphic designer, be certain to show him/her your favorite picture book sample(s) and proposed mock-up. These tools are viable templates for the layout and design elements of your self-published children's picture book. Your graphic designer will inform you of any flaws inherent in your mock-up—and can address any related questions/concerns about the layout and design process.

The Scoop!

Choose your graphic designer wisely! He/she is critical to the success of your children's picture book project.

Quality In Equals Quality Out

Optimal illustration dimensions are contingent upon the design and layout of your picture book. A square children's book requires proportionally square illustrations; a rectangular children's book requires proportionally rectangular illustrations. Without proportionally sized illustrations, images must be stretched/distorted or cropped to suit your selected trim size. For illustrations that "bleed" off the edges of your pages, an extra 1/8" of art is required on each side of your illustrations—due to the inadvertent cropping that is inherent in the printing process.

Artists utilize an array of techniques for their prized illustrations. Some create and transfer their digitized illustrations via computer. Others are more comfortable with traditional hand-made illustrations. Non-digitized images must be scanned on a flat bed scanner if 11" x 17" or smaller, or on a drum scanner if larger than 11" x 17". A scan digitizes the continuous tone of an image into dot formation—an essential step in the printing process.

THE SCOOP!

To produce a quality picture book, your scans must be at least 300 dots per inch (DPI). If you do not have an adequate home scanner, your graphic designer or book manufacturer can generate the necessary scans for you.

Whereas scans are typically used for flat, standard-sized art pieces, digital photography is used for oversized, dimensional, and rigid illustration surfaces—such as rippling watercolor paper, dimensional collage, or uneven mosaic. It is imperative that you seek advice from your graphic designer prior to initiating the critical illustration phase of your self-published picture book. Otherwise, you risk illustrations that are non-proportional to your overall trim size and margin allotments. Case in point: For my picture book, *The Zebra-Striped Whale with the Polka-Dot Tail* (an oversized 11″ x 11″ hardcover children's picture book with dust jacket), I created eighteen collages on inconsistently-sized surfaces—over the course of a ten year period. Due to significant surface and sizing irregularities, it was necessary to spend literally thousands of dollars on film transparencies and electronic resizing.

The Communication Factor

Your graphic designer is a gold mine of invaluable information—and is likely to save you time, effort, and money! He/she thoroughly comprehends the nuances of translating original artwork to the printed page, and can communicate directly with your illustrator to solidify final art size and page formatting constraints. Once your graphic designer has verified illustration specifications, finalize all aspects of your pre-negotiated illustrator agreement. Obtain assistance from an attorney, if necessary. Be specific and concrete so that your illustrator fully understands the agreed upon terms including:

* Illustration fee structure

* Artistic style

* Approximate timeline to completion

* Payment terms and conditions

* Optional royalty percentage

* Illustration ownership rights

Forecast your illustration completion date and arrange payment installments. Once the illustrator contract is signed, manage your project effectively. Encourage your illustrator to stay on task and work as quickly as possible. Review illustrations as they are completed—making any necessary changes in a timely fashion.

Book Covers Sell Books

An attention-grabbing cover is critical to the success of your children's picture book. Because 82% of all children's picture book consumers are women, the key to an effective cover is an intriguing blend of illustration and text—with a component of feminine appeal. Using a discerning eye, determine the elements that you find most appealing in a cover including:

* Colors

* Special effects (such as embossing)

* Typeface

* Characterizing illustration

* Overall design components

Choose your favorite picture book covers as models to study and emulate. Work with a graphic designer who has had ample experience creating picture book covers. Obtain cover samples to ensure the quality of his/her work. This individual may or may not be the graphic designer who is responsible for the interior layout/design of your picture book.

The Scoop!

For your all-important children's picture book cover, you may re-use a favorite illustration from the interior—or commission your illustrator to produce a separate cover illustration.

Choosing Your Title

Do not underestimate the powerful combination of your cover illustration and title! Once you have decided upon your cover illustration, take sufficient time to formulate a winning title. To generate title ideas—utilizing synonyms, antonyms, and related words—visit www.rhymezone.com. To uncover other title possibilities, visit www.namingnewsletter.com. Though this Web site was constructed specifically for branding company names, you may be able to glean helpful titling strategies.

Brainstorm at least a dozen title ideas. Share your favorites with friends and family—young and old alike. Choose your top three. Once again, obtain input from friends and family of all ages and/or a professional publishing consultant. Your graphic designer will ultimately overlay the cover illustration with your selected title—leaving ample space for the names of the author and illustrator, of course!

Determining Your Cover Price

To maximize sales of your title, select a retail price that falls within the range of similar books in its category. Determine your optimal price point by sampling 12–18 children's picture books having comparable trim size, page count, and cover type. Though some independent publishing houses subscribe to a formula of multiplying production costs by a predetermined factor of 8—for example—overpriced picture books are doomed to face major obstacles in a saturated marketplace. It is difficult to justify non-competitive pricing in a market that is characterized by over-supply and under-demand—unless your title serves a very unique niche. The price typically appears on the back cover and/or on the upper right hand corner of the front dust jacket flap. It is best to include both the USA and converted Canadian prices on your children's picture book.

Creating a Winning Cover

Your graphic designer should provide you with a minimum of three original cover samples for your children's picture book. Proudly show these samples to your family members, friends, teachers, children's librarians, and other industry professionals. Gather as many objective opinions as possible. Include young children and their moms in your research. Observe all responses—even subtle ones—very carefully. Do not rush the cover selection process. Which of your picture book cover samples appeal to grown-ups as well as to young children? Visit your local bookstore. Place your mock cover samples on the bookshelf, and see for yourself! View your cover samples at close range, as well as at a distance. Which cover "stands out" amidst the hundreds of other children's books lining the shelves? Follow your instincts. Remain flexible and open to all feedback. Work closely with your graphic designer to make any necessary improvements. It may take a few go-rounds—sometimes more—prior to achieving the quality professional cover that you desire.

The Scoop!

A colorful, child-friendly front cover—geared towards the feminine buyer—is likely to increase sales of your self-published children's picture book!

Cover Cohesiveness

Your talented cover designer will extend the look and feel of your front cover ... to the back cover ... to the spine ... to the dust jacket and flaps—through color consistency and spot illustration. The back cover of your children's picture book is prime location for the following:

* Highly regarded testimonials and reviews

* Spot illustration

* Donation information, if applicable

The back covers of two of my religious titles include the following statement: "10% of the profits derived from the sale of this title will be donated to MAZON—A Jewish Response to Hunger," followed by a brief organization description. The back cover of the second printing of *The Zebra-Striped Whale with the Polka-Dot Tail* features a thematic spot illustration, as well as four favorable media reviews, publicized after the first printing.

If you are self-publishing a casewrap (hardcover), the paper that "wraps" the front and back cover boards is printed with images and text that are replicated on the protective, removable dust jacket. The dust jacket also provides precious front flap space for your title synopsis, publisher contact information (with logo), and optional suggested retail price—in the upper right hand corner. The back flap of the dust jacket features brief author/illustrator biographies with accompanying photos.

Complying with Compliance Codes

As a self-publisher, it is essential that you adhere to the strictest standards and placement of compliance codes. Ensure that your graphic designer places the following information on the copyright page of your children's picture book:

* ISBN

* Library of Congress Control Number

* Copyright date

* © symbol

* Name of copyright owner

* Rights protection clause—"All rights reserved. No portion of this book may be reproduced in any form or by any means without prior written permission."

* Publishing company contact information—address, e-mail, fax, and phone number

* Company logo

* Web site

* Optional dedications/credits

* Geographical printing location—if the title has been printed outside the USA i.e. Printed in Hong Kong

To enable your children's picture book to be recognized by the bookstore cash register, you must order an internationally compatible Bookland European Article Number (EAN) bar code. Your graphic designer is responsible for applying your EAN bar code with ISBN and optional retail price—in black for readability—on the lower right hand corner of your back cover (and dust jacket, if applicable).

Library of Congress ... Impressive!

If you plan to sell your picture book to the library market, it is necessary to obtain a unique identification number—known as the Pre-assigned Control Number (PCN). Self-publishers are required by the Library of Congress to utilize the PCN in response to the increasing demand for official registration. The PCN program assigns a Library of Congress Control Number (LCCN) to your picture book—in advance of its publication—to facilitate cataloging and other book processing activities.

Submit an online pre-assigned control number request form through the Library of Congress Web site: http://pcn.loc.gov/pcn. Upon acceptance—approximately within one week—the Library of Congress will electronically forward you an account number and original password. Utilize the account number and password to submit your online PCN application, via the same Library of Congress Web site. When you click on the "Log On" button, you will be provided with three options:

* "PCN Application"—to request your Pre-assigned Control Number

* "PCN Change Request"—to report a change to a work for which a PCN has been assigned

* "Publisher Information Change Request"—to update or to change previously submitted information

Expect to receive your LCCN—with copyright page placement instructions—via e-mail. Your LCCN must appear on the copyright page of your picture book. If you have further questions regarding the LCCN, call the Library of Congress at 202-707-5000.

The Scoop!

As dictated by the Library of Congress, a U.S. place of publication must appear somewhere on the title page or copyright page of your picture book.

Cataloging Your Title

There is no charge for your LCCN; however, you are obligated to forward a complimentary copy of your picture book to the Library of Congress—immediately upon publication. If you are mailing your picture book via U.S. Postal Service, use the address:

Library of Congress, Cataloging in Publication Division
101 Independence Avenue, S.E.
Washington, D.C. 20540-4320

If you are shipping your picture book via commercial carrier, use the address:

Library of Congress, CIP 20540-4320
9140 East Hampton Drive
Capitol Heights, MD 20743

Upon receipt, your title will be reviewed by Library of Congress selection officers for possible addition to the Library of Congress collection. Selected titles are assigned a cataloging priority, and cataloged according to that priority status. The Library of Congress database lists priority-cataloged titles via its Web site: www.loc.gov. (If you are determined to obtain cataloging priority for your title, your local librarian can assist you!)

Books submitted to the Library of Congress on behalf of PCN compliance are not returned. As self-publisher, you must be readily available to answer any bibliographic questions regarding your title.

Cataloging-in-Publication: Traditional & Publisher's Version

U.S. publishers who represent titles by at least three different authors have the option of applying for either the Pre-assigned Control Number (PCN) or Cataloging-in-Publication (CIP). Librarians are more likely to purchase CIP-designated titles than PCN-designated titles, as a result of the expanded cataloging information. CIP-designated titles offer librarians extensive acquisition and processing data as follows.

Cataloging-in-Publication Data

* Distinctive heading in bold typeface
* Name of author
* Book title
* ISBN
* Specific Library of Congress subject headings
* Classification Numbers: Library of Congress catalog card number and Dewey Decimal

An optional, "non-sanctioned" publisher's version of CIP—known as PCIP—has been established to provide librarians with the more desirable title cataloging format. For a peek at an actual PCIP, refer to the copyright page located at the front of this book. According to the May 2006 *SPAN Connection* newsletter, as stated in the "News You Can Use" section, "If self-publishers would courageously commit to obtaining their own PCIPs, perhaps the Library of Congress would lose their self-appointed clout, leaving books to be judged strictly on their own merit." If you are interested in attracting the attention of librarians and participating in the vanguard of change, consider purchasing your own PCIP. Fees range from $50 to $150 for the exact same service. Compare PCIP pricing from the following companies:

* The Donohue Group, Inc.
  www.dgiinc.com

* Quality Books Inc.
  www.quality-books.com

* Cataloger-At-Large
  www.cipblock.com

ISBN: Huh?

To facilitate title tracking and fulfillment for the life of your picture book, you are required to obtain an International Standard Book Number (ISBN) from R. R. Bowker Company—the U.S. agency licensed to sell ISBNs—in conjunction with the International Standards

Organization (ISO). The ISBN is a universal numeric identifier that permits publishers, bookstores, consumers, and the media to identify and/or order a title. ISBNs—purchased in groups of ten ($249.95) or as singles ($125 ea.)—are available from R.R. Bowker Company. Prices are subject to change. When self-publishing both a softcover and hardcover version of the same children's picture book, you must utilize two different ISBNs.

The Scoop!

As of January 1, 2007, the 10-digit ISBN was replaced with the 13-digit ISBN—to increase ISBN system capacity, and coordinate with the EAN.UCC global consumer goods code.

Older 10-digit ISBNs can be converted to 13-digit ISBNs with the 978 prefix. Visit www.isbn.org for easy conversion instructions. Since January 1, 2007, only the ISBN-13 is mandatory for all published titles. (During transition year, 2006, published titles required use of both the ISBN-10 and converted ISBN-13.)

The new 13-digit ISBN is comprised of 5 sections of numbers that are separated by dashes:

* The first section is one of two added prefixes (978 and 979)—the default prefix for books.

* The second section consists of just one digit that specifies the language of the book. The digit—0 or 1—is utilized for books that are published in English.

* The third section, usually consisting of six to seven digits, identifies the publisher.

* The fourth section consists of digits that correspond to the number of publications released by the publisher.

* The fifth section consists of an automatic algorithmic "check" digit—0 to 9, or X—to ensure that the ISBN is indeed correct.

A sample ISBN follows.

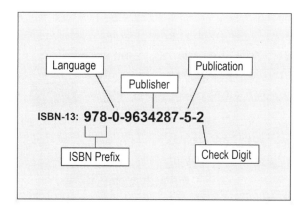

If you have not yet purchased your ISBNs, register online at www.isbn.org with your credit card—or download the forms and mail with your check or money order to:

R. R. Bowker Company
121 Chanlon Road
New Providence, NJ 07974

Standard ISBN processing time is approximately ten business days by mail, or three days for a rush order. When ordering an entire set of ten ISBNs, select the first in line for your first picture book—and the remaining nine, consecutively, for future publications! If you have questions regarding the ISBN, call R. R. Bowker Company at 800-521-8110.

Registering Your ISBN

At least six months in advance of your official publication date, report your ISBN-associated title information to R. R. Bowker Company for use in *Books in Print*—the industry's most comprehensive bibliographic database. Fill out the online Advance Book Information (ABI) form at www.bowkerlink.com. For registration access, utilize your *Books in Print* user name and password—included with your ISBNs. Your title specifications and ordering information—listed free of charge—will be readily accessible to thousands of booksellers, distributors, wholesalers, and publishers nationwide. R. R. Bowker Company publishes *Books in Print* twice per year in June and December. If you have any questions regarding *Books in Print*, call R. R. Bowker Company at 800-521-8110.

EAN Bar Code

The EAN (European Article Number) bar code behaves as your title's unique fingerprint for standard order processing at all U.S. bookstore chains—and most independent bookstores—throughout the U.S. The internationally compatible EAN bar code is translated into a scanner-readable format from your ISBN. The actual ISBN is listed above the bar code "as is"—and repeated below—with a three-digit prefix (identifying code for books) and an altered final check digit.

The book's smaller retail price extension bar code is situated to the right of the ISBN bar code. The first of five digits typically appears as a 5, designating U.S. currency. The remaining four digits indicate the retail price of the book in dollars and cents. For example, the number, 51995, represents the retail price of $19.95 in U.S. currency. The EAN bar code may or may not include the book's retail price. If no price is formally listed in the book, the bar code reads 90000. A sample EAN bar code follows.

You can easily create your own EAN bar code via a simple software program. If you do not have access to the software, consider purchasing your EAN bar code online. Obtain a comprehensive list of EAN bar code suppliers via www.isbn.org/standards/home/isbn/us/barcode.asp. For a fee of approximately $20–$25, your bar code will be electronically transferred to your e-mail address—sometimes in less than five minutes! (Refer to Appendix D for a listing of EAN bar code suppliers.)

Designating Your Copyright Date

A new release—commonly designated by the copyright year on the copyright page—receives the greatest attention from book buyers, media, and reviewers. Larger publishers use the terms, "front list," for new titles released in the spring/fall, and "back list," for previously introduced titles that continue to be promoted in their line-up.

Take advantage of "new title" promotional status! If introducing your children's book in January through August of the current calendar year, establish the current calendar year as your copyright date. If your children's book is not time-sensitive in nature, a January release enables you to benefit from a full twelve months of new title promotional status. If introducing your children's book in October through December of the current calendar year, establish your copyright date as the forthcoming calendar year—to effectively leverage new title promotional status.

THE SCOOP!

Publishers typically release double the quantity of titles in the fall than in the spring to gear up for the winter holidays. Forty to fifty percent of total bookstore sales occur during the month of December!

To Officially Copyright ... Or Not

Your published children's book is legally copyright-protected by its sheer existence—and protected under U.S. law (Title 17, U. S. Code). It is unnecessary to officially copyright your work with the government. Upon a book's completion, government form TX is a formality adhered to by the majority of publishers (self-publishers and traditional publishers) to establish public record of the copyright claim in protecting against infringement. For statutory damages and attorney's fees in the case of court action, it is essential that copyright is registered within three months following the date of publication. Formal copyright registration beyond the three month period will result in court awarded damages (actual) and profits only. Talk to your attorney about the legal benefits/drawbacks of copyrighting your children's picture book under your personal name versus your business entity.

THE SCOOP!

Copyright law dictates that book titles cannot be copyright protected. The same title may be used by multiple publishers—with the stipulation that there is no intent to manipulate buyers into believing that a like-title book is the product of another publisher.

Submitting Your Copyright Form

For further details regarding copyright, visit the Web site of the copyright office at www.copyright.gov/register/literary.html. Send a completed downloaded form along with a copy of your picture book to:

Library of Congress, Copyright Office
101 Independent Avenue S.E.
Washington D.C. 20559-6000

If you have additional questions, call 202-707-3000 to speak with a U.S. Copyright Office representative.

Prototype Protocol

Your graphic designer will provide you with a full color sample prototype of your completed children's picture book from his/her desktop printer. Compare your full color sample prototype to your original mock-up. Your exciting picture book project is likely to have evolved considerably since its inception. Verify that your designated title page, copyright page, text/illustration pages, and any additional pages are in proper order. Make all necessary changes—prior to the actual printing of your title. Hopefully, at least one round of reasonable changes is included in your graphic designer's fee structure. Otherwise, your anxiety is likely to grow with mounting change fees!

Wrapping It Up

Invite at least three trusted individuals (paid or unpaid) to review your full color sample prototype for any mistakes, glitches, and/or typos. Consider all serious comments and/or recommendations. Note that substantial changes beyond this point may significantly impact production costs and the ultimate completion date of your children's picture book. Wrapping up the layout and design phase of your picture book can be difficult—especially if you are a perfectionist. At the risk of alienating an increasingly impatient graphic designer—who is likely to be up to his or her eyeballs in other projects—you must approve your final design concept and make subsequent payment in a timely fashion.

Your book manufacturer requires the following to proceed with production:

* Portable document format (PDF) files with "for position only" low resolution illustrations

* Separate high resolution scans of original illustrations (300 DPI)

* Sample composite of your finalized children's picture book (utilizing a standard desktop printer)

Request a copy of your picture book files—both editable and print-ready versions—as well as your high resolution illustration scans for back-up purposes.

The Scoop!

Your graphic designer will be eager to have an autographed copy of your children's picture book—"hot off the press." What an effective tool for demonstrating his/her graphic designing expertise to future clients!

CHAPTER 4

The Birth of a Children's Picture Book

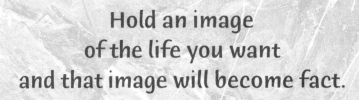

Hold an image
of the life you want
and that image will become fact.

-Author Unknown

Decisions ... Decisions

Because of limitations inherent in expensive printing machinery, book manufacturers cannot afford to be everything to everyone—and specialize in one or more areas of printing, such as digital, web, or sheet-fed. Your selected printing method depends on your desired picture book quantity, materials utilized (paper, ink, special effects, etc.), and trim size. SPAN, in conjunction with publisherssurveys.com, has created a Web site that enables publishers to openly evaluate printing companies and services. Visit www.BookPrinterRankings.com to participate in this free service. In addition to your own research, your experienced graphic designer is likely to offer book manufacturing recommendations.

Solidifying Your Book "Specs"

Per your requests, book manufacturers will evaluate the specifications of your picture book—and bid to win your business. Book specifications—commonly referred to as "specs"—characterize the details of your finished picture book as follows:

* Trim size

* Ink

* Page count

* Interior paper type and weight

* End sheets

* Binding type

* Exterior cover specifications

* Proof type

* Lamination/UV coating/varnish

* Special effects

* Shrink wrap

> **THE SCOOP!**
>
> In a hardcover book, trim size refers to the dimensions of interior pages—not the exterior hardcover case.

Picking Your Paper

Prices greatly fluctuate in book manufacturing from company to company—sometimes from week to week—often depending on the cost of paper. Paper accounts for approximately 40% of the costs of manufacturing a full color children's picture book. Like butter, paper is a commodity that is sold by the pound. As paper weight increases, cost increases.

> **THE SCOOP!**
>
> In the United States, text paper poundage is based on the weight of five hundred sheets measuring a "basis" size of 25" x 38". Five hundred 25" x 38" sheets of 70# text paper weigh 70 pounds whereas five hundred 25" x 38" sheets of more expensive 80# text paper weigh 80 pounds. Self-supporting cover stock—such as the stock on "perfect bound" softcover books—is based on the weight of 500 sheets measuring a basis size of 20" x 26". Five hundred 20" x 26" sheets of 70# cover stock paper weigh 70 pounds whereas five hundred 20" x 26" sheets of more expensive 80# cover stock paper weigh 80 pounds.

In addition to weight, paper pricing is impacted by the following:

* Color

* Brightness

* Opacity

* Type of finish

* Composition

Because of manufacturing differences, paper weight does not always correlate with the number of pages per inch (PPI)—the determining factor of picture book thickness. For a quality picture book, paper must be opaque enough to minimize see-through on the reverse side. Glossy paper is not recommended due to the glare factor; the higher the gloss, the greater the reflective sheen. For a comprehensive overview of paper options, review the *Buyer's Paper Encyclopedia*.

The Scoop!

Veer away from expensive paper selections—or your book manufacturing costs will skyrocket unnecessarily! Make a point to request estimates for "house" paper when comparing pricing from book manufacturers. House paper is typically 70# or 80# matte coated stock that is purchased in bulk—a practical way to reduce printing costs without compromising quality.

Going Green

To save trees and reduce greenhouse gases, many printers are currently phasing out of papers that contain fibers from endangered forests—and substituting cost-effective recycled paper. Though recycled paper is more expensive to purchase than virgin paper, it actually requires 60% less energy to produce.

According to an article in the PMA *Independent* newsletter, entitled "The Pluses of Printing on Recycled Paper," by Rudy Shur, "A first-time publishing effort might use about a ton of paper. Switching that much to post consumer recycled would save 24 mature trees, the equivalent of the total energy used for one home in a year, and of greenhouse gases from one car driven for a year. ...If printers think they can get more business by using recycled sheets, then we all win."

If you are interested in printing on recycled paper, it is wise to obtain quotes from Canadian book manufacturers. The Canadian government subsidizes Canadian book manufacturing companies that utilize recycled paper. As a result, printing on recycled paper is more competitively priced in Canada than in the U.S.

Minding Your Binding

Selecting the cover and binding type for your prized picture book is an incredibly exciting experience! Your options include:

* Hardcover (Case)—choice of side, Smythe, or thread sewn reinforcements

* Softcover—choice of perfect bound, saddle stitch, spiral, or Wire-O

Visit the Bang Printing Web site, www.bangprinting.com, for a visual presentation of binding types; click "Capabilities," then "Binding."

■ ■

The Scoop!

Picture book publishers often produce both a hardcover and softcover version of the same book. When this occurs, two different ISBNs are required—one for each version.

■ ■

Hardcover Picture Books: Hard to Resist!

With protective hard case, display spine, and optional dust jacket, hardcover picture books are highly valued by bookstores, libraries, and schools alike. Though hardcover picture books are expensive to purchase, they are aesthetically appealing and durable.

"End sheets" hold the front and back sections of the hardcover case firmly in place—and may be printed as an option. In self-ended hardcover picture books, end sheets are included in the signature page count—making use of the same paper stock. When end sheets are not included in the signature page count, heavier end sheet stock is typically selected.

Both adhesive and sewn reinforcements are required in the hardcover picture book binding process. Adhesive alone is NOT adequate. Types of hardcover sewn reinforcements include side sewn, Smythe sewn, and thread sewn (thread seal) as follows.

Hardcover Sewn Reinforcements:

Side Sewn: All signatures are sewn together approximately 3/8″ from the spine prior to being glued into the cover for maximum durability (a consideration when planning illustration spreads). Though side sewn picture books do not open as flatly as Smythe or thread sewn versions, librarians prefer this option to withstand heavy borrower usage.

Smythe Sewn: Each printed signature is sewn down the center; individual signatures are then sewn together at the folds prior to being glued into the cover.

Thread Sewn (Thread Seal): Each printed signature is sewn down the center with heat-sealed, plastic-coated thread—but signatures are not sewn together prior to being glued into the cover. Thread sewing—both the least durable … and least expensive option—may suffice for a 32-page picture book comprised of only two signatures.

Evaluate your needs when considering sewn reinforcement options. If your picture book is being used primarily by friends and family, thread sewn reinforcements may be adequate. Likewise, if you are self-publishing your picture book for heavier commercial usage, I recommend that you select side or Smythe sewn reinforcements. It's always better to be safe than sorry! Book buyers will be less apt to purchase your inventory in the future if pages loosen from the spine.

THE SCOOP!

Not all book manufacturers are capable of side, Smythe, and thread sewn options. Because of variations in binding equipment, pricing for hardcover sewn reinforcements can range significantly. Do comparison shopping!

Softcover Picture Books: The Price Is Right!

Softcover picture books are less expensive to produce than hardcover (case bound) picture books. Because of the lower price point, they are in high demand at bookstores and other commercial outlets, such as K-Mart and Walmart. Softcover picture book binding methods include perfect bound, saddle stitch, spiral, and Wire-O as follows.

Softcover Binding Methods

Perfect Bound: Pages are stacked and bound to the cover with a durable adhesive—creating a prized flat spine to feature the title, name of author/illustrator, and publisher logo.

Saddle Stitch: Pages are laid over a piece of metal that resembles a horse's saddle, and fastened at the fold via staple-like metal stitches.

Spiral: A spiral-like wire—sometimes covered in colored plastic—is inserted through tiny holes across the binding edge.

Wire-O: A double series of wire loops—usually plastic coated—are threaded through punched slots across the binding edge.

Perfect bound picture books (like hardcover picture books) are favorites among bookstores, libraries, and schools—as a result of the value-added display spine. Lower cost saddle stitch picture books are typically sold in mass through discount stores, supermarkets, and drugstores (typical retail price: $2.95) … and peddled by book vendors on bustling city street corners.

The Scoop!

Spiral and Wire-O binding methods are less frequently used than perfect and saddle stitch binding methods in commercial picture book publishing.

Selecting Your Print Run

Do extensive soul searching prior to determining the initial print run that works best for you—and your current lifestyle! Your personal/financial commitment is likely to increase with the quantity of picture books that you elect to self-publish.

Understand that fixed costs associated with producing your children's picture book—including illustration and graphic design charges—are identical whether you're printing 1 copy, 1,000 copies, or 7,500 copies. For example, if you pay a fee of $3,000 for original illustrations and $1,000 for graphic design, these fixed costs amount to $4,000—regardless of the quantity of books printed.

* If you digitally print 25 copies, your fixed costs per book are: $4,000/25 = $160 plus printing costs.

* If you print 5,000 books in Hong Kong, your fixed costs per book are: $4,000/5000 = $0.80 plus printing costs.

THE SCOOP!

Your cost per book actually decreases as the quantity of books printed increases. Rule of Thumb: The higher the print run ... the lower the unit cost ... the greater your total financial expenditure.

More ... or Less than Enough

It is difficult to estimate printing variables, such as spoilage, during the book manufacturing process. You will be billed the difference for overruns, or credited the difference for underruns—up to a 10% margin. This percentage typically appears adjacent to the proposed quantity on each book manufacturing bid. If you require a minimum quantity due to a guaranteed sale (lucky you!), then your calculated overrun percentage will double to potentially 20% of your overall print run.

Printing on Demand ... with Purpose

If your intended book trim size is 8 1/2" x 11" or smaller—and your objective is to proceed cautiously—consider full color print on demand (POD). This digital print technology enables you to self-publish as little as one copy of your title at a time—in saddle stitch, perfect bound, and casewrap/dust jacket versions. Though high unit costs and lack of significant quantity discounts are associated with POD technology, the nominal financial investment required to publish small quantities of your title is extremely advantageous.

The Scoop!

POD printers are **NOT** the same as POD publishing service providers. Unlike POD publishing service providers—such as Xlibris, AuthorHouse, and Trafford—POD printers claim no ownership of your self-published title.

POD requires a 24-page minimum, usually with no signature constraints. Consider designing your POD picture book as an industry standard 32-page format—for easy transitioning to traditional print methods ... as the need arises.

Full color POD books are currently printed at a lower DPI than the 1,200–2,560 DPI of most traditional presses. As print quality improves and unit costs decrease, POD will more effectively compete with traditional printing for volume print runs.

If you are interested in controlling your publishing process in its entirety—from layout and design to sales, marketing, and distribution—POD printers can offer you the following advantages:

* You own the ISBN (International Standard Book Number) and LCCN (Library of Congress Control Number).

* The name of your publishing company—not the publishing service provider— appears on the copyright page and cover of your picture book.

* All rights belong to you.

Digital printing offers fast turnaround time, and is widely used to:

* Self-publish limited copies for personal use

* Revise picture book text/illustrations

* Establish the existence of a larger market

* Predict future sales activities

* Acquire testimonials

* Stimulate the interest of a traditional publisher

* Keep a title in print indefinitely

Previewing Full Color POD Printers

The full color POD printing process is relatively easy to execute:

1. Your graphic designer forwards a portable document format (PDF) of your children's picture book to the digital printer.

2. A full color digital proof of your children's picture book arrives at your door—often within five days. Make all necessary changes/corrections. (Change/correction fees as well as new proof output are billed to your account.)

3. Return your signed and approved proof to the digital printer.

4. Your digitally-printed children's picture books are shipped to your door within 3-6 weeks.

POD picture book capabilities vary from printer to printer. Be certain to request full color POD samples from at least three printers prior to making your decision.

Is a Full Color POD Picture Book Expensive to Produce?

Publishers' Graphics (www.pubgraphics.com) manufactures an $8^{1/2}''$ x 11", 32-page, full color POD picture book in both a hardcover and softcover option:

Hardcover (Casewrap)

* $14.50 ea./25 copies

* $10.77 ea./50 copies

* $9.68 ea./75 copies

* $9.28 ea./100 copies

Perfect Bound Softcover (12 pt. C1S Smooth)

* $7.02 ea./25 copies

* $5.38 ea./50 copies

* $5.08 ea./75 copies

* $4.85 ea./100 copies

RJ Communications (www.selfpublishing.com) offers an 8" x 8", 24-page, full color POD saddle stitch picture book as follows:

* $6 ea./100 copies

* $2.75 ea./1,000 copies

* $1 ea./5,000 copies

* $0.65 ea./10,000 copies

    (A 24-page format—not the standard 32-page format—is required.)

Traditional Volume Printing

Economy of scale web and sheet-fed presses specialize in large print runs with steep volume discounts; the higher the print run, the lower the unit cost. Web presses are fast and efficient—printing at 25,000 impressions per hour. Sheet-fed presses are slightly slower than web presses—printing at 5,000 impressions per hour. Both types of presses print at 1,200–2,560+ DPI (dots per inch). Historically, sheet-fed presses were known for producing higher quality children's picture books than web presses, but this is no longer the case.

Web versus Sheet-Fed Presses

Web press: utilizes large rolls of coated or uncoated paper for print runs of 5,000–10,000+, standard trim sizes, and certain binding specifications.

Sheet-fed press: utilizes flat sheets of coated or uncoated paper for print runs of 1,000+, non-standard or standard trim sizes, and certain binding specifications.

As a result of rapid technological changes, picture book manufacturers use a varied array of web and sheet-fed presses. Printing constraints are contingent upon individual press capabilities. Whereas one web press may print 10,000+ copies, another web press may print only 5,000+ copies.

The Scoop!

A full color picture book is printed on a traditional four-color printing press, utilizing CMYK colors: Cyan, Magenta, Yellow, and Black. During the printing process, each of the four CMYK colors is overlaid on the page—resulting in the illusion of full color.

PDF-file based direct-to-plate printing/proofing is the primary method utilized in the U.S. today. Overseas printers are likely to offer both film-based and direct-to-plate printing/proofing options. Direct-to-plate printing is generally more cost effective than film-based printing. Whereas book reprints are less expensive than initial print runs in film-based printing, first and subsequent print runs are comparably priced in direct-to-plate printing.

Investing in Yourself

With money available to invest in yourself … and your dreams, consider printing quantities of 1,000+ picture books. Traditional volume printing is the appropriate choice under any of the following circumstances:

* You are printing a larger than 8 1/2″ x 11″ children's picture book.

* You already have a large quantity of pre-sold books.

* You tend to be a bit of a risk-taker with sufficient investment money to spend.

* You are transitioning to higher print quantities from your successful digital version.

Self-publishing on a grand scale is indeed a rewarding, challenging, and exciting experience; however, it is not for the faint of heart. Know thyself, thy interests, thy passion, and thy customers—*before* you commit to printing excessive quantities of your children's picture book. As your print run increases, the more time and effort you are likely to spend selling books— not writing books—in order to recoup your costly up-front publishing investment.

The Scoop!

A wise, conservative measure is to produce 1,000 to 3,000 copies of your title for starters—depending on your perceived risk factor—and reprint as your need arises.

Major publishers print massive quantities of low cost, softcover titles—typically 50,000–100,000 copies—and can afford to charge a retail price as low as $1.95 per copy. Unless you have a non-price sensitive, niche, softcover picture book, it is difficult for you to compete in this market.

It is important to note that even major publishers print a relatively small quantity of expensive-to-produce hardcover children's picture books—as low as 5,000–10,000 copies per title. Because operational costs are significantly lower for self-publishers than for major publishing houses, self-publishers can more readily compete on hardcover price, especially when printing 1,000+ copies.

Persistence, Determination ... & Deep Pockets

Larger quantity print runs require deep pockets to attract fickle consumer attention. Creating and sustaining sales volume—with or without the assistance of hired experts—can be daunting! If your objective is to print 1,000 or more children's picture books, it is essential to build a comprehensive marketing strategy to promote sales of your title. Every publishing-oriented task, no matter how simple, is likely to take longer than expected. (In heeding the advice of an old friend, multiply your expected task time by four to predict a more realistic completion date. It really works!)

Know that it is your passionate enthusiasm that separates you from the other publishers. According to Carl Sams II, famed self-published co-author of *Stranger in the Woods*, shameless self-promotion is critical to the success of your self-publishing career. This wise guerilla marketer turns a simple task—such as paying a utility bill—into a powerful promotional campaign. He encloses a *Stranger in the Woods* flyer/order form in the payment return envelope! Carl Sams II acknowledges that even the lowest paid clerk is a potential customer for his prized children's book. Your ability to communicate sheer enthusiasm for your picture book at every turn is the key to multiplying sales.

The Scoop!

Use your wits, not your wallet, to fulfill your role as a shameless self promoter! Acquaintances, colleagues, teachers, doctors, attorneys, dentists, store clerks, mail carriers—and all other service providers in your path—are your potential customers.

Predicting Demand

Proceed cautiously prior to committing to aggressive reprints. A first-time children's picture book self-publisher excitedly sold her entire print run of 2,500 copies to a major chain—and immediately reprinted 25,000 additional copies to optimize book manufacturing costs. Within several months, copies from the first print run were returned by the chain—an all-too-common occurrence in the publishing industry. The astonished author/self-publisher was left with a portion of books from the first print run … as well as the entire second print run!

The over-abundance of books in the marketplace causes the #1 downside of traditional publishing: returns … returns … returns! Traditional print runs are usually based on projected demand versus actual demand. According to Kent Sturgis, past PMA President, as stated in the March 2006 PMA *Independent* newsletter, "Too many of us have our precious cash tied up in the form of books gathering dust in the garage, or in a distributor's warehouse. ...Optimism will motivate you but does not necessarily translate into sales."

The magnitude of paper utilized by the book returns driven publishing industry is truly staggering! According to Environmental Defense estimations (2004), book publishing required the consumption of as many as sixty million trees over a three year period.

Book Production ... All in the Details

Of the approximately forty traditional U.S. book manufacturers, only a handful are capable of printing and binding full color 32-page children's picture books. Book manufacturing costs include labor and material. The majority of U.S. book manufacturers specialize in printing one color interiors on uncoated stock—with full color covers—due to the following:

* Less production labor is required.

* Uncoated paper is abundantly manufactured in North America.

Labor rates are significantly lower in many other countries—including China, Mexico, and Switzerland. In some instances, children's picture book publishers may save up to 30% by manufacturing large quantity print runs overseas, despite the hefty shipping costs. Overseas book manufacturers are typically represented by U.S.-based, English-speaking brokers who personalize the publishing-at-a-distance process. Realize that if you choose to print overseas and would like to be on press, there is the added expense of hotel and airfare—as well as travel time considerations.

Choosing Your Book Manufacturer/Broker Wisely

Obtain at least six book estimates—known as Requests for Quotation (RFQ)—from your targeted list of picture book manufacturers/brokers. (Refer to Appendix D for a listing of U.S./overseas children's picture book manufacturers/brokers.) Book estimate guidelines are designated by the National Association of Printers and Lithographers and the Printing Industries of America. Following is a sample hardcover picture book quotation from a print broker, RJ Communications:

R J
COMMUNICATIONS L.L.C.
The Print Buyers' Alternative

51 East 42nd Street, Suite 1202
New York, NY 10017
Tel 800-621-2556
Fax 212-681-8002
http://www.booksjustbooks.com

ID:	201823
Title:	The Bouncing Book
Trim Size:	8 X 8
Number of Pages:	32
Prep:	Customer to furnish separate PDF files for text, casewrap and jacket (if applicable). Digital proofs sent by printer for approval.
Paper:	**Text:** 80# matte **Dust Jacket or Casewrap:** 80# C1S Litho
Ink:	**Text:** Four color process **Dust Jacket or Casewrap:** 4-color process 1 side plus gloss film lamination
Bind as:	Thread sewn hardcover with jacket. 110 pt (3 mm) boards wrapped with printed casewrap. Endpapers are printed 1 color 1 side on 80# uncoated offset stock.
Packing:	Bulk Cartons
Shipping:	FOB Factory (No freight included in price)
Schedule:	To be agreed (generally 4 weeks from an OK'd proof)
Quantity:	5000 (+/-5%)
Price:	$2.35 ea.

When filling out on-line book estimates, specifications that you do not actually select may sometimes appear. In the example above, thread sewn binding had been automatically inserted into the "bind as" space by the print broker; however, thread sewn binding may or may not be the best option for you. Always feel free to request another option, if necessary. Verify that you are receiving pricing for specifications that best suits the needs of your particular project.

Do not be misled by low-ball estimates that result from disparities in your book specifications. Remain constant when obtaining book manufacturing estimates. Request identical book quantities, page count, paper type/weight, color usage, trim size, binding type, shipping costs, etc. Do your homework, and compare pricing. Take your time. Do ample research. Always compare "apples to apples" options.

The Scoop!

Visit www.selfpublishing.com, RJ Communications' Web site, for useful self-publishing information and a copy of *Publishing Basics for Children's Books*. The complimentary guide—a clever company promotional tool—is formatted as a hardcover picture book with samples of coated gloss and matte stock.

Show Me the Proof

The book manufacturer that you ultimately select will utilize 300 DPI scans of your illustrations to create a full color proof of your picture book. This is your final chance to tweak color prior to the printing process. If major alterations to color, saturation, and/or tone are required, your graphic designer must prepare new files for the printer—and patiently await a new set of digital proofs. Even minor changes to color at this phase may prove to be quite costly.

Proofing paper is typically glossier and brighter than other types of paper. With direct-to-plate printing technology, your digital proofs may appear somewhat richer and/or darker in color than the printed pages of your book. Full color proofs should be calibrated to the printing press for optimal results.

Prior to printing your children's picture book, the book manufacturer will send you a final one-tone special process proof, called "line proof" or "blue line." This proof provides you with the final opportunity to make necessary changes to text or placement. Examine your line proof extremely carefully. It is wise for you to garner a few extra pairs of objective eyes. It will behoove you—and your pocket—to keep changes to a minimum!

THE SCOOP!

Your graphic designer is pivotal during the proofing process. Be certain to utilize his/her expertise. The professionalism of your children's picture book is at stake!

Being on Press: An Exhilarating Experience

I highly recommend that you experience the birth of your self-published children's book firsthand. During production of my first hardcover children's book, *Celebrate Hanukkah with Me*, I worked closely with Worzalla—an employee-owned book manufacturing facility located in Stevens Point, Wisconsin. The patient guidance demonstrated by Worzalla staff, during the printing process, has given me a fascinating glimpse into the world of picture book manufacturing. Being on press enables you to tweak color and tone saturation while your picture book is actually printing. Otherwise, subjective coloration is left strictly to the eye of the print technician. If at all possible, don't miss being on press to observe the printing of your children's book in vibrant, living color. The experience is exhilarating—and certain to be one of the highlights of your self-publishing career!

A, B, Cs ... F & Gs

Once your approved cover and signatures are printed, you can request samples of the actual printed pages of your children's book in the form of unbound "folded and gathered" signatures, known as "F & Gs." If you are dissatisfied with the printed color for any reason, you may make changes at your own expense. Though quite costly, it is considerably less expensive to reprint a signature at this stage rather than starting over once books are bound. I initially published 5,000 copies of *The Zebra-Striped Whale with the Polka-Dot Tail* in 2001. When the book quickly sold out, I ordered a second print run of 7,500 books incorporating some minor changes to three interior pages. With the arrival of F & Gs at our doorstep, my husband noticed that the copyright page was lacking the required "second printing" designation. I had totally missed this deletion at the earlier blue line phase! As a result, I was forced to have a new copyright page with appropriate dates quickly prepared by my graphic designer ... who in turn forwarded the new file to the printer ... who in turn created a new line proof for my signed approval. This little oversight cost me $1,300 plus additional graphic designer fees—not to mention the time delay in distributing my book to the marketplace!

The Scoop!

An objective set of eyes is always helpful! Sometimes we become so immersed in our own projects ... that it becomes difficult to see the forest through the trees.

Remembering the Extras

Always remember the extras when producing your children's picture book. I recommend that you order at least a dozen approved F & Gs from your printer to be used as "pre-pub" submission samples for journal review purposes. If your children's picture book is a hardcover with dust jacket, purchase approximately 20% extra dust jackets to be used as replacements for damaged dust jackets resulting from the returns process. Simply replace the old dust jacket— and your hardcover children's picture book is as good as new! If your children's picture book is bound with a quality varnished softcover, consider the purchase of extra covers for use as promotional folders.

Some publishers request shrink-wrap for their children's picture books—in bundles of five to twenty-five. Shrink-wrap helps to maintain a dry, dust-free environment, and prevents covers from scratching against the interior of the carton. Discuss shrink-wrap options with your children's picture book manufacturer.

The Scoop!

Book manufacturers sometimes recommend single copy shrink-wrap to prevent full color, heavily glossed dust jackets/ covers from scuffing. Single copy shrink-wrap may actually result in decreased sales because it deters potential customers from further examining the book. When is the last time you turned the pages of a shrink-wrapped book at a bookstore?

Picking a Publication Date

With your book manufacturing specifications resolved, select a publication date—month and year—for your children's picture book. Your title's publication date should fall within your title's copyright year, determining when your book will be introduced to the marketplace. A title generally receives its greatest fanfare within the three months before and after its scheduled publication date. Because you are the publisher of your title, the publication date is left completely to your discretion—and may, or may not, correspond to your print run completion date.

The Scoop!

Postpone your picture book publication date by at least four months from your print run completion date—leaving ample time to garner pre-pub reviews and establish viable sales channels.

Time-Sensitive Children's Picture Books

If your children's picture book is seasonal or "holiday" in scope (Christmas, Hanukkah, Kwanzaa, Easter, Passover, Mother's Day, Father's Day, etc.), the calendar date of the specified season/holiday will guide your publication date/market introduction. The general rule of thumb is that you introduce your time-sensitive title to bookstore buyers 6–9 months prior to the upcoming holiday/season.

Welcoming Your New Arrival

The day has finally arrived—and the glorious truckload of children's picture books appears before you! Boxes upon boxes of your creation fill you with awe. What now? Believe it or not—your garage (if you have one!) is the best place to store your prized inventory. Heavy books are a nightmare to haul up and down steps—to and from the basement. Most garages, even without climate controls, offer adequate storage capability and driveway access for easy loading/unloading of books. Carefully stack the unopened cartons on wooden pallets in your garage—leaving room between the floor and your books, and between the wall and your books—to maximize air circulation. The pages of your books will remain flat if your inventory is stored safely in their tightly sealed cartons. Guard against dampness and sunlight. High humidity curls corners and ripples pages. Sunlight fades color. If you do not have ample space at home, consider renting a low cost storage facility nearby.

THE SCOOP!

Plan accordingly! Books can be drop-shipped from your book manufacturer directly to a storage facility, wholesaler, or distributor—to avoid unnecessary re-shipping charges from your home.

Picking, Packing & Pampering

The process of fulfilling book orders is comprised of:

* Inventory storage/maintenance

* Picking

* Packing

* Shipping

* Invoicing

If you are shipping product from your garage or some other storage facility, place a long work table, as well as all supplies—cartons, sealing tape, padded envelopes, staplers, razor knife, rubberized postal stamps, plastic book enclosure bags, scales, heat sealers, and stuffing materials—within easy reach. Book orders, generated by mail/phone/fax/e-mail, are fulfilled via your own "in-house" staff (in other words … you!) or optional distribution intermediary. Ship whole unopened boxes whenever possible. To fulfill smaller orders or the remainder of larger orders, remove specified quantity of books from the original storage carton—depleting one carton at a time. Pack books carefully for shipment in padded bags or cartons, using a plastic bag enclosure to protect against cover scratches, as necessary.

Adventures in Shipping

Visit www.usps.gov for a listing of domestic and international United States Postal Service rates including expedited, first class, and media mail (book) rates. For small package delivery up to 250 pounds, FedEx, UPS, and Airborne Express offer an array of express services, regular parcel air, ground, and multi-weight shipping to businesses and residences. The SPAN and PMA-affiliated freight program, Partnership (www.partnership.com), provides substantial discounts on small package shipments without required minimums or obligation. When in a pinch, consider utilizing the packing/shipping services of a convenient—but costly—neighborhood mail-house, such as Mail Boxes, Etc. For freight shipments over 250 pounds that comprise one large box, or multiple stacked boxes shrink-wrapped on pallets, consider utilizing the services of freight companies including Yellow, Overnite, R & L, and Roadway. Consolidate your "Less Than Truckload" (LTL) shipments whenever possible to yield a savings of up to 35%. Beware of add-on carrier fees charged to your invoice including:

* Residential/inside pick-up or delivery

* Fuel surcharges (up to 15% of net transportation charge)

* Liftgate delivery

* Declared insurance

* Express pick-up

* Single shipments

* Pre-delivery notification

* Address correction

* Weight

* Inspection

Research your freight options carefully. (Refer to Appendix D for a listing of shipping companies.)

The Scoop!

When shipping inventory, deplete the contents of one carton of your picture books prior to opening the next. Your children's picture books are best left undisturbed in their tightly sealed cartons!

Remainder Reminder

As books are returned due to overstock or damage, store them in a separate holding area—away from your salable books. As time permits, carefully examine your returned stock. Whenever possible, replace damaged dust jackets with new ones on hardcover books. Return all resalable stock to your fresh book inventory for future shipping.

To cut losses or earn a profit on unsold inventory—including returns, hurts, remainders, and overstocks—it is wise to consider the following options:

* Donate books to a non-profit organization in support of a good cause.

* Sell books to retail "bargain book" buyers or wholesale remainder dealers.

* Sell books to the general public via online channels or special events.

Donation outlets include:

* Literacy programs

* Struggling school libraries

* Churches/synagogues

* Military families

* Prisons

A charitable non-profit arm of PMA, Lifetime Literacy Foundation (LLF, www.lifetimeliteracy.org), accepts tax-deductible donations of books for beneficial literacy projects throughout the U.S.

The Scoop!

Tax deductions on donated books include original book value in addition to storage, handling, and shipping costs.

"Bargain book" sales have grown into a lucrative business! Popular bargain book expos include:

* CIROBE (Chicago International Remainder and Overstock Book Exposition, www.cirobe.com)—in the fall

* BEA (BookExpo America, www.bookexpoamerica.com)—in the spring

* The Spring Book Show (www.springbookshow.com)—in the spring

Exhibit table rentals typically start at just under $1,000. The Spring Book Show rents an 8-foot exhibit table for $945. CIROBE rents a 6-foot exhibit table for $1,175.

The Scoop!

Bookstore remainder buyers tend to purchase unsold publishers' stock for approximately 5% of the retail price—2%-4% higher than the price offered by wholesale remainder dealers. Remainder terms are usually net 30 days, with a no-returns policy and FOB warehouse shipping.

Remainder dealers can be found in the following publications:

* *Literary Market Place*

* *American Book Trade Directory*

* *Publishers Weekly*

(Refer to Appendix D for a listing of remainder dealers.)

Your excess inventory may also be sold online through Amazon.com, Abebooks, and/or your own Web site. PMA provides a remainder listing Web site that includes children's books; the cost is currently $25 per quarter, per title. Book fairs and street fairs can also be lucrative venues for selling off excess inventory. An informative article, entitled "Beyond Remainders," may be accessed through Dan Poynter's Web site at www.parapublishing.com.

Invoice Forms Mean Business

It is common industry practice for traditional and self-publishers to invoice their customers once product has been shipped. Payment terms—typically 30–180 days—vary according to the following customer types:

* Wholesaler

* Retailer

* Library

* School

* Private individuals

A 100% refund guarantee is common industry practice. Be certain to add sales tax to all end-user merchandise purchased within your state. Resellers, such as wholesalers and bookstores, are not subject to sales tax. Shipping fees are not taxable. Depending on the account, you may or may not be responsible for paying the costs of shipping and/or returns. Some whole-salers/distributors offer freight-collect services and require the use of specified carriers i.e. FedEx Ground Collect. It never hurts to ask for shipping cost reimbursement!

According to the Federal Trade Commission (FTC), orders that are accompanied by payment must be processed within thirty days of receipt. Visit www.ftc.gov for transaction guidelines.

Create easy-to-read invoice forms on your computer incorporating the following information:

* Company name and logo

* Address, phone number, e-mail, and Web address

* Purchase order number and date

* Invoice number

* Payment terms

* Title

* ISBN

* List price

* Quantity

* Discount

* Subtotal

* Shipping fees

* Total (including shipping)

A sample invoice form follows.

ARIMAX, INC. Invoice

2865 S. Eagle Rd., PMB #399, Newtown, PA 18940   ph: 215-205-2227   fax: 215-862-7005   e-mail: sharidonahue@justselfpublish.com

INVOICE #_____   P.O. #_____   P.O. Date_____

PAYMENT TERMS_____

Arimax, Inc. Book Title	ISBN	Price	Quantity	Discount	Sub-Total
The Zebra-Striped Whale with the Polka-Dot Tail	0-9634287-3-X	$18.00			$
Celebrate Hanukkah with Me	0-9634287-2-1	$12.95			$
My Favorite Family Haggadah	0-9634287-1-3	$5.95			$
Children's Picture Books: How to Self-Publish Your Way to Success!	978-0-9634287-5-2	$19.95			$
SUBTOTAL					$

BILL TO:

Company:	
Address:	
City, State:	
Zip Code:	
Attention:	

SHIP TO:

Company:	
Address:	
City, State:	
Zip Code:	
Attention:	

SHIPPING: $_____

TOTAL DUE: $_____

www.arimaxbooks.com

The Power of Three

Make three copies of each invoice form, and use as follows:

* ✻ Copy #1 for a shipping label/packing slip

* ✻ Copy #2 for an invoice

* ✻ Copy #3 for your records

Upon receipt of your purchase order, immediately ship requested quantity as directed to the "Ship To" address. Slip the first copy of your invoice form—folded in thirds—into a 4.5" x 8.5" clear packing list envelope (available at office supply stores). Adhere to package, with "Ship To" address exposed, for use as a combination shipping label/packing slip. If you prefer, use a non-gloss generic or customized shipping label. (Ink smears on glossy labels.) Customized labels may be purchased from label manufacturers such as Discount Labels at www.discountlabel.com. Always mark the purchase order number on each carton of books shipped. Once product has been shipped, mail the second copy of your invoice form to the "Bill To" address on the purchase order form. (Some customers accept faxed copies.) Date-stamp the third copy of your invoice form upon receipt of payment, transfer to a binder or file cabinet for storage, and update your computer file, if applicable. Follow up, follow up, follow up—if payment is not remitted as expected!

CHAPTER
5

Distribution Sales
Channels

Nothing will take
the place of persistence.
Talent will not;
nothing is more common than the
unsuccessful person with talent.
Genius will not;
unrewarded genius is almost a proverb.
Education will not;
the world is full of educated derelicts.
Persistence and determination
alone are omnipotent.

–Calvin Coolidge

Leveling the Playing Field

Like any traditional publishing house, you have the power to "even" the playing field by becoming affiliated with one or both of these national wholesaler giants:

* Baker & Taylor

* Ingram Book Company

Market accessibility of your children's picture book, through Baker & Taylor and/or Ingram Book Company, is your major springboard into the publishing industry. Major wholesalers operate on a non-exclusive basis—and account for the most significant dollar flow into publishing houses.

Wholesalers are utilized to:

* Fulfill book orders

* Consolidate publisher-related order processing and returns procedures

Both Baker & Taylor and Ingram Book Company own multiple warehouses throughout the U.S., and offer easy product accessibility—usually within 1–2 days. Their customers include:

* Independent bookstores

* Mass retailers

* Gift stores

* Children's museums

* Book fairs

* Public libraries

* School libraries

* Specialty stores

The wholesaler process behaves like a consignment business—and the publisher is forced to bear the risk. Unlike any other industry, the publishing industry mandates a full returns privilege for a period of six months … from the time a title goes out of print.

Wanted: A Wholesaler ... Or Two

Become affiliated with at least one wholesaler if you are planning to extend the reach of your children's picture book beyond:

* Personal use

* Local bookstore consignment

* Direct sales to a specified niche market

Your decision to work with more than one wholesaler is solely based on your preference as a small publisher. Most retailers, libraries, schools, review journals, and award committees request wholesaler affiliation prior to serious title consideration.

A wholesaler—known as the publisher's "vendor of record"—behaves as a passive, demand-driven fulfillment entity—and typically earns 15% of the retail price per quantity of books sold. Until consistent title demand is established—and your picture book is "stocked" by the wholesaler—the ordering process for self-publishers is likely to operate as follows:

1. The national wholesaler receives demand for a specified title quantity.

2. The national wholesaler submits a purchase order to the self-publisher, if a direct relationship exists.

3. The self-publisher ships the ordered quantity to the national wholesaler; the national wholesaler in turn ships the product to the account's "Ship To" address.

4. The self-publisher invoices the national wholesaler.

5. The national wholesaler pays the self-publisher a contracted percentage of the title's retail price within 90–180 days of being invoiced.

6. The wholesaler ships all book "returns" back to the self-publisher. If the wholesaler has not yet paid the self-publisher's invoice, a credit is taken against the quantity of books returned. If the self-publisher has already been paid for the returned books, the wholesaler may establish a credit against future purchases—or invoice the self-publisher for books returned. The self-publisher is ultimately responsible for paying the sum back to the national wholesaler, within a specified time frame.

Betting on Baker & Taylor

Baker & Taylor—second in size to Ingram Book Company—ships more than one million titles with unique ISBNs to:

* Domestic and international retail stores

* Public and academic libraries

* Educational institutions

Request a "Vendor Profile" form by accessing www.btol.com, or by calling the Baker & Taylor buying department at 908-541-7425. Sign your publishing company up to either the "Standard" or "Partner Package":

* The Standard Package lists your picture book title on the Baker & Taylor database for a fee of $75. Baker & Taylor will purchase your children's picture book to fullfill customer backorders, but will not stock your book—unless consistent demand is established.

* The Partner Package offers the following for a fee of $295 (less $50 as a SPAN or PMA member):

    1. Advertising in Baker & Taylor's print catalog—entitled *Books and More for Growing Minds*

    2. Guaranteed stocking of at least twelve copies of your title in each of Baker & Taylor's four service centers

    3. Access to Baker & Taylor's online database for inventory and demand information

Within a week of submitting the proper forms, your publishing company will be officially affiliated with Baker & Taylor. You will receive a confirmation letter indicating that your account has been established. Baker & Taylor does not require an exclusive relationship with your publishing company. Typical terms are as follows:

* 55% discount

* 100% full returns privilege

* Publisher-paid inbound freight

* 90-day net payment

The following chart depicts a typical Baker & Taylor revenue distribution model.

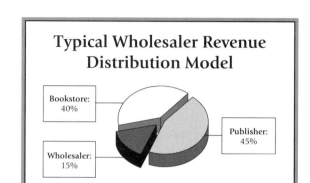

Typical Wholesaler Revenue Distribution Model

Bookstore: 40%

Publisher: 45%

Wholesaler: 15%

Affiliating with Ingram Book Company

Though your affiliation with Baker & Taylor is all that is needed to make your children's picture book accessible to the retail, school, and library markets, you may also consider working with the largest national wholesaler—Ingram Book Company (www.ingrambook.com). Ingram currently carries 1.3 million titles! Whereas Baker & Taylor works directly with publishers of any size, Ingram Book Company requires the small/self-publisher—with less than ten titles—to obtain representation indirectly, though an Ingram-approved distributor. (Visit www.ingrambook.com for a listing of Ingram-approved distributors.) The role of distributors is to consolidate book fulfillment and returns processing. The publisher-supported wholesaler/distributor team works hand-in-hand to "move" books—each earning a percentage of sales as follows.

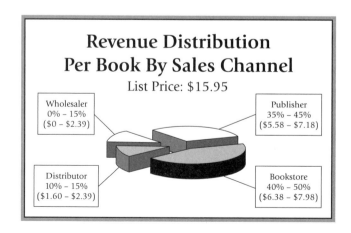

Revenue Distribution Per Book By Sales Channel

List Price: $15.95

Wholesaler
0% – 15%
($0 – $2.39)

Publisher
35% – 45%
($5.58 – $7.18)

Distributor
10% – 15%
($1.60 – $2.39)

Bookstore
40% – 50%
($6.38 – $7.98)

The #1 complaint among self-publishers is book distribution—and Ingram's new model has sent this group scrambling. Ingram's demands for distribution partnerships could significantly reduce self-publishers' profits.

The Scoop!

To facilitate a remedy, the PMA/Ingram Wholesale Acceptance Program permits committee-approved publishers, with less than ten titles, to work directly with Ingram. Acceptance is based on the publisher's ability to sell $20,000 worth of books—at cost, net of returns—over a two-year period. Visit the PMA Web site at www.pma-online.org for program specifications.

Daunting Distribution

Partnering with an Ingram-approved distributor may be worth the added costs—if you can sell more books. It is difficult to make the determination at the onset of your self-publishing endeavor. Hindsight is "twenty-twenty." If you are interested in working indirectly with Ingram Book Company, consider your distribution options carefully. Restrictive legal agreements force publishers to bear the risk of an unsuccessful distributor relationship during the critical book launching phase. If an Ingram-approved distributor cannot generate substantial demand for your picture book, direct partnering with Baker & Taylor is likely to be your most profitable scenario.

Distributor Overview

All Ingram-approved distributors are not created equally! Distributors wear many hats—having their origins in independent publishing, printing, and/or inventory storage/fulfillment. Some Ingram-approved distributors concentrate strictly on basic warehousing/fulfillment services. Examples of these distributors include:

    ✻   Book Clearing House
        www.bookch.com

    ✻   BookMasters, Inc.
        www.bookmasters.com

The following distributors actively market titles via an array of national sales and marketing programs (including telemarketing, Internet/e-mail/snail mail promotional campaigns—and, in some cases, feet-on-the-street sales reps):

    ✻   AtlasBooks (a division of BookMasters, Inc.)—absorbed Biblio Distribution
        www.bookmasters.com

    ✻   Greenleaf Book Group
        www.greenleafbookgroup.com

    ✻   Independent Publishers Group (IPG)
        www.ipgbook.com

    ✻   Midpoint Trade Books Inc.
        www.midpointtrade.com

    ✻   National Book Network (NBN)
        www.nbnbooks.com

    ✻   Perseus Distribution—absorbed Publishers Group West (PGW)
        www.cdsbooks.com

    ✻   SCB Distributors
        www.scbdistributors.com

Perseus Distribution and NBN are now the two largest marketing/distribution companies in North America. The distributor—with connections—is critical in obtaining invaluable shelf space at the mass retail level. The more selective Ingram-approved distributors tout only a 1%–3% publisher acceptance rate, and may require exclusivity from their publisher base. In an exclusive distribution arrangement, all orders must be funneled through the specified distributor for the contracted period—usually a one-year minimum.

IPG is a sales-based distribution company that considers submissions from one-title children's picture book self-publishers. Approximately eleven months preceding your publication date (prior to the book's actual printing), submit a finalized prototype, with cover letter, to IPG. If your title is accepted for distribution, IPG staff will work closely with you on any recommended changes. IPG prefers to distribute niche children's picture books, with a subtle moral, that can be sold in specialty shops … as well as bookstores.

■ ■

THE SCOOP!

Twice per year, Publishers Marketing Association (PMA) convenes a committee of representatives from the major bookstore chains and wholesalers to select completed titles for trade distribution through IPG. Titles of consideration must have been published within the past twelve months by PMA members, and have no previous history of being connected to another exclusive distributor. Publishers of selected titles are offered a distribution agreement by IPG that includes all backlist titles. Publishers of non-selected titles receive a brief explanation for the committee's decision.

■ ■

Small Publishers: Limited Options

The current market supply of children's books far outweighs demand—fueled by an increase of 80.11% in new juvenile titles/editions during 2003. With approximately 50,000 publishers currently in existence, publisher competition for distributors is fierce. Powerful Ingram-approved distributors—with sales representation—can afford to be discriminating in the publisher selection process. Distribution companies, operating as marketing/sales forces in retail, specialty, school, and library markets, collaborate primarily with deep-pocketed, multi-title publishers—leaving limited distribution options for the vast majority of self-publishers.

The Scoop!

Due to severe competition, self-publishers typically partner with distribution companies that "accept" just about anyone who is willing to pay for services. The less selective the Ingram-approved distributor, the more likely it is to function as a passive warehousing/fulfillment arm, versus a proactive marketing/sales arm.

A self-publisher who can generate his/her own sales may benefit from working with a reputable fulfillment-oriented distribution company that offers the following:

* Warehousing

* Order-taking (toll-free number/credit card capability)

* Accounting

* Invoicing

* Shipping

Writing children's books can indeed be a challenge—when you spend your time boxing and shipping books from your garage all day!

The Truth about Distributors

Ingram-approved distributors are likely to charge a percentage of net or retail book sales plus substantial administrative, storage, marketing, distribution, and/or fulfillment fees. Though there is no distribution industry standard, publishers typically earn 35% of retail sales—with no guarantee of books sold. Payments to publishers could take more than 270 days depending on projected returns. It is common for distributors to be forced out of business—due to insufficient funding—only to be replaced by new ones. At this time, two of the nineteen distributors listed on Ingram's Web site respond with a pre-recorded "out of service" message when telephoned.

I urge you to research your distributor options for your protection. Contact each of the general Ingram-approved distributors listed on Ingram's Web site (www.ingrambook.com). Comparing Ingram-approved distributors is a challenging endeavor. Services vary greatly from distributor to distributor. Create a chart that summarizes distribution services, fee structure (including any extraneous fees), and title submission guidelines—based on the following screening questions.

Distributor Screening Questions:

✔ Do you distribute children's picture books?

✔ Do you partner with self-publishers? (If yes, continue the interview process.)

✔ Do you offer a fee-based publisher program—or are earnings based on the percentage of net or retail sales? What is the publisher/distributor earnings ratio?

✔ Do you have mandatory set-up or marketing fees for publishers?

✔ Who are your primary customers ... independents, chains, libraries, specialty sales?

✔ What type of distribution services do you offer?

✔ Do you require exclusivity?

✔ How long have you been in operation?

✔ Do you have feet-on-the-street sales reps? How many?

✔ Do you have inside telemarketing reps? How many?

✔ Do you actively market/advertise titles?

✔ Do you promote titles through catalogs?

✔ Do you offer a customer toll-free phone number for ordering purposes?

✔ Do you warehouse books? What is the storage fee? Is there a pallet price reduction?

✔ Who pays for shipping from publisher to the distributor—and vice versa ... and from distributor to the customer—and vice versa?

✔ How do you ship books to customers? Do you accept credit card payments?

✔ Do you offer publishers a Web presence? What is the fee?

✔ Can book orders be driven through your Web site?

✔ Can book orders be driven from my Web site to yours?

✔ How do you handle returns?

✔ Is there a fee per returned book?

✔ What is your publisher payment schedule?

✔ Are publisher earnings withheld as a result of projected future book returns?

✔ Do you require a signed publisher contract?

✔ What is the duration of the contract?

✔ Can the contract be terminated immediately upon request?

✔ What is the contract termination procedure ... if termination is requested by the publisher ... if termination is requested by the distributor?

Be a Skeptic

Some distributors refuse to provide industry newcomers with solid answers to posed questions —and may even misinform. Any discomfort that you experience during your initial telephone encounter with a distributor is only likely to worsen once the contract is signed. Proceed cautiously! A distributor-publisher relationship is much like a marriage; do not just "jump in." Consider working with distributors who take the time to answer your questions directly and concretely—to your satisfaction. Obtain as many references as possible, including current publisher clients and distribution customers. Interview all references in depth.

If you choose to affiliate with an Ingram-approved distributor, I urge you to hire an attorney prior to signing your contract. Do not be fooled by sparse one-page contracts or complicated multi-page contracts. Read the fine print! Understand that you are agreeing to relinquish control of all day-to-day accounting and fulfillment functions in the majority of cases. Your earnings will be forwarded to you by your distributor, usually on a monthly basis—with ample funds withheld based on projected future returns. Beware of hefty set-up fees that benefit the distributor, not the publisher! With no guarantee of sales, the publisher often writes checks to the distributor at the end of the month—not vice versa.

The Scoop!

Not all distributors are reputable. Due diligence is required prior to "signing" with a distribution partner. Relationships do not always prove to be a match made in heaven!

Carefully review all detailed distributor sales reports that you receive during the course of your distribution contract. Stay abreast of all potential disparities. If you are discontent with distributor services and opt to terminate the contract, it can take up to ninety days from your termination request date to be legally "released." The distributor is in the driver's seat—and you may not enjoy every aspect of the ride. I worked with an Ingram-approved distributor several years ago to assist with the warehousing and fulfillment of my children's book titles. As book sales increased, reports became increasingly difficult to decipher and the small company owner became increasingly unavailable. Earnings checks were inaccurate. I uncovered so many sales report "glitches" that I demanded contract termination. I also enlisted the services of an accountant who confirmed the obvious—the distributor withheld $13,000 in payments over the course of eighteen months that I still have not received to this day.

A Word about Publishers' Sales Reps

Non-exclusive, independent sales reps earn a 10% commission by successfully leveraging impressive lists of publishers' titles through the following channels:

* Chains

* Independent retailers

* Specialty stores

* Libraries

These feet on the street sales reps—with buyer contacts—neither warehouse inventory nor fulfill orders. Their role is to simply sell books. Actual orders are fulfilled through national wholesalers, such as Ingram Book Company and Baker & Taylor. Many mid-sized and large publishers opt to forego distributor involvement, and hire the same non-exclusive sales reps used by distributors to stimulate sales. The non-exclusive independent sales reps for mid-sized publishers—such as Kane/Miller, Barefoot Books, and Brimax—appear on the final pages of their catalogs. In some instances, independent sales reps may represent a self-publisher directly if his/her title fills a void or enhances a particular category selection. For a comprehensive listing of independent publishers' representatives by region, visit www.naipr.org, the Web site of the National Association of Independent Publishers Representatives (NAIPR). For consideration, forward a review copy of your children's picture book with cover letter and promotional material.

The Role of Regional Wholesalers

Regional wholesalers—including Bookazine, The Distributors, Partners Book Distributing, Southern Book Service, and Sunbelt Publications—provide non-exclusive sales representation in targeted regions throughout the country. Unlike major wholesalers, smaller regional wholesalers are more apt to stock and sell highly demanded regional titles. Regional bookstore buyers (chain and independent) enjoy working with nearby regional wholesalers—whose staff can provide personalized attention, and respond quickly to their inventory needs.

THE SCOOP!

To fill demand—in a pinch—Ingram Book Company and Baker & Taylor actually purchase hard-to-find regional titles from well-stocked regional wholesalers!

As a supplement to your affiliation with Baker & Taylor and/or Ingram Book Company, it may behoove you to sign up with at least one regional wholesaler. Remember that the role of both national and regional wholesalers is to fulfill incoming orders. It is up to you to stimulate demand for your title! For consideration by regional wholesalers, follow submission guidelines. (Refer to Appendix D for a listing of regional wholesalers.)

Many regional wholesalers employ a children's book specialist to assist children's book buyers in selecting revenue-producing titles. Children's books are BIG business! For this reason, Bookazine wisely features its enthusiastic and knowledgeable children's book specialist, Heather, in an attention-grabbing ad campaign.

Bookazine's "Together with Heather" Ad Copy
Fall 2006 NAIBANEWS
(The New Atlantic Independent Booksellers Association's Newsletter)

✳ Talk to a children's book expert with over 10 years of experience and an enthusiasm that is contagious!

✳ Learn about the newest and best titles. (If it's out there, she's read it.)

✳ Have your questions answered, get helpful reviews and bestseller lists, and hear about appropriate titles for your store, every Thursday afternoon.

✳ Whether you're an established bookseller with a special customer request or a new bookseller with lots of questions, together with Heather, you will find what you need.

The Distribution Dilemma

As mentioned previously, the publishing industry mandates a full returns privilege for a period of six months … from the time a title goes out of print! The liberal book returns policy creates a major setback in accounting and inventory procedures for wholesalers, distributors, and publishers alike. As a result, wholesalers or distributors can be forced into bankruptcy—if they are unable to collect refunds from publishers for excessive inventory returns.

* On December 29, 2006, Publishers Group West (PGW)—the largest independent distributor for independent publishers—was forced by the courts to cease operations due to the bankruptcy of its parent company, Advanced Marketing Services. PGW, in business for 30 years, has recently been absorbed by Perseus Distribution.

* Koen Book Distributors operated as a fulfillment/returns warehouse for decades, prior to recently declaring bankruptcy. The company restructured as Koen-Levy Book Wholesalers LLC—operating from the same southern New Jersey location —and quickly closed its doors once again.

The Scoop!

In a typical wholesaler/distributor warehouse, cellophane bundled boxes of book returns—arranged by publisher— are stacked 8-15 feet high. Returns include overstocks and damages of popular titles, such as *Harry Potter* and *Pat the Bunny*—as well as less popular titles that do not live up to publishers' expectations. Whenever possible, publishers replace wrinkled or torn dust jackets on hardcover children's picture books with new ones. Revamped and non-damaged returned books replenish wholesaler or distributor stock for yet another round of sales. Damaged books, having bent corners, scratched/scuffed surfaces, or tears, are written off by publishers as donation—or sold at a severely reduced rate.

Library Distribution Channels

In addition to Baker & Taylor and Ingram Book Company, libraries purchase titles through wholesalers and distributors specializing in the public and school library markets. Visit http://acqweb.library.vanderbilt.edu/pubr/vendor.html for a comprehensive directory of library wholesalers/distributors. Library-specific wholesalers include:

* BWI

* Follett

* Brodart

* Emery-Pratt

* Ambassador Book Service

* Midwest Library Service

* Coutts Library Service

* Blackwell Book Services

* Academic Book Center

* Book House

* Eastern Book Company

* Perma-Bound

* Bound To Stay Bound Books, Inc.

BWI and Follett are sister companies; BWI sells to public libraries whereas Follett sells to school libraries. Library distributors include Quality Books and Unique Books. Seek representation from multiple non-exclusive library wholesalers/distributors. Visit library wholesaler Web sites for general information and title submission guidelines. Negotiate wholesaler/distributor-paid freight, whenever possible. Notify library wholesalers and distributors of your picture book release—at least three months prior to its publication date.

The Scoop!

Baker & Taylor caters to 80% libraries versus 20% retailers.
Ingram caters to 80% retailers versus 20% libraries.

Seeking Quality Representation

In operation for over forty years, Quality Books is a self-publisher-friendly library distributor —highly regarded by both public and school libraries for "unique and unobvious" titles. According to Wendy Steck, Publisher Relations Manager, Quality Books accepts approximately 80% of all current year picture book submissions—regardless of review status. Selected titles are promoted throughout the U.S. and Canada by a sales force of thirty. Approximately thirty new publishers are added per month. Titles are purchased on a fully returnable basis at a 55%–65% discount. For title consideration, submit F & Gs or a review copy of your finished picture book to the Quality Books selection committee. Visit www.quality-books.com for submission guidelines. If your title is accepted at least 90 days prior to publication, Quality Books Inc. may forward your F & Gs or review copy to *Booklist* for review on your behalf. Unique Books, another self-publisher-friendly library distributor, is similar in scope to Quality Books. Visit www.uniquebooksinc.com for submission guidelines.

Not All Library Wholesalers Are Self-Publisher Friendly

The vast majority of library wholesalers select titles based on the highly competitive journal review process. Title desirability increases with the number of favorable reviews and awards. Because self-published titles are frequently overlooked or unfavorably reviewed by traditional reviewers, library wholesalers are more apt to stock and promote titles by mainstream publishers. Without the support of library wholesalers' sales reps, self-publishers must rely on their own ability to generate library sales activity. The following library wholesalers may list nominally-reviewed self-published titles in their database only to fulfill incoming orders:

* BWI
  www.bwibooks.com

* Follett
  www.follett.com

* Brodart
  www.brodart.com

Terms are likely to include:

* 20%–55% discount

* Full returns policy

* Negotiable incurred shipping costs

The library wholesalers, listed below, specialize in the sale of durably bound books to the school and library markets:

* Perma-Bound
  www.perma-bound.com

* Bound To Stay Bound Books, Inc.
  www.btsb.com

In a special process, interior pages are torn apart from the original cover and rebound with more sturdy materials. Selected titles are purchased on a non-returnable basis at a 50%–60% discount.

The Scoop!

To increase book sales, library wholesalers provide librarians with recommended reading lists that feature forthcoming children's titles 1–2 months in advance of market introduction.

CHAPTER

6

Your Online Presence
is Priceless!

I long to accomplish
a great and noble task,
but it is my chief duty
to accomplish small tasks
as if they were great and noble.

–Helen Keller

Amazon.com & BarnesandNoble.com

Once your publishing company is affiliated with Baker & Taylor and/or Ingram Book Company—at no cost to you—your title information will be automatically "fed" to the following online retail giants:

* Amazon.com (www.amazon.com)

* Barnesandnoble.com (www.bn.com)

* Borders.com (www.borders.com)—"teamed" with Amazon.com

What an incredible bonus for publishers of all sizes! The online retail system is a WIN-WIN-WIN for all involved parties:

* Publisher/author

* Wholesaler/distributor

* Online retailer

Each entity benefits by receiving a percentage of the sale. When the consumer makes an online book purchase, the order is typically channeled through the publisher's vendor of record i.e. Ingram Book Company, Baker & Taylor. Over time, with a proven sales history, the online retailer may opt to purchase stock directly from the publisher—at a more favorable discount rate.

These phenomenal online retailers are responsible for selling millions of books per year. Your picture book will be available for consumer purchase 24 hours a day, 7 days a week. In addition to a twenty-word summary of your title, a full color image of your cover will be displayed—followed by media and consumer reviews. If temporarily unavailable, your title will be listed as "out of stock," until replenished.

THE SCOOP!

As a self-publisher, you are responsible for verifying the accuracy of your online title information. Stay current. Online retail giants require you to make necessary changes via e-mail. For example, to expedite change requests, BarnesandNoble.com suggests the use of two different e-mail addresses:

- corrections@barnesandnoble.com—for title corrections
- titles@bn.com—for adding title-related content.

For Amazon.com marketing advice, read *How to Make Your Book an Amazon.com Bestseller and Sell Tons of Copies Even if You're a Book Marketing Novice* by Steve Harrison—publisher of *Book Marketing Update* and *Radio-TV Interview Report*.

Online sales make up 12% of total book sales. According to the Book Industry Study Group (BISG), over 11.1 million used books were purchased by consumers in the U.S. for a total of $2.2 billion in 2004, representing 8.4% of consumer spending; $609 million of used books were sold online—a one-year increase of 33%.

Promoting Your Children's Book Online

Optimize the online salability of your children's picture book. Ask your satisfied customers—including friends and family—to write heartfelt online reviews of your children's picture book when they access your title. Favorable reviews sell books. In addition, request that your customers give your book a "5-star" rating by responding to the "Rate This Item" function.

The "Make a Recommendation" tool helps to increase online sales. Suggest that your avid supporters recommend your title by pasting your ISBN in the "Make a Recommendation" box and clicking the on-screen "Submit" button. To further enhance your title's visibility, create a "Favorites" list by adding your title to a list of other complementary, bestselling titles. As online sales increase, the associated product ranking number improves. Though online customers may not fully comprehend product ranking, Amazon.com and Barnesandnoble.com—as well as bookstores, libraries, wholesalers, distributors, and the media—keep abreast of fluctuations. I received a call a couple of years ago from a *New York Times* journalist who was researching the responsiveness of our churches and synagogues to the growing base of time-challenged congregants during religious Easter/Passover holiday ceremonies. She requested my opinion for her article because my Passover book, *My Favorite Family Haggadah*, had been ranked #1 on Amazon.com during that time period. Do not underestimate the power of online retailers in bringing awareness to your title!

Amazon.com Book Marketing Programs

Without affiliation to Baker & Taylor or Ingram Book Company, Amazon.com charges self-publishers an annual fee of $29.95 for inclusion in its Amazon Advantage consignment program. If there is demand for your title, Amazon.com may:

* Waive the annual fee

* Bypass the national wholesaler

* Improve your designated discount structure

For specific questions regarding the Amazon Advantage program, access the contact link at http://advantage.amazon.com/gp/vendor/public/join.

All publishers who maintain Web sites are invited to join the Amazon Associates program—a successful online affiliate program with over 1,000,000 members world-wide. As an Amazon Associate, you may earn up to 10% in referral fees while increasing your Amazon.com title sales rank. Visit www.amazon.com and click the "Make Money" link on the home page to learn more about the Amazon Advantage and Amazon Associates programs.

The Scoop!

A new free service, Amazon Connect, enables authors to create personal profiles—and viewers to post author-specific messages—on Amazon.com book pages. This interactive program is likely to increase internet traffic to authors' Web sites. Visit www.amazon.com/connect for details.

Building a Worthwhile Web Site

Develop your interactive company Web site as the cornerstone of your picture book promotion program. Provide online visitors with an appealing reason to visit your Web site. Keep your information fresh!

Because you are likely to self-publish more than one title, keep your options open when selecting a viable Web address. Unless you are promoting a brand i.e. "The Zebra-Striped Whale," or publishing a series, it is not wise to use a particular title in your domain name. To research domain names, visit www.netsol.com. Submit your Web address to as many search engines as possible—including Yahoo! and Google—so that potential customers can find you. Visit www.searchengine.com to obtain a comprehensive list of search engines. Include your Web address in all of your marketing materials.

THE SCOOP!

An effective Web site behaves as both a marketing and sales tool that adds credibility to your offering. Your Web site should reflect your personality and the type of book(s) that you publish.

Checking Out the Online Competition

Research the host of Web sites produced by other children's picture book publishers. On my Web site, www.arimaxbooks.com, for example, the tail of the zebra-striped whale is animated to create a sense of whimsy. Both the Nick Jr. Web site (www.nickjr.com) and PBS Web site (www.pbskids.org) are fun, interactive—and highly effective at attracting an endless stream of mesmerized online visitors! Visit www.barnesyardbooks.com, an information-packed Web site developed by Laura Barnes, self-publisher of the popular *Twist and Ernest* series (Barnesyard Books). She effectively attracts parents, teachers, children, librarians—and even the media—to her Web site by providing content of interest to each category of online visitor. Her Web site features several graphic buttons including:

* ✷ "Ernest Series"

* ✷ "Meet the Author"

* ✷ "Fun Stuff"

* ✷ "Talk to Ernest"

* ✷ "Order"

* ✷ "What's Happening"

* ✷ "Author Visits"

Web site visitors can easily access the following:

* ✷ Calendar of upcoming school, library, and bookstore events

* ✷ Downloadable coloring pages and games

* ✷ Event photographs

* Fee specifications

* Testimonials

* E-mailed responses by Ernest himself

Cornerstone of Promotion

Consider hiring a Web specialist to create your site. Web site specialists advertise in both the SPAN and PMA newsletters. Obtain bids and referrals. As an inexpensive alternative, find a high school student to develop your Web site—or if you have technical capabilities, enjoy the experience of implementing your own! To optimize your Web site, incorporate audio and video capabilities. Feature a full color image of your picture book cover as well as author/illustrator head shots. Your company contact information—including address, phone (include a toll-free number, if possible), fax, e-mail, etc.—must be readily available to your Web site visitors. Add the following components to your Web site as they become available:

* Activity kit pages

* Downloadable sticker sheets

* Press release content

* Testimonial sheet

* Author/illustrator bios

* Publication sheet

* Reviews

* Feature articles to your Web site

Create a downloadable brochure to easily and effectively promote your school author visits. Betty Tatham, author of several traditionally published non-fiction children's books—including the award-winning *Penguin Chick* (Henry Holt and Company)—provides information regarding her national and international school visit program via a full color downloadable brochure; visit www.bettytatham.com. Include a lesson plan, teaching guide, bibliographies, and student workbook. Incorporate a calendar of upcoming events—featuring dates, times, and locations. Share recent photographs and testimonials relating to your successful events. Consider the use of free online articles and ever-changing children's games and activities. Develop your Web site as your publishing company evolves. Experiment with different approaches to attract a full array of online visitors:

* Children

* Teachers

* Parents

* Librarians

* Book buyers

* Media

Both fiction and non-fiction children's picture book self-publishers can build entire communities around their subject matter via the following:

* Message boards

* Newsletters

* Video vignettes

* Associated product lines

* Links to other informational sites

Sell your children's picture book online, "direct" to the consumer, by offering secure credit card payment (refer to Appendix D for a listing of credit card merchant companies)—or link to a sales affiliate, such as Amazon.com, via the Amazon Associates program. To partner with Amazon.com, visit www.amazon.com and click the "Make Money" link on the homepage.

THE SCOOP!

Drive more visitors to your Web site through Big Universe (www.biguniverse.com)! This exciting, new online children's book community offers traditional and self-publishers a host of "no-fee" services including: complete "browse-through" capability of online picture books, a link to the book-buying Web site of choice, author spotlights, blog discussions, and global awareness features. Check it out!

Accessing Your Online Universe

E-mail friends and family as soon as your picture book is available for purchase. At the bottom of your e-mail, include an automatic signature file—known as "sig file"—that includes:

* Contact information (your name, company name, address, phone number(s), e-mail, fax, and Web site)

* Brief, descriptive marketing sound-bite

* Optional photograph

"Hot link" your e-mail address to your Web site for easy accessibility. To build a viable customer database, capture the e-mail addresses of your target audience as they visit your Web site. Find creative ways to encourage your online guests to share their contact information

with you. Laura Barnes, self-publisher of the *Twist and Ernest* series, for example, enables her young Web site visitors to "interact" with Ernest, the lovable little donkey—if they leave an e-mail address … and answer a few brief questions; visit www.barnesyardbooks.com. If you prefer, a "Weblog" feature may be designed for your Web site that ensures automatic registration of online visitors. For a definition of e-marketing terms and lingo, visit www.marketingterms.com.

The Scoop!

Consider joining popular e-mail discussion groups to target your children's book prospects. Create relevant online links with fellow publishers and other appropriate companies to optimize the benefits of symbiotic marketing.

Blogging ... Podcasting ... What Next?

Self-publishers frequently share their information on a dynamic Web page known as a "blog." Through blogging, subscribers and other blog publishers are able to cross-promote each other's content by linking to one another. Free accounts may be offered by hosting services, including Yahoo! and Hotmail. For additional blog information, visit the following Web sites:

* www.weblogger.com

* www.angelfire.lycos.com

* www.livejournalk.com

"Podcasting" is considered to be the audio form of blogging. The self-publisher downloads information in audio form (MP3). Subscribers are required to download the audio communications on their computers, burn files to CD, or transfer the files to a MP3 player. The term, podcasting, emanates from iPod—created by Apple Computer. As acceptance continues to grow, podcasting is capable of becoming a powerful, inexpensive marketing tool. Visit www.podcastalley.com to preview a sample show.

It's the Craze: Digital Book Previews

To spark a pre-release buzz, feature your picture book in an enticing, digitally formatted book preview video. Post on blog sites, and distribute to targeted consumer e-mail lists as well as to Internet sites such as:

* MySpace.com

* MSN Video

* Yahoo!

Book preview videos are also effectively used to attract consumers via:

* In-store book promotion teasers

* Cable television advertisements

* Pre-film movie theatre trailers

According to Sarah Bolme, owner of Crest Publications, in the December 2006 PMA *Independent* newsletter, "Having four trailers on thirty-two movie screens for one month—a total of 1,000 showings—cost about half as much as purchasing a full-page color ad in one issue of a popular magazine."

A two-minute book preview video typically includes an author interview—and costs approximately $3,000 to $4,000 to produce, depending upon complexity. There are several companies that offer book preview production services including:

* Circle of Seven Productions
  www.cosproductions.com

* Book Stream, Inc.
  www.bookstreaminc.com

* Expanded Books
  www.expandedbooks.com

* Vidlit
  www.vidlit.com

Online Search for Copyright Material

Online users can access the millions of books that exist worldwide through Google Book Search at www.google.com. Via the Partner Program, publishers of all sizes—in addition to major libraries—may submit their book text for digitization, free of charge.

To protect online book content, Google disables all printing, copying, and saving functions. Users—interested in learning more about a title—may link directly to the publisher's Web site. Titles can be purchased via online links to both publisher and retailer Web sites. Google is planning to offer online access to entire books through its own secure credit card transactions.

Online content competition is growing. Microsoft is offering a version of searchable, digitized book content through its Windows Live Books Publisher Program. Unlike Google—a system that accepts text from libraries as well as publishers—Microsoft deals with content rights holders only to avoid copyright-related issues. Book publishers, such as HarperCollins, can now digitize and display their controlled book content online via LibreDigital Warehouse by NewsStand, Inc.

Googling for Gold

Earn extra revenue by permitting ads for related products/services to appear on your Internet content pages. Google pays you each time that a user clicks on one of the ads. Through the Google Ads program, you can have your publishing company's banner/text ad placed on the Internet content pages of other commercial Web sites. Google AdWords enables you to choose pre-selected search terms for optimized ad placement. Visit www.google.com for further advertising/promotional information.

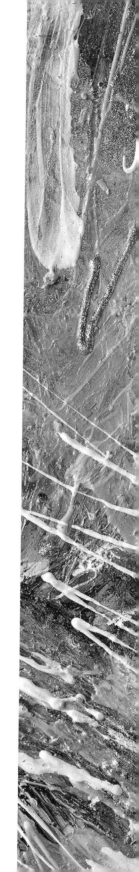

CHAPTER

7

Making Waves in the Industry

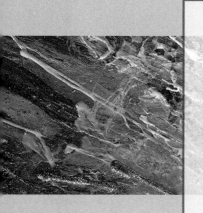

**Success
is that old ABC—
ability, breaks, and courage.**

–Charles Luckman

"Pub" Sheet Prowess

With distribution channels firmly established, use your company letterhead to produce a single page bibliographic publication sheet—known as a "pub" sheet—to inform reviewers and book buyers about your new picture book. In addition to your contact information (company name, address, phone, fax, e-mail, and Web site), include the following:

* Title specifications

* Book synopsis to "hook" the reader

* Author biography that features your credentials

Excerpts from both the synopsis and author biography are frequently synthesized into review copy by pre-pub and post-pub reviewers. A sample bibliographic "pub" sheet follows.

Arimax, Inc. Publishing

2865 S. Eagle Rd., PMB #399, Newtown, PA 18940 ph: 215-205-2227 fax: 215-862-7005 e-mail: tomdonahue@zebrastripedwhale.com

New Title: *The Zebra-Striped Whale with the Polka-Dot Tail*

Author/Illustrator: Shari Faden Donahue
Publication Date: January 2, 2001
ISBN: 0-9634287-3-X
LCCN: 98-93673
Type: Children's Picture Book
Binding: Hardcover
Dimensions: 11.4" x 11.4" x .05"
Page Count: 48 pages
Trade Price: $18.00

Age Range: All Ages
Distribution Channels: Ingram, Baker & Taylor, Koen, Quality, Follett
Supplementary Materials: 16-page Activity Kit
Merchandising Items: Imprinted Mugs, Tee Shirts, Pins, Balloons & Stickers
Public Relations Coordinator: Marci Shander
World Rights: Available

Synopsis: Two sisters, Maxime and Ariele, discover the magical attributes of the zebra-striped whale with the polka-dot tail—and pink and purple octopus. As they journey to a space where all trues are false ... and all falses are true, the girls grow to understand that "all that glitters is not gold."

Author/Illustrator Bio: Shari Faden Donahue utilizes fabric, paper, cellophane, paint, clay, and other dimensional materials to enhance her enlightening, rhyming text. Donahue is the founder and president of Arimax, Inc. Publishing—and has written several popular titles, including *Celebrate Hanukkah with Me*, *My Favorite Family Haggadah*, and *Philly's Favorites Recipe Collection*.

www.arimaxbooks.com

Designating Your Public Relations Contact

Your public relations coordinator can range from a professional publicist—having many media contacts—to a friend or family member who is willing to assist you with the more basic publicity functions. Though a highly regarded children's picture book publicist—with contacts —is worth his/her weight in gold, he/she is truly a challenge to find. Publicists veer away from most picture books that lack a powerful angle or "hook." Those who actually commit to working with children's book authors are extremely selective, quite expensive (approximately $100+ per hour), and eager to represent the major publishing houses. If you are unable to affiliate with a children's book publicist, due to lack of availability or expense, a handful of general public relations firms can provide partial assistance. (Refer to Appendix D for a listing of marketing and public relations specialists.)

The Scoop!

If you are willing to manage your own public relations campaign, ask a friend or family member to serve as your public relations contact. This individual's name should be listed as public relations coordinator on your bibliographic publication sheet, as well as other marketing material. (Refer to sample "pub" sheet on previous page.) Accompanying cover letters to reviewers, media, and/or buyers should emanate from your public relations contact—not "author"—for optimal professionalism in your public relations campaign.

Hear Ye ... Hear Ye: Book Announcements

The *Publishers Weekly* Children's Announcement Issue—published each spring and fall— features new children's titles from publishers of all sizes, and designates a children's picture book bestsellers list. Though inclusion in the issue is not guaranteed, *Publishers Weekly* attempts to list as many new titles as possible. If your picture book is selected, your listing will include the following information:

* Name of your publishing company

* Book title

* Author

* Illustrator

* Retail price

* Recommended age of reader

* Brief description of twenty words or less

For consideration by *Publishers Weekly* for the spring or fall Children's Announcement Issue (based on your title's publication date), fax your request to Children's Books Senior Editor Diane Roback at 646-746-6738. *Publishers Weekly* Children's Announcement Issues also feature a sampling of picture book illustrations. If you are interested in submitting illustrations from your picture book, send one set of your F & Gs to:

Diane Roback
Senior Editor, Children's Books
Publishers Weekly
360 Park Avenue South
NY, NY 10010

Visit www.publishersweekly.com for further information.

In the Forefront

Publishers Weekly—with a circulation of 40,000—is considered by many to be the single most important publication in the book industry. Subscribers include:

* Bookstore owners and managers

* Librarians

* Publishers

* Media outlets

* Literary agents

* Movie industry executives

PMA offers cooperative advertising opportunities for its members in *Publisher's Weekly* Small Press Issue—as well as the spring and fall *Publishers Weekly* Children's Announcement Issues. In each of these popular issues, PMA purchases a highly visible block of advertising space for its members' cooperative use. Cost is $495 per ad. This highly cost-effective advertising program is a phenomenal way to "get noticed" by *Publishers Weekly's* vast reading audience.

In addition, *Publishers Weekly* e-mails a free weekly newsletter, *Children's Bookshelf*—every Thursday—featuring juvenile title information to more than 17,000 newsletter subscribers. The newsletter presents children's book news that has not been selected for publication. Submit your children's book press release and contact information to Children's Books Senior Editor Diane Roback at droback@reedbusiness.com. For a complimentary newsletter subscription, visit www.publishersweekly.com/bookshelf.

Reviews by the Movers & Shakers

Industry "movers and shakers" include highly selective "pre-pub" journal reviewers who greatly influence the buying decisions of retailers and librarians alike, including:

* *Booklist*

* *BookPage*

* *School Library Journal*

* *Horn Book Magazine*

* *Horn Book Guide*

* *Kirkus*

* *ForeWord*

* *Publishers Weekly*

Booklist alone receives more than 2,500 submissions per month! Some highly demanded pre-pub journals review less than 10% of submissions—and are likely to support the major presses. To make those industry movers and shakers aware of your picture book, submit F & Gs 3–4 months prior to your title's publication date—followed by an actual review copy, as it becomes available. It is imperative that you have at least one designated wholesaler/distributor.

Do not include reviews and/or testimonials by any other reviewers. Submissions must be received—prior to the publication date—to be considered. In addition to pre-pub journals, submit review copies of your children's picture book to important "post-pub" review sources including:

* *The Bulletin of the Center for Children's Books*

* *The Bloomsbury Review*

* *Midwest Book Review*

I recommend that you also submit a review copy to *Book Links*, an American Library Association journal, featuring focused bibliographies of available trade children's books for the classroom—kindergarten through eighth-grade. (Refer to Appendix C for a listing of pre-pub and post-pub review/bibliographic sources.)

THE SCOOP!

Visit the Horn Book Web site, www.hbook.com. The "Authors & Artists" link leads you to an array of insightful articles—by and about authors and illustrators—in all stages of their careers.

Reviewers Are Unique

The unique submission requirements of each review source must be evaluated on an individual basis, as indicated below.

* *Publishers Weekly* and *Booklist* consider self-published titles with established national distribution channels.

* *School Library Journal* and *Kirkus* do not accept self-published titles as a rule; however, it can be difficult for a reviewer to ascertain whether a quality title has been published by a small versus self-publisher.

* *ForeWord*, a pre-pub journal, reviews submissions from the "best of the independent press," but does not review submissions from the major publishing houses.

＊ Unlike *Horn Book Magazine*, *Horn Book Guide* considers only titles by publishers listed in *Literary Marketplace*.

＊ *The Bulletin of the Center for Children's Books*, *The Bloomsbury Review*, and *Midwest Book Review* embrace independent publishers—including self-publishers!

It is essential to obtain individual rules and guidelines from each pre/post-pub review source—prior to submission. Requirements can change. Reviewer submission guidelines from *The Bulletin of the Center for Children's Books* follow.

The Bulletin
of the Center for Children's Books

If you are interested in submitting materials to the *Bulletin* for review consideration, please refer to the following guidelines.

Information for Publishers

The Bulletin of the Center for Children's Books is a book review journal for librarians, teachers, parents, and others interested in new children's books. *The Bulletin* is a selective journal, reviewing approximately 900 of the over 5000 trade books published for children and young adults annually. Books reviewed include both recommended and not-recommended titles.

If you are interested in submitting a book to *The Bulletin* for review consideration, please keep in mind the following:

Only trade and mass-market books are considered. We do not review textbooks, curricular materials, cassettes or book/cassette combinations, videos, software, electronic publications, or magazines.

While we do not review "vanity press" books, we encourage submissions by small and alternative publishers. We do not review books that are only available by mail-order from the publisher, so please include distribution details with review copies.

We do not review or publish notice of reprints. Paperback originals are welcome and encouraged.

The Bulletin aims to review books within a few months of publication, beginning one month before the publication date. We prefer to review from bound galleys or f&g's, which means we prefer to receive review copies at least three months prior to publication date. We do not review from flat galleys, manuscript, or non-print (electronic) sources. Only one copy of the galley, f&g, or bound book needs to be submitted, and a bound copy must follow upon publication. All materials submitted become property of *The Bulletin* and will not be returned.

Please include the following with review copies: price and ISBN for each edition, estimated pagination, publication date, and contact person and phone number. It is most helpful if this material is printed on the galley or securely attached. If a catalog is available, please send that as well.

Please do not call to ask if and when a book is going to be reviewed, although a call to check that we have received a title is OK. If a book is reviewed, a copy of that review is sent to the publisher approximately three weeks before the review is published (so don't forget to include your address!).

Submission Guidelines Continued ...

Professional, scholarly, and adult trade books about children's books, reading, and librarianship are listed and/or reviewed monthly in a section called "Professional Connections" Submission requirements are the same as for children's books.

Send review copies and any editorial correspondence to:

Deborah Stevenson, Editor
The Bulletin of the Center for Children's Books
501 East Daniel St.
Champaign, IL 61820

Subscription information is available from:

Mail
The Johns Hopkins University Press
2715 North Charles Street
Baltimore, Maryland 21218-4363

Phone
1-800-548-1784
Outside the U.S. and Canada call 410-516-6987

Fax
410-516-6968

Online
www.press.jhu.edu/journals

Email
jlorder@jhupress.jhu.edu

Information about advertising and rate cards are available from:

Monica Queen
The Johns Hopkins University Press
2715 North Charles Street
Baltimore, Maryland 21218-4363
410-516-6984. Her e-mail is
myq@press.jhu.edu

Questions about submitting books for review should be directed to Deborah Stevenson, Editor by phone at (217) 244-0324, via e-mail at *bccb@alexia.lis.uiuc.edu* or by mail to *The Bulletin of the Center for Children's Books,* 501 East Daniel St., Champaign, IL 61820.

Thank you very much.

Realistic Expectations

Have realistic expectations. With more than 9,000 children's picture books published this past year, competition for reviews is fierce. Though your title may not be reviewed as a result of the quantity of new titles published, submit your title anyway. You have nothing to lose—except some time, effort, and postage! Precisely follow all submissions procedures. (Larger distributors are likely to assist with the review process.) Pre-pub reviewers typically require

F & Gs prior to the review copy. When submitting your review copy, place a "For Review Only" sticker—including contact information—on the outside front cover; insert a brief cover letter with your "pub" sheet inside the front cover.

Reviewer preferences vary. According to James A Cox, Editor-in-Chief of *Midwest Book Review*, the practice of attaching something foreign to a review copy—via tape, adhesive, staples, etc.—should be avoided because it detracts from the pristine quality of a freshly printed book.

Rockin' & Rollin' with Reviews

Whereas the majority of review journals focus on "recommended" reviews, be aware that others—including *School Library Journal* and *The Bulletin of the Center for Children's Books*—print negative reviews as well. Though a "good" SLJ review is likely to encourage its audience of librarians and retail buyers to purchase a recommended title, a "bad" review is deemed worthy by many who believe the following:

* All publicity is good publicity.

* There is no such thing as a bad review.

The opinions of reviewers—typically librarians throughout the country—are indeed respected … but also subjective. For every poor review a title receives, favorable reviews are likely to appear in other sources. Well-reviewed titles, even from large publishing houses, have been known to flop. Don't take bad reviews or good reviews too seriously! Even with no reviews whatsoever, a solid children's title can achieve success—with favorable media publicity, enthusiastic hand-selling, and good old-fashioned word of mouth.

Awards ... Wow!

To achieve recognition in the children's picture book publishing arena, consider submitting your published title—"hot off the press"—for professional state, regional, and national publishing awards. Though numerous award competitions exist, be selective. Some awards have greater significance than others. For the majority of professional award competitions, your children's picture book must be published during the year preceding the actual award nomination.

The Scoop!

Award competitions are usually sponsored by review magazines as well as national and state associations. Though some require a registration fee of up to $100, many are free.

The most coveted children's picture book award is the Randolph Caldecott Medal—awarded by the American Library Association (ALA)—to honor the artist of the most distinguished picture book for children, published in the United States. This award is held in such high esteem that a winning Caldecott title remains in print indefinitely. Other children's picture book awards include:

* Jane Addams Children's Book Award

* ASPCA Henry Bergh Children's Book Award

* Benjamin Franklin Award

* Black-Eyed Susan Award

* The Irma S. and James H. Black Book Award

* Book Sense Book of the Year Award

* Boston Globe-Horn Book Award

* Buckeye Children's Book Award

* Children's Booksellers Choices Award

* Christopher Award

* ✳ Gold Medallion Keats/Kerlin Fellowship

* ✳ Kentucky Bluegrass Award

* ✳ Kerlan Award

* ✳ The National Book Award

* ✳ Newbery Award

* ✳ Once Upon a World Children's Book Award

* ✳ Orbis Pictus Award for Outstanding Non-fiction for Children

* ✳ Patterson Prize for Books for Young People

* ✳ Please Touch Museum Book Award

* ✳ The Sugarman Family Award for Jewish Children's Literature

* ✳ Treasure State Award

* ✳ *Writer's Digest* International Self-Published Book Award

* ✳ Young Hoosier Book Award

* ✳ Charlotte Zolotow Award

The Scoop!

Consider submitting your picture book to noteworthy children's book lists in your title's category. Popular children's book lists include: ALA (American Library Association) Notable Books for Children, Children's Choices, International Reading Association, National Science Teacher Association, Notable Social Studies, Parents' Choice, and end-of-year compilations by *Publishers Weekly* Round-Up, *Booklist* Editor's Picks, and the *Boston Globe/Horn Book* "Best Books of the Year." Did you know that Oprah promotes children's books through the Oprah's Book Club Kids Reading List? Visit www.oprah.com/obc/kids/obc_kids_20000803.jhtml for details.

Award Submission Guidelines

You must adhere to all rules and regulations when submitting your children's picture book for awards and noteworthy list competitions. Award Web sites offer access to competition deadlines and requirements. Children's picture book awards are based on proposed mission objectives. Study submission guidelines carefully to determine if your title effectively meets award criteria. For example:

* The Please Touch Museum's Book Award is presented on behalf of a children's book that is imaginative, exceptionally illustrated, and helps foster a child's life-long love of reading.

* The Jane Addams Children's Book Award is presented on behalf of a children's book that most effectively promotes peace, social justice, world community, and the equality of the sexes and all races.

* The ASPCA Henry Bergh Children's Book Award is presented on behalf of a children's book that promotes the humane ethics of compassion and respect for all living things.

Depending upon the award, judging committees may be composed of librarians, media specialists, booksellers, or other children's literary specialists. Though winners may be awarded gifts—including cash, honor medal, statue, small gift, or certificate—it is the validation/recognition factor that makes the award competition truly worthwhile.

The Scoop!

PMA's Benjamin Franklin Award competition is beneficial to both winners and non-winners alike—because judges' title evaluation forms are actually shared with the publishers of record (self-publishers included!). Each publisher is offered a rare glimpse into the highly subjective judging process. A submitted title may receive a rave review by one judge, and a terribly harsh review by another.

Ready ... Aim ... Submit!

To select awards that are of particular interest to you, review *Children's Books: Awards and Prizes* compiled by Children's Book Council—in print or online; visit www.cbcbooks.org. Other sources include:

* *Literary Market Guide*

* *Children's Writer's & Illustrator's Market*

* *Children's Writer Guide*

Contact your local library or school district regarding state or regional children's picture book competitions in your area. Visit http://childrensbooks.about.com/cs/stateawards for links to state awards that celebrate picture books selected by the children of those states. Stay abreast of new awards and lists that emerge each year.

Some award competitions necessitate an actual written nomination of your children's picture book. When a nomination is required, ask a favorite teacher/librarian in your community to make the submission on your behalf. Carefully follow award submission guidelines.

Children's Book Clubs

Popular national children's book clubs include:

* Weekly Reader

* Scholastic

* Grolier

* Book-of-the-Month Club

* Junior Library Guild

Whereas Junior Library Guild targets librarians, Grolier and Book-of-the-Month Club target parents and their children. Weekly Reader and Scholastic market their children's titles through elementary schools.

THE SCOOP!

Scholastic features several book clubs including: Firefly, SeeSaw, Lucky, Arrow, and Tab. Teachers distribute Scholastic book club catalogs in the classroom—and place their students' orders online, or by phone/fax/e-mail. Accrued bonus points earn loyal teachers an array of desirable classroom resources. Student orders and teacher bonus gifts are conveniently delivered—right to the classroom!

Large national book clubs either print their own copies of a selected title or join the publisher's print run—providing the publisher with 10% savings in production costs. Exclusivity must be guaranteed by the publisher. The publisher is typically paid a royalty of 10% of the book club's list price. The book club's list price can be 20%–30% lower than actual retail list price. Profitable book clubs strive to keep costs under 25% of their proposed selling price.

As with every other form of children's book publishing, national book club competition is fierce. Though there is little probability that your title will be accepted by national award/review-driven book clubs, consider trying anyway—if you have the time and tenacity! Review *Literary Market Place* for national book club guidelines. To be considered by a national book club, submit your F & Gs with a cover letter of intent and "pub" sheet—at least twelve months in advance of your publication date. To prevent "pub" sheet loss during the lengthy submission process, attach an adhesive-backed label—imprinted with "pub" sheet specifications —to the inside front cover of your F & Gs. If you receive no response within approximately two months, resubmit. Include a copy of your finished title and all favorable reviews/feature articles as they become available.

Special Interest Book Clubs

For niche children's titles, opportunities may be available through special interest book clubs that typically purchase 500–1,000 copies at a 55%–60% discount. Special interest book clubs tend to offer no more than 25% of the heavily discounted member price for limited title quantities. A Google search can prove helpful in obtaining applicable special interest book clubs and community reading programs for children. For consideration, submit your F & Gs—

with cover letter of intent and "pub" sheet—6–12 months prior to your publication date. To prevent "pub" sheets from being misplaced during the special interest book club consideration process, attach an adhesive-backed label—imprinted with "pub" sheet specifications—to the inside front cover of your F & Gs. If you receive no response within a two-month period, resubmit. Forward a review copy of your finished title, in addition to all favorable reviews/feature articles, as they become available. Selection by an interest-related book club or community reading program for children grants an added independent endorsement—and is likely to lead to greater overall sales of your picture book.

The Scoop!

Some universities feature book clubs to promote publications by their alumni. Contact your university for information regarding alumni book club availability.

CHAPTER

8

Standing Out
from the Crowd

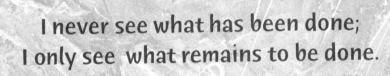

I never see what has been done;
I only see what remains to be done.

—*Marie Curie*

Actualizing Your Activity Kit

Develop an activity kit to complement the theme of your children's picture book. Include one or more of the following components:

* Coloring sheet of your main character—or favorite illustration

* Word search

* Word scramble

* Maze

* Game idea

* Recipe

* Craft idea

* Illustrated name tags

Staple or ribbon-tie black & white (or color) copies of your activity kit pages together—with a cover page—or produce a professionally bound version with the assistance of a promotional printing company. (Refer to Appendix D for a listing of promotional printing companies.) Request assistance from your graphic designer, as needed. If you do not have the time to design a full-blown activity kit, one or two thematic coloring sheets will suffice. To further promote your title, consider the purchase of imprinted thematic specialty items such as:

* Stickers

* Latex balloons

* Pins

(Refer to Appendix D for a listing of advertising specialty companies.)

THE SCOOP!

Add your activity kit pages to your Web site for easy downloading. Bookstore staff, librarians, and teachers may use your activity kit during a pre-scheduled story hour—even when you're not present—if downloadable games and activities are stimulating, interactive, and age appropriate.

Creativity Counts

A creative activity kit is an effective promotional tool that celebrates the release of a promising new children's title. For example, the picture book, *If You Take a Mouse to the Movies*—published by HarperCollins—has a corresponding high gloss, sixteen-page activity kit (two-color interior, full color cover) that features activities, games … and even a bag of microwavable popcorn! When I introduced my picture book, *The Zebra-Striped Whale with the Polka-Dot Tail*, I designed a unique, fun-filled black & white activity kit—with the following components:

1. Polka-Dot Party Premiere Invitations

2. Zebra-Striped Whale Name Tags

3. Great Job Award Certificates

4. Polka-Dot Delight Ice Cream Dessert Recipe

5. Polka-Dot Eruption Balloon Game

6. Zebra-Striped Whale Maze Fun

7. Character Coloring Sheets

8. Drawing Fun: What Can You Create from Just One Polka-Dot?

9. Word Scramble Fun

10. Word Search Fun

11. Zebra-Striped Whale Bookmark

12. Musical Polka-Dots Game

13. Polka-Dot Pals Collage Craft & Parade

14. Giveaway Items (Stickers, Latex Balloons, Pins)

The activity kit opens with a letter to the bookstore's children's event coordinator. See sample activity kit pages below.

Dear Children's Event Coordinator:

The Zebra-Striped Whale with the Polka-Dot Tail is certain to make a huge splash this spring! Bursting with explosive collage illustrations, whimsical characters, and verse that begs to be read aloud, this colorful picture book inspires children to enthusiastically express their creativity. In this easy-to-use Polka-Dot Party Activity Kit, you will find everything you need to fill your upcoming event with imagination, excitement and wonder!

- **Hints and Ideas** for making your event a success
- **Invitation/Flyer** to notify all your little polka-dot fans
- **Giveaways** including Zebra-Striped Whale pins, balloons & stickers
- **Name Tags** for the kids
- **Polka-Dot Pal Collage Craft & Parade** with special **Award Certificates**
- **Zebra-Striped Whale Balloons** for Polka-Dot Eruption Activity
- **Fun Polka-Dot Party Games**: Musical Polka Dots & Follow the Polka-Dot Trail
- **Reproducible Handouts**: Drawing Fun, Coloring Fun, Word Search Fun, Word Scramble Fun, Maze Fun, Bookmark Fun and Recipe Fun
- **Colorful stickers** for the kids to wear home
- **Author/Illustrator Bio**
- **Ad Slick** to promote your event

The Polka-Dot Party Activity Kit is brimming with suggestions for activities guaranteed to captivate your young audience. We hope you enjoy this kit, and look forward to learning about your own unique Polka-Dot Party event ideas. As always, we welcome your questions or comments.

With polka dots and zebra stripes,

Children's Marketing Department
Arimax, Inc.

P.S. Be sure to stock up on **The Zebra-Striped Whale with the Polka-Dot Tail** before the big event (ISBN: 0-9634287-X)!

Don't Miss ...

Zebra-Striped Whale's

"POLKA-DOT PARTY PREMIERE"

featuring

Author/Illustrator,

Shari Faden Donahue's newest book:

The Zebra-Striped Whale with the Polka-Dot Tail

"POLKA-MANIA"

GAMES, CRAFTS, ACTIVITIES ...

& LOTS of GIVEAWAYS TOO!!!

DATE: _____

TIME: _____

PLACE: _____

FOR MORE INFORMATION ...

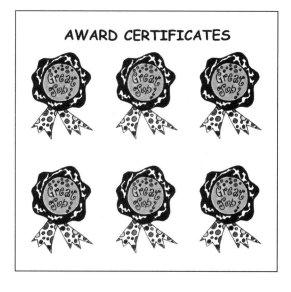

AWARD CERTIFICATES

Hello! My name is:

Hello! My name is:

Hello! My name is:

Hello! My name is:

RECIPE FUN

With just a little help, you'll have fun preparing
Zebra-Striped Whale's favorite dessert,
"Polka-Dot Delight!"

Ingredients:

2 of your favorite cookies, homemade or store-bought

1 scoop of your favorite ice cream, softened

Zebra-Striped Whale's "Polka-Dots"
(m & m's, Skittles, colored nonpareils or jelly beans)

Here's what to do!

Place ice cream on flat side of first cookie. Top with
flat side of second cookie. Squeeze cookies together
gently. Coat ice cream layer with Zebra-Striped
Whale's "polka-dots" by pressing candy lightly onto ice
cream. Zebra-Striped Whale says, "Eat right away!"

BALLOON ACTIVITY FUN

"Polka Dot Eruption"

Here's what you'll need to play!

Zebra-Striped Whale with the Polka Dot Tail Balloons
(Enclosed in "Polka-Dot Party" Activity Kit)

Activity Instructions:

Distribute one balloon per child. After each child's balloon has been inflated by accompanying adult, instruct the children to create a "polka dot eruption" by tapping their balloons up in the air for as long as possible, without letting the balloons touch the ground. Encourage the children to count aloud with every tap. Challenge the children to a higher tap count each time they start again!

Zebra-Striped Whale cannot find its polka-dots and
some zebra stripes too! Can you help by coloring them in?

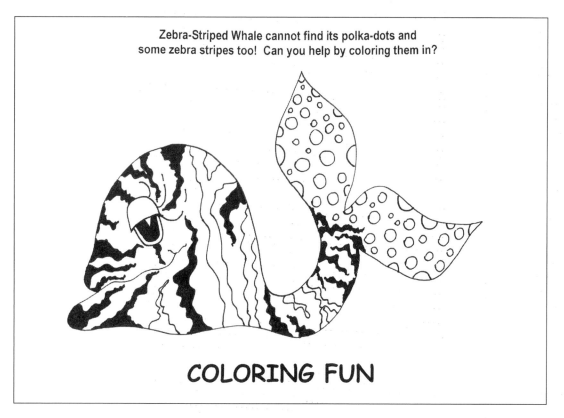

COLORING FUN

MAZE FUN

Travel inside the zebra-striped diamond, on the white path, to
discover Zebra-Striped Whale at the center!

Dive in ...
and color the Polka-Dot Tail of Zebra-Striped Whale!

COLORING FUN

DRAWING FUN

Zebra-Striped Whale loves to ask,
"What can you create from just one POLKA DOT?"

Is it the nose of a ... clown ... dog ... happy face, the center of a flower,
an eye of a ... monster ... Martian ... fish, a cherry on a sundae?
Use your imagination ... You decide!

WORD SCRAMBLE FUN

Unscramble the mixed-up words below ... Ready 1, 2, 3, GO!
Zebra-Striped Whale is curious ... How many do you know?

RZABE PETDSIR _ _ _ _ _   _ _ _ _ _ _

APKLO TDO _ _ _ _ _   _ _ _

AMMEXI _ _ _ _ _ _

REEILA _ _ _ _ _ _

OWW _ _ _

STRTELIG _ _ _ _ _ _ _

DLGO _ _ _ _

CLMAIGA _ _ _ _ _ _ _

Answers: zebra-striped, polka-dot, maxime, Arielia, wow, glitter, gold, magical

WORD SEARCH FUN

Find words diagonally, up, down & in all directions too
from *the Zebra-Striped Whale especially for you!*

POLKA DOT	RAINBOW
WHALE	TRAIL
OCTOPUS	TRUE
WOW	FALSE

```
P  W  D  J  W  Q  E  F
Z  O  C  T  O  P  U  S
H  B  L  T  W  U  R  J
B  N  K  K  C  V  T  Q
T  I  W  H  A  L  E  M
Q  A  V  W  A  D  Z  Z
T  R  A  I  L  C  O  C
F  A  L  S  E  G  K  T
```

BOOKMARK FUN

Use a scissors to carefully cut out your very own one-of-a-kind
Zebra-Striped Whale with the Polka-Dot Tail bookmark!

Engaging Young Children

In addition to attracting the attention of book buyers and the media, the role of your activity kit/sheets is to engage young children during your bookstore, library, and school events. Use your imagination. Be creative, and have fun! Derive your ideas from pre-existing games and activities—adding your own thematic component. It is not necessary to re-invent the wheel. The "Musical Polka-Dots" game that I utilize is a variation of the simple "Musical Chairs" game. Tactile activities, such as the "Polka-Dot Pals Collage Fun & Parade," as described below, are popular among young children.

Polka-Dot Pals Collage Craft

Materials: Googly Eyes, Cotton Balls, Glitter, Fabric Scraps, Pipe Cleaner, Curly Hair, Yarn, Paper Plates, Water Soluble Glue, Markers

Instructions to Children: Create your own Polka-Dot Pal masterpiece by gluing your favorite materials to a paper plate. Use markers to add your special artistic touches. Will your Polka-Dot Pal be a dog, cat, clown, lion, tiger, girl, boy, gorilla, fish, monster, Martian, whale, octopus ... or something altogether different? You can decide!

Polka-Dot Pals Parade

Coordinator Directive: As soon as the children have completed the above collage activity, invite them to participate in their very own "Polka-Dot Pal Parade." Play lively music as the children march in a circle—proudly holding their Polka-Dot Pal masterpieces for all the grown-ups to see. Present each collage artist with a special "Great Job" award certificate (illustrated in activity kit) for his or her unique artistic skill and creativity.

Mastering Your Media Kit

The media kit—also known as press kit—is your self-publishing company's image-building vehicle. Its role is to solidify your marketing platform, and disperse timely information about your exciting new title to book buyers and the media. Your physical media kit should consist of the following components:

* Cover Letter

* Press release

* Testimonial sheet

* Author/illustrator biography (bio)

* Sample media questions

* Premium promotional material

* Author photograph—typically a black & white head shot (5″ x 7″ or 8″ x 10″)

* Favorable reviews/articles

* Sample book review

* Thematic book launching device

Be aware that media kit contents may be unintentionally dispersed throughout the offices of hectic editors and book buyers. Verify that your contact information—including publishing company name, public relations contact, address, phone number(s), fax, and e-mail—appears on all items. Neither book buyers nor the media have the time to shuffle through reams of material to uncover your contact information—even when interested. Make yourself accessible every step of the way!

Composing Your Cover Letter

Use your cover letter as a venue for:

* Presenting your media kit in the form of benefits to the recipient

* Building enthusiasm for your picture book

* Offering assistance if review copy, author interview, or further information is requested

Personalize your cover letter to maximize reader impact. Your cover letter must be clear, concise, and well-edited. If you are donating all or a portion of your picture book proceeds to a non-profit organization, specify details. Be certain to refer the media kit recipient to your online media kit and other Web site content.

Writing Your Press Release

Prepare a concise, attention-grabbing one- to two-page communiqué known as the press release. It announces the introduction of your picture book via the use of a "hook" or angle—and answers the questions: who, what, when, where, and how. Use "third person" when writing your press release content. Never use "I" unless included in a direct quotation. Place the phrase, "FOR IMMEDIATE RELEASE," at the top of your press release—followed by your public relations contact information and attention-grabbing headline. Add a small image of your book cover to the page. Center three pound signs, ###, at the bottom of your press release to designate the end of your final paragraph.

Spark the interest of book buyers and the media by telling the story behind the story. "Spin" the contents of your press release accordingly—emphasizing your unique selling proposition (USP). For optimal results, your message must respond clearly and directly to the needs of the recipient. Develop multiple press releases to attract multiple target audiences. Add substantial data as needed to stimulate interest. For example, if your children's picture book is entitled *Peter's Pet Pig*, include statistics regarding pigs as popular household pets. The more exciting your press release, the better the response! Your children's picture book is likely to receive the greatest word of mouth "buzz" during its initial release. Your title is new only once. Spread the word to book buyers and the media as quickly as possible. Present yourself and your children's picture book in the best possible light! Accentuate the positives!

According to author and public speaker, Joe Vitale, the press is always in need of interesting material to create news. He states, "About 80% of what you see in the papers and on TV is planted by people like you and me sending out news releases! ...You can't send out self-serving announcements and expect media coverage, however. You have to hunt for the news angle, and then send out a riveting release conveying your news angle to the appropriate media."

Visit Joe Vitale's Web site, www.mrfire.com, for an array of insightful marketing tips and articles including:

* "Inside Secrets to Writing News Releases"

* "The 5 Biggest News Release Mistakes"

If your funds permit, consider hiring the exuberant Joe Vitale (known as Mr. Fire!) to assist you in press release preparation. Publicist Paul Krupin provides samples of several children's book press releases on his Web site, www.directcontactpr.com. He also publishes an eBook, entitled *Trash Proof New Releases*—composed of strategy, tactics, and 120 effective news releases. A beneficial Para Publishing Special Report, entitled "News Releases and Book Publicity," is available through www.parapublishing.com. Visit www.prwebdirect.com to find helpful tips, guidelines and templates for writing an effective press release.

Creating Your Testimonial Sheet

Testimonials and endorsements stimulate interest in your title as a result of the credibility factor. The header, *Testimonials*, should boldly flank the top of your testimonial sheet—just above the title of your children's picture book. Place your contact information in the footer located at the bottom of your page. Compile an easy-to-read testimonial sheet on behalf of your children's picture book. Hire a graphic designer to assist you with page design, if necessary.

Politely request a 1–2 sentence endorsement from at least six peer contacts—colleagues, relatives, friends, and even friends of friends—with professions such as:

* Elementary school teacher

* Principal

* Librarian

* Book store owner/manager

* Psychologist

* Social worker

* Organization head

Don't be shy. Your testimonial providers are likely to feel flattered! As a gesture of appreciation, present your avid supporters with a signed copy of your title for their enjoyment. Invite each of your testimonial providers to sign a release—granting you permission to utilize his/her direct quotation. A sample Testimonial Permission Form follows.

Testimonial Permission Form

In completing this form, you grant the absolute right and permission for <u>PUBLISHING COMPANY</u> to include your testimonial as outlined below in the promotion and advertisement of the children's picture book, entitled <u>CHILDREN'S PICTURE BOOK</u>, in all of its published forms.

Name _____ Phone _____

Company _____ Fax _____

Title _____ E-mail _____

Address _____

City _____ State _____ Zip Code _____

Testimonial _____

_____

_____

Published Works _____

_____

Signature _____ Date _____

Please sign completed form, and return to <u>ADDRESS</u> by <u>SPECIFIED DATE</u>. If you have any questions, call <u>PHONE NUMBER</u>. Keep an autographed copy of <u>PICTURE BOOK TITLE</u> for your enjoyment.

If you feel confident regarding the professionalism of your work, consider soliciting endorsements from prestigious authors, actors, and politicians. Their contact information may be uncovered via the Web or through personal contacts—of personal contacts. Be bold. Shoot for the stars! The worst possible outcome is a polite, "No." Be patient. Over time, your sources are likely to emanate from journalists, reviewers, satisfied customers … and perhaps even the famous! Endorsements blossom into a truly impressive list. As you receive your incoming testimonials and endorsements, add them to your testimonial sheet. Replace one endorsement with another, if your testimonial sheet becomes unwieldy. Visit www.parapublishing.com to obtain a Special Report, entitled "Blurbs for Your Books: Testimonials, Endorsements and Quotations."

Building Your Bio

Now that you have completed both your press release and testimonial sheet, write your one-page (or partial page) author biography—known as author bio—to detail your credentials. Your author bio adds a personal touch to your media kit that can ignite the response of book buyers and the media alike. Use "third person" when writing your author bio. Never use "I" unless included in a direct quotation. Keep your bio concise and to the point. Content may mirror the author-related text located on your rear book flap—if you are self-publishing a dust jacketed hardcover. Your author bio should contain interesting background information such as:

* Education

* Work experience

* Family

* Hobbies

* Other published titles

The header, *About the Author*, should boldly flank the top of your bio sheet. I recommend that you place a scanned headshot in the upper left corner. (A picture is worth a thousand words!) Place your contact information in the footer located at the bottom of the sheet. If necessary, hire a graphic designer to assist you with page layout.

The Scoop!

Illustrations are an integral part of your picture book. Remember to include in your media kit a one-page (or partial page) bio—and photograph—on behalf of your illustrator. If you are both author and illustrator, compile your content under one heading, "Author/Illustrator Bio."

Compiling Your Sample Media Questions

Hectic editors and radio/TV hosts respond favorably to intriguing capsules of news—conveyed in a concise question/answer format. Prepare a list of 6–12 author interview questions with brief, corresponding answers for use by the media. Your objective is to simplify the job of the media by providing a relevant framework for an engaging interview forum. Utilize your press release, testimonial sheet, and author bio content to customize interview questions that are unique to you.

Sample Media Interview Questions:

✔ What inspired you to become a children's picture book author?

✔ How did the idea for your children's picture book emerge?

✔ What message does your children's picture book convey?

✔ How did you create the concept for the main character?

✔ Who illustrated your children's picture book?

✔ How did you select the organization that benefits from title proceeds?

✔ Have you always had an interest in writing for young children?

✔ Do your future plans include writing more children's picture books?

The header, *Sample Media Interview Questions*, should boldly flank the top of your sheet. Place your contact information in the footer located at the page bottom. Hire a graphic designer to assist with page layout, if necessary.

Materializing Your Mock Book Review

Your time-constrained media contacts have little time to write an original book review. Make their lives easier by writing a fabulous review on behalf of your own picture book! Remember that reviews grant tremendous credibility to small/self-publishers. To encourage media review of your picture book, use enticing, quotable language. A paragraph format enables media outlets to quickly seize informational segments that suit their particular needs. Develop targeted paragraphs that are brief, organized, and credible. The header, *Sample Book Review*, should boldly flank the top of your page. Consider placing a scanned image of your cover in the upper left corner. Place your contact information in the footer located at the bottom of the page. If necessary, request page layout assistance from your graphic designer.

Designing Your Premium Promotional Material

Promotional printing can add a touch of priceless pizzazz to any title. Utilize a professionally printed full color, glossy flyer (sell sheet) to enthusiastically introduce your children's picture book. Your flyer/sell sheet should contain the following components:

* Cover image of your picture book

* Unique sales pitch

* Brief author bio

* Endorsements

* Availability specifications including: price, binding, ISBN, wholesaler/distributor, and process for requesting review copies

* Contact information

* Reference to your Web site (featuring your downloadable activity kit, if applicable)

* Order form—if targeting your media kit to book buyers

According to Toni Albert of Trickle Creek Books, in the December 2006 PMA *Independent* newsletter, "When producing mock reviews and book flyers, it's critical to use exciting, quotable language, interesting blurbs, and short, catchy descriptions, because many reviewers for niche publications or smaller periodicals and Web sites will use your material verbatim."

In addition to flyers, premium promotional materials—including brochures, postcards, and bookmarks—make effective media kit enclosures, package/mail stuffers, and hand-outs for book fairs, expos, trade shows, and retail stores. Some savvy authors distribute them—whenever, wherever possible:

* Medical/dental offices

* Hair salons

* Supermarkets

* Drug stores

* Craft stores

* Children's clothing stores

* Party stores

* Pet stores

* Community bulletin boards

* Seat pockets of busses, trains, and planes

* Taxicabs

* Public restrooms

* Hotel lobbies

The look and feel of your promotional material should complement the unique style of your picture book. Uphold the highest professional image to achieve success. Re-work content from your press release, testimonial page, and author bio to formulate your cohesive promotional text. "Spin" the text of your message accordingly to maximize response from your targeted recipients—independent booksellers, librarians, teachers, niche outlets, retail customers, etc. Text that "grabs" sells books. Your promotional message must respond clearly and directly to the needs of your specified markets. A "one-message-serves-all" promotional campaign is unlikely to obtain optimal results with desired niche audiences. Work in conjunction with a graphic designer and promotional copywriter to create premium promotional material with "high impact." (Refer to Appendix D for a listing of graphic designers and promotional copywriters.)

Promotional printers offer specialty printing, graphic design, and direct mail services—with fast turnaround time. Affordable options are available through an array of promotional printers including:

* TWIG
Phone: 561-740-9901/Web site: www.twigonestop.com

* Simply Postcards
Phone: 800-770-4102/Web site: www.simplycatalogs.com

* Tu-Vets Corporation
Phone: 800-894-8977/Web site: www.tu-vets.com

* PostcardMania
Phone: 800-628-1804/Web site: www.postcardmania.com

* ModernPostcard
Phone: 800-959-8365 x2500/Web site: www.modernpostcard.com

* Growl.com
Phone: 877-678-6537/Web site: www.growl.com

Do your homework and diligently compare prices. TWIG, for example, offers a publisher package which includes 5,000 2″ x 7″ bookmarks, 5,000 business cards, and 5,000 4″ x 6″ postcards—all with full color on both sides—for $525.

The Scoop!

To reduce your postcard/bookmark production costs, print your book cover image in full color on the front side and text in one color (black) on the back side. If you self-publish a second picture book in a related category, consider printing a two-sided, full color bookmark that features one book per side.

Samples of bookmarks and postcards follow.

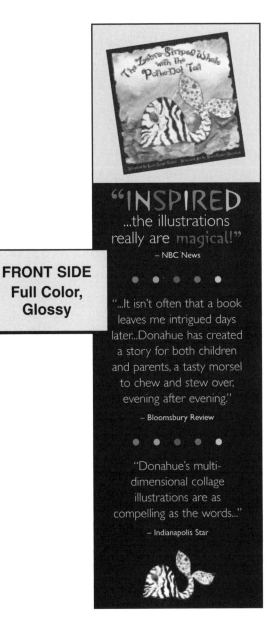

FRONT SIDE
Full Color,
Glossy

"The luminous colors
are splendid!
THE ZEBRA-STRIPED WHALE
WITH THE POLKA-DOT TAIL
is a book I have read more
than once. Each time I find that
the book speaks to me more.
The message is on a spiritual
level that both little people and
older people can grasp. The art
is stunning and enhances the
uplifting, inspirational text itself."

– NAIBA Independent Bookseller,
Sheilah Egan,
A Likely Story Children's Bookstore

• • • • •

ISBN: 0-9634287-3-X
$18.00
Hardcover with dust jacket/48 pgs.

Available through:
Ingram, Baker, & Taylor, Koen

PO BOX 53
Washington Crossing, PA 18977
Ph: 215-862-5899
Fax: 215-862-7005
arimax1@aol.com

www.arimaxkids.com

BACK SIDE
One Color,
Glossy

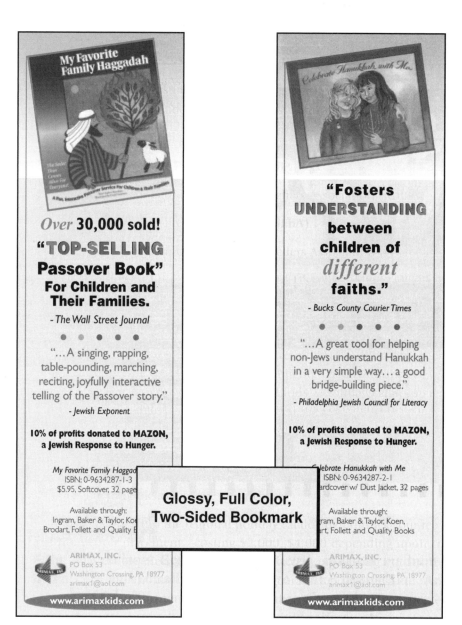

Featured on the front covers of

NAIBA **NEBA** **GLBA** **PNBA** **SCBA**

As well as the children's section of
NCIBA and **Book Page** **2001 Holiday Catalogs.**

"**...INSPIRED**

...the illustrations really are magical!"
– NBC News

The Zebra-Striped Whale with the Polka-Dot Tail

"**Inhabits a rare sea** where children
and adults swim together in deep
reflection...**lavishly illustrated**...
a **cornucopia of textured color**..."
– Times Chronicle

"**...INSPIRED**

...the illustrations really are magical!"
– NBC News

The Zebra-Striped Whale with the Polka-Dot Tail

Oversized Promotional Postcards

Target Customer Base:
Independent Book Retailers (left)
vs. General Audience (right)

Front Side (above): Full Color, Glossy
Back Side (below): One Color Black, Non-Glossy

Producing Your Thematic Book Launching Device

Give your picture book the edge that it deserves through a powerful product launch! With over 27,000 new and reprinted juvenile titles published last year, it is imperative that you think "outside the box" when addressing book buyers—and the media. Consider a thematic book launching device to make your media kit stand out from the crowd! Be creative. You can generate excitement on a shoestring, as exemplified in the three contrived examples below:

* The picture book, *Sally's Special Sock*, can be bundled with a cute pair of socks —imprinted with title, publishing company name, and Web address.

* The picture book, *Sonny's Sensational Sunflower Seeds*, can be bundled with a packet of sunflower seeds—imprinted with cover image, publishing company name, and Web address—as well as a mini spade for added zest.

* The picture book, *Mike's Miraculous Marbles*, can be bundled with a small, see-through bag of colorful marbles—sealed with a computer-generated sticker featuring title, publishing company name, and Web address.

THE SCOOP!

Your thematic book launching device is designed to capture the attention of important book buyers and media contacts. With nominal investment, this clever tool can promote enthusiasm for your title ... and get the contents of your package noticed!

When I self-published *The Zebra-Striped Whale with the Polka-Dot Tail*, I decided to make a HUGE splash with thematic, imprinted mugs, stickers, pins, and latex balloons. For an enticing book launching device, I utilized clear cellophane and zebra-striped ribbon to wrap a colorful gumball-filled mug—simulating my title's polka-dot theme—with an autographed copy of my picture book. I shipped the entire media package—including my media kit folder (cover letter, press release, author bio, testimonial sheet, promotional bookmark/postcard, pin, latex balloon, sample activity kit pages, and favorable articles/reviews)—in an inviting zebra-striped whale sticker-embellished box.

Preparing Your Media Package

Aside from your thematic book launching device (depending on its size and shape), media kit components (cover letter, press release, author bio, testimonial sheet, premium promotional material, activity kit/pages, favorable articles/reviews, etc.) typically fit nicely into a standard pocket folder. Overruns of your picture book cover or dust jacket, if available, may be glued onto the front and back sides of the plain folders for greater visual impact.

Another option is to use a distinctive, self-assembly style portfolio that can be personalized with the name of your publishing company on your home computer—such as the *Pendaflex* Print & Present Custom Portfolios #5, Letter Size, Glossy White 48725—readily available at office supply stores. Visit www.printandpresent.com for product details. If you prefer to order professionally printed portfolios instead of designing your own, contact promotional printing companies for details. (Refer to Appendix D for a listing of promotional printing companies.) Insert your publishing company business card into the business card slot of your folder/portfolio.

If you have ample picture books on hand, add a review copy to your media package as follows:

* Place a "Review Copy" sticker—with your complete contact information—on the outside front cover.

* Insert a loose "pub" slip just inside the front cover.

    (Option: Attach a reduced-size "pub" sheet to your inside front cover via double-sided tape—or use an adhesive-backed label imprinted with the same information.)

The Scoop!

Take measures to make your media package stand out from the crowd. Use enticing, book-related stickers and/or stamps to ensure that your shipping box or mailing envelope "begs to be opened!"

Refer to "Adventures in Shipping" on p. 107 for cost effective media package shipping options. The reality is that shipping hundreds of media packages—with review copies—can be an expensive endeavor! If your budget is tight, consider substituting the review copy of your picture book with a stamped, pre-addressed Review Copy Request Card, as depicted below.

Review Copy Request Card

Picture Book Title:

ISBN: Cover Price: Page Count: Binding Type:

_____ **Please forward a complimentary review copy.**

_____ **I am interested in scheduling an interview with the author.**

_____ **Please provide me with additional information:**

_____

_____

_____

Contact Information: Publisher Name, Address, Phone, Fax, E-mail, and Web site

---

Use Review Copy Request Cards sparingly. Be as generous as possible with your review copies for optimal response.

Your Online Media Kit Matters!

The truth is that, today, a physical media kit alone is simply not enough to capture book buyer and/or media attention. It is wise to produce your media kit in both a physical and online version. Feature your online media kit throughout your physical media kit materials. In addition to your press release, testimonial sheet, bio, sample media questions, and sample book review, your online media kit should contain the following:

* High and low resolution formats of your picture book cover

* High and low resolution formats of author photographs (head and action shots)

* High and low resolution formats of selected interior illustrations

* Current press releases in downloadable format—tailored to specified audiences

* PDF file of promotional sell sheet/flyer

* List of past and upcoming media coverage and reviews—with hotlinks

* Downloadable activity kit pages

* Downloadable visiting school author brochure

* Sample media interview video clip

* Sample bookstore event video clip

* Sample visiting school author video clip

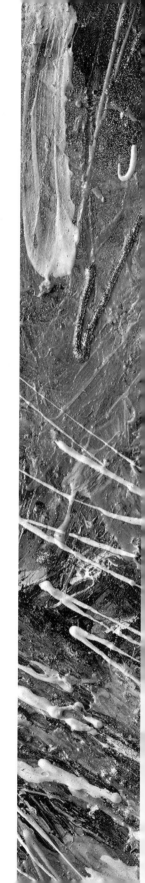

CHAPTER

Leveraging
Libraries

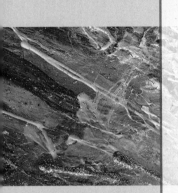

Life is like a grindstone—
whether it grinds you down
or polishes you up
depends on what you're made of.

—Anonymous

Libraries Revealed

According to *Book Industry Trends 2007*, $1.679 billion worth of books were purchased by libraries in 2006. Over one-tenth of publishers' net book sales are derived from libraries. Libraries purchase titles through an array of wholesalers and distributors including:

*   Baker & Taylor

*   Ingram Book Company

*   BWI

*   Follett

*   Brodart

*   Emery-Pratt

*   Ambassador Book Service

*   Midwest Library Service

*   Coutts Library Service

*   Blackwell Book Services

*   Academic Book Center

*   Book House

*   Eastern Book Company

*   Perma-Bound

*   Bound To Stay Bound Books, Inc.

*   Quality Books

*   Unique Books

Visit http://acqweb.library.vanderbilt.edu/pubr/vendor.html for a comprehensive directory of library wholesalers/distributors. Refer to "Library Distribution Channels" on p. 131 for further information. Public and school libraries are most likely to purchase your children's picture book if it is the recipient of consistently positive reviews in several classic review journals such as:

*   *School Library Journal*

*   *Kirkus*

*   *Horn Book Magazine/Guide*

*   *Booklist*

*   *Book Link*

*   *Publishers Weekly*

*   *The Bulletin of the Center for Children's Books*

*   *New York Times*

*   *Child Magazine*

*   *Parenting Magazine*

The budgets of school librarians typically permit the purchase of books only once or twice per year. Children's books that have received glowing pre-pub journal reviews—followed by prestigious awards—are immediately embraced by the library market, and translate to hefty publisher sales.

THE SCOOP!

ONEBOOKAZ for Kids is a highly publicized school program supported by Arizona libraries—in conjunction with Barnes and Noble and other partners—encouraging every child throughout the state of Arizona to read and discuss the same children's book. This year's selected title is *Danger in the Desert*, written by Terri Fields and published by Rising Moon Books. A book-selling opportunity of this magnitude is paramount to winning the lottery!

Powerful Associations

The American Library Association (ALA, www.ala.org), based in Chicago, is the oldest and largest library association in the world—with approximately 65,000 members from academic, public, school, government, and special libraries. ALA has incorporated specialized sections and divisions since 1889. Today, ALA is composed of eleven membership divisions, each with a type-of-library—or type-of-library-function—specialization. For example, the American Association of School Librarians (AASL, www.ala.org/aasltemplate.cfm?section=aboutaasl) is in existence to:

* Impart leadership and actively participate in the entire education process

* Promote life-long learning and the love of reading

* Facilitate the use of information technologies by developing leaders in the school library media field

The Association for Library Service to Children (ALSC, www.ala.org/alscTemplate.cfm?Section=alsc) is the division that presents the Caldecott and Newbery Medals. The ALSC is responsible for:

* Evaluating library materials for children

* Improving and expanding all children-related library services

* Advocating the rights of children within and beyond libraries

* Supporting the professional development of members

* Implementing research and study in these areas

One of the fastest growing divisions of the American Library Association is the Public Library Association (PLA, www.pla.org)—with more than 10,000 members. The mission of PLA is to:

* Strengthen public libraries

* Respond to community needs

THE SCOOP!

"Every Child Ready to Read @ Your Library" is a joint project of the PLA and ALSC—based on research by Dr. Grover C. Whitehurst and Dr. Christopher Lonigan, in the areas of early literacy and brain development. The project supports the premise that it is never too early to prepare children for reading success! Early literacy information is disseminated to parents, child care providers, early childhood educators, children's advocates, and political decision makers—via workshops and resources.

Examining Examination Centers

To further capture librarian attention, consider forwarding a review copy of your children's picture book to examination centers throughout the country. Examination centers are accessible to all local public and school librarians who wish to review physical copies of titles for acquisition purposes. Located at public libraries and universities in major cities (Chicago, Milwaukee, New York, Miami, etc.), examination centers review titles from publishers of all sizes—including self-publishers—and compile recommended reading lists on behalf of parents, teachers, and librarians.

The Scoop!

The Charlotte Zolotow Award is presented annually to the author of the best picture book text—published in the U.S. in the preceding year—by the Cooperative Children's Book Center (CCBC). Established in 1996, the award is named for the distinguished Harper Junior Books children's book editor, Charlotte Zolotow. A recipient of the University of Wisconsin writing scholarship (1933-1936), Zolotow is the author of 70+ picture books—including *Mr. Rabbit and the Lovely Present* (Harper, 1962) and *William's Doll* (Harper, 1972). Visit www.education.wisc.edu/ccbc for The Charlotte Zolotow Award submission guidelines. Call Kathleen T. Horning, Director of CCBC, at 608-263-3721, to obtain a complete roster of committee members.

Extending Your Library Reach

As your budget permits, advertise your newly released children's picture book in a pre-pub or post-pub review journal—especially if the journal has reviewed your title favorably. Because of the power of repetition, it is best to invest in a series of smaller ads over a 4–6 week period versus a single, large "hit-or-miss" ad that runs only once.

Also, consider participating in PMA's publisher-pooled direct mail library program. The cost is $215 to send 3,500 pre-printed promotional flyers to K–12 acquisition librarians throughout the U.S. Contact PMA at 310-372-2732—or visit www.pma-online.org for more information. Atlantic Publishing distributes a targeted library mailing of 25,000 ($.07 per piece) to libraries four times per year through its cooperative marketing program; call 352-622-1825 for further information.

THE SCOOP!

To rent a mailing list of children's librarians for your own marketing purposes, call the American Library Association (ALA) at 800-545-2433—or visit www.ala.org.

Building Local Library Interest

Even a title lacking in consistent favorable reviews—or any reviews—from traditional review sources may be considered for library acquisition under any of the following circumstances:

* The author is local, and receives favorable local press. (Articles by the local media "count" as reviews!)

* There is sufficient demand for the title among library patrons.

* The subject matter of the title is rare and fills a unique library niche.

THE SCOOP!

With sufficient demand from friends, family, and the public at large—as a result of word of mouth and media publicity—local libraries are apt to reduce their emphasis on book review status when purchasing a title.

Libraries can pay full retail price for limited quantities of a title. Public library collection development is moving toward centralization. One staff member dictates purchasing decisions for multiple libraries within a particular system. The objective of the collection development specialist is to maximize title circulation among library patrons. Circulation—easily tracked via library management technology—determines title effectiveness. Poorly circulating titles underutilize precious shelf space, and are ultimately destined for the library's used book sale bin. Because the role of the collection development specialist is to serve the literary needs of patrons, individual title requests can indeed impact library purchasing decisions.

Growing a Grass-Roots Local Library Campaign

Contact local public libraries within a fifty mile radius of your home, and encourage collection development specialists to purchase your title for their collections—if they have not done so already! Your local author status and personal touch can add tremendous leverage to the title selection process. Send or hand-deliver the appropriate individuals a review copy of your finished picture book, "pub" sheet, and media kit—complete with any favorable reviews/articles. Bina Williams, children's librarian at Bridgeport Public Library (Connecticut), urges new authors/self-publishers to be cognizant of the growing number of children's books published each year—and to have realistic expectations. Be persistent, patient, and polite! An over-zealous author/self-publisher may be construed as demanding—inadvertently causing a local librarian to disregard his/her new title.

According to Penny Haff, Children's Program Director at the Village Library of Wrightstown in Bucks County, Pennsylvania, a children's librarian is more likely to respond favorably to a new local author/self-publisher if his/her title complements a pre-selected library book theme i.e. jungle animals, seasons, dinosaurs, etc. Participate in the library's pre-established toddler story time program—if one exists—or create a book event that is appropriate for a young library audience. If applicable, utilize your special talents as an artist, musician, magician, puppeteer, etc. to enhance the value of your program.

THE SCOOP!

Story time for children is a popular event! The Village Library of Wrightstown Tales for Toddlers Program was advertised in the *Newtown Gazette* (December 8, 2006 issue) as follows: "As the holidays approach, enjoy a break in the quiet of the Village Library of Wrightstown. ...Stories, movement, songs, finger-play and fun will make the time fly...as the 10:00 AM session explores winter and polar bears."

Some libraries extend author honorariums and permit the sale of books during special events—without partaking of author's profits. Consider requesting an honorarium in the amount of $50 to $400+ for your special event, if one is not offered. I recently presented my titles to a young pre-school audience on a Saturday afternoon at the Village Library of Wrightstown. Not only was it great fun interacting with the children and library staff, but I received a generous honorarium for sharing just an hour of my time. A great event will help generate a "buzz" about your title—and YOU!

THE SCOOP!

Librarians consistently share information regarding books, authors, and programming with one another during local/regional meetings—and through simple e-mail communications. Word of mouth endorsements among librarians can be quite powerful in promoting your title!

CHAPTER

10

Bookstores
& Beyond

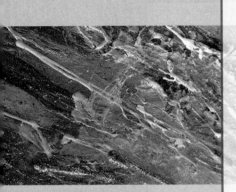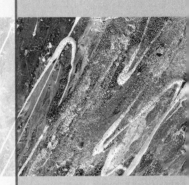

It is good
to have an end
to journey toward;
but it is the journey
that matters,
in the end.

-Ursula K. LeGuin

Chains: Staking Your Claim

Chains, such as Barnes & Noble, Borders, Waldenbooks (owned by Borders Group, Inc.), Books-A-Million, and Hastings, consider a title for acquisition—upon completion—with distribution channels firmly in place. F & Gs are not accepted for acquisition purposes. A vendor of record i.e. Ingram Book Company, Baker & Taylor is required by chains for all stock book purchases and returns. Buying decisions are based on factors such as:

* Author's sales history

* Title marketing plan

* Book cover

* Genre sales trends

A title's perceived potential earnings significantly impact the purchasing decisions of corporate chain buyers. Precious in-store shelf space is saved for profit-bearing titles. Unless a children's book author is already famous—with thousands of flocking fans—the corporate chain buyer rarely places a massive book order. A chain is more likely to "test the waters" in stores that are local to the author—approximately 2–3 returnable copies per store. If demand proves to exist, the chain responds by purchasing greater quantities of the title, on a returnable basis.

Visit the bookstores that stock your title, and introduce yourself to the children's book department managers. Offer to sign the store's inventory of your title. Autographed books are typically marked with "Autographed by the Author" stickers, and placed in a more prominent location of the children's book section. Make the most of these opportunities—and schedule promotional events at bookstores of interest. The personal touch is amazingly powerful!

THE SCOOP!

Bookstores are always searching for new and innovative ways to sell books! The Paradies Shops—an independent chain of airport book/retail stores—actually grants its patrons a unique "read and return" policy. A book may be returned within six months to any airport location for a refund of 50% of the purchase price. That's a frequent flying book lover's dream!

Chain Submission Process

For consideration by mega-book chains, such as Barnes & Noble (www.barnesandnobleinc.com) and the Borders Group, Inc. (www.borders.com), submit a non-returnable copy of your finished children's picture book for review. To the outside front cover, adhere a "Review Copy" sticker that includes your contact information. To the inside front cover, attach a size-reduced "pub" sheet via double-sided tape—or make use of an adhesive-backed mailing label that is printed with the same information. In addition to your media kit—complete with favorable reviews and articles—include a sample activity kit and one-page marketing plan outlining your strategy for product "sell-through." Use your marketing plan to concisely describe all efforts to "move" your picture book, such as:

* Media promotion

* Paid advertisements

* Awards

* Reviews

* Feature articles

* Children's book events/signings

* Supplemental activity kit

Be as specific as possible. Chain buyers demand good reasons for lining their shelves with copies of your children's picture book. Update the buyers often—by fax or e-mail—to provide the most current marketing information. A sample marketing plan update follows.

FAX

TO: **D. Somalsky, Barnes & Noble**
FR: **Thomas W. Donahue**
RE: **Marketing Plan Update, 9/27/01**
     ISBN 0-9634287-3-X
     The Zebra-Striped Whale with the Polka-Dot Tail

HOLIDAY MARKETING PLAN UPDATE:

- **MORE FAVORABLE REVIEWS:** Bloomsbury Review, Midwest Book Review, Bacon's, Copley

- **T.V. APPEARANCES:** NBC Philadelphia Morning Show with Steve Levy (May)

- **FRONT COVER ADS:** NEBA, NAIBA, NCIBA and SCBA Independent Bookseller Holiday Catalogs
  Note: These catalogs are also circulated in a variety of newspapers including the LA Times.

- *BOOK PAGE HOLIDAY CATALOGS:* November and December Issues

- *NEW YORK IS BOOK COUNTRY EXPO:* Book Kiosk on 5th Avenue

- *NEW YORK TIMES* **CHILDREN'S BOOK FEATURE AD:** Fall 2001

- *PUBLISHERS WEEKLY* **ADS:** Spring 2001 Children's Book Issue; March 12, 2001; May 7, 2001; June 11, 2001 (BookExpo America Issue); Fall 2001 (PMA inside front cover ad)

- **COLLAGE CRAFT ACTIVITY & BOOK SIGNING EVENTS:** Philadelphia vicinity bookstores

- **AUTHOR/ILLUSTRATOR VISITS:** Philadelphia vicinity schools and libraries

Arimax, Inc. Publishing

2865 S. Eagle Rd., PMB #399, Newtown, PA 18940   ph: 215-205-2227   fax: 215-862-7005   e-mail: tomdonahue@zebrastripedwhale.com

"Booking" the Chains

Title acquisition information for national and regional chains of interest may be obtained via:

* *American Book Trade Directory*

* Corporate chain Web sites

It can take 90 days to receive a written response from the chains regarding acquisition status of your children's picture book. Remember, patience is a virtue!

To be considered by Barnes & Noble, mail your submissions package to:

Barnes & Noble
Small Press Department
122 5th Avenue
NY, NY 10011

Include the following items in your submissions package to Barnes & Noble:

* Review copy of your finished book—including review copy sticker and "pub" sheet (as described on p. 208)

* Cover letter summarizing the uniqueness of your title

* Marketing plan

* Media kit with favorable reviews and/or articles

* Sample activity kit

To be considered by Borders Group, Inc., on behalf of Borders and Waldenbooks, mail your submissions package to:

Borders Group, Inc.
Attention: New Vendor Acquisitions
100 Phoenix Drive
Ann Arbor, MI 48108

Include duplicates of the following items in your submissions package to Borders Group, Inc.:

* Downloadable Product Submissions Form (www.borders.com)

* Review copy of your finished book—including review copy sticker and "pub" sheet (as described on p. 208)

* Cover letter summarizing the uniqueness of your title

 ✻ Marketing plan

 ✻ Media kit with favorable reviews and/or articles

 ✻ Sample activity kit

Book Acquisition Equals Consignment

Do not judge your publishing success on the quantity of books ordered by the chain. The acquisition of mass quantities of books is not synonymous with "guaranteed sale," but is synonymous with "consignment." Though rare, bookstore buyers may opt to initially stock large quantities of your children's picture book based on perceived demand. If sales prove disappointing over a 3–4 month period, unsold books are returned to your wholesaler/distributor (vendor of record) for a 100% refund. The opposite scenario could also hold true. Bookstore buyers, tentative regarding your "new author" status, may initially opt to stock limited copies of your title at selected stores. As demand drives sales, corporate buyers are likely to respond by stocking additional copies of your title. Regardless of the quantity of books purchased by the corporate chain buyer, whether 0 or 5,000, you have the opportunity to stimulate demand for your own title! Even if the chain does nothing more than add your children's picture book to its corporate database, you can still have a future bestseller. Your title may be "special ordered" by interested customers at individual chain stores. If sales prove exceptionally strong, your title may be scheduled for automatic reorder.

THE SCOOP!

Make no mistake! Bookstores operate to increase their bottom line. Precious shelf space is given freely to proven profit-generating titles only.

With ample publicity, grass-roots marketing, and good old fashioned word of mouth, sales of your title can soar! That was my experience with my second title, *My Favorite Family Haggadah* (1st printing, 1994; 2nd printing, 1996; 3rd printing, 1998). When I initially presented this book to Barnes & Noble for consideration prior to the Passover holiday in 1994, I received written word that the title was unacceptable for acquisition due to its saddle stitch spine. (At the time of publication, all top-selling Passover Haggadahs in its category incorporated this binding type.) Because my distribution channels were in place through Ingram, Baker & Taylor, and Koen Book Distributors, *My Favorite Family Haggadah* was listed on the Barnes & Noble corporate database. Since I was unable to alter the chain's buying decision, I focused my attention on getting publicity for this unique Passover title. Numerous feature articles appeared in local community newspapers and regional Jewish newspapers throughout the country with headlines such as, "A new book is helping families keep Passover traditions alive" and "Telling it her way: Singing, rapping and rocking with new Haggadah." Title sales were stimulated at independent bookstores, Jewish bookstores, and mega-book chains around the country. This Passover book found its niche, and word of mouth spread. Five months prior to the following Passover, based on proven sales history, Barnes & Noble informed me that *My Favorite Family Haggadah* ($5.95 retail) was indeed worth acquiring— even with its saddle stitch binding. Thirty-thousand copies of this title are currently in print!

Co-op: A Chain Reaction

Larger publishers actually provide the chains with substantial cooperative marketing funding, known as "co-op," to feature their titles in well-merchandised, attention-getting book displays throughout desired store locations. Co-op opportunities are typically buyer-driven— approximately four months in advance—and cost publishers from $5,000–$30,000 to participate. Premier front-of-store table space and end cap placements are saved for books that the buyers believe will sell the greatest number of copies. For advertising co-ops, publishers provide a 75% credit in the form of  future book purchases (not to exceed 10% of the value of books received by the store), while the bookstore pays the remaining 25%. Regularly advertising stores benefit from better media rates.

Though expensive buyer-driven co-op programs are geared to large, financially-backed publishing houses, there may be a rare exception—if your title "speaks" to the corporate chain buyer and complements a particular buyer-selected co-op theme. If you are a self-publisher with ample co-op dollars to spend, write a detailed letter of request to the chain's acquisition department (separate from your initial book submission), at least four months prior to your proposed cooperative marketing program.

> ## The Scoop!
> Proceed with caution. Based on a ruling by the Federal Trade Commission, a co-op marketing opportunity that is granted by the publisher to one bookseller must be made available to all like business entities. The reality is that most self-publishers simply cannot afford co-op demands.

Sell More Books: Special Chain Events

The objective of bookstores is to sell books—and you can help to make this happen by creating a successful in-store children's book event! The chain thrives on talented authors, like you, to stimulate customer demand through exciting FREE event programming. If you are a musician, interact with your bookstore audience while playing the guitar or keyboard. If you are a magician, create a magic show. If you are a puppeteer, present a puppet show—starring some of the characters from your book. If you are the illustrator of your title, or simply an art lover, build your event around a unique age-appropriate craft project. If you are an expert on a topic that relates to your title, prepare an in-store presentation geared toward young families. Betty Tatham, popular author of *Baby Sea Otter* (Henry Holt and Company), shares interesting facts about otters during her successful bookstore events. Regardless of your technique, your objective is to fully engage your audience—and bolster store level sales of your title.

> ## The Scoop!
> Utilize your talents! Don't just sign books. Have fun promoting your title during a 30-minute, interactive event in the vibrant and alluring children's section of the chain bookstore.

Scheduling Your Event

Introduce yourself—by phone or in-person—to the general or community relations manager of several local chain stores in your region, 3–4 months in advance of your desired event. Forward your media kit (complete with favorable reviews/articles), sample activity kit, and a detailed description of your proposed in-store event. Be persistent and follow up.

In many cases, the marketing/community relations manager will actively market your picture book event via:

* Free local publicity

* Customer event calendar listings

* In-store promotional easels

He/she may even merchandise your children's picture book, "face out," in a prominent store location for several days surrounding your event. Plan to sign all stock copies of your title.

The Scoop!

Customers are more apt to purchase signed children's books—well beyond the event itself. Autographed books are less frequently returned to publishers.

The Audience Factor

For a "built-in" audience, develop your children's picture book event around the chain's popular morning or afternoon story hour program. A story hour typically attracts an audience of 20–30 toddlers. The majority of story hour participants are below the age of three. Make your event age appropriate.

If you believe that you can generate a large audience on your own, coordinate a children's event that is completely independent of the scheduled story hour. Communicate with the marketing/community relations manager regarding maximizing event publicity. In some cases, it may be necessary to invest in your own local newspaper/radio ads.

Be certain to participate in FREE community announcement services offered by your local newspapers, radio/cable stations, and online billboards. At least 3–4 weeks prior to your children's event, e-mail or fax all details—including time, date, location, and contact information—to your targeted list of community announcement providers. Public service announcements are typically listed on a "first come–first serve" basis. Whether you are participating in the pre-designated story hour program or creating your own independent event, the marketing/community relations manager depends upon you to stimulate customer enthusiasm—and increase the chain's bottom line.

THE SCOOP!

To guarantee an audience for an in-store event, extend invitations to family, friends, and friends of friends. It is up to you to spread the word! An event can flop without ample audience turn-out!

As your picture book is praised by bookstore personnel and/or customers, invite them to fill out a Testimonial Permission Form. (Refer to p. 181 for a sample Testimonial Permission Form.) Use the endorsements as both Web site and press kit testimonials.

When autographing a book for a particular customer during your event, verify the proper spelling of the recipient's name. Inscribe your picture book with a brief, thoughtful message. Take a photograph with your enthusiastic audience and/or the bookstore staff—and forward a copy to the community relations manager along with a note of appreciation for hosting the event.

The Stronghold of Independent Bookstores

Do not underestimate the powerful stronghold of independent booksellers! According to Curt Matthews, CEO of both Independent Publishers Group and Chicago Review Press, as quoted in the January 2006 PMA *Independent* newsletter, "The terrible attrition among small retail booksellers has dramatically slowed. The stores that remain are run by battle-hardened veterans with the savvy to succeed in a very difficult business."

Whereas chain superstores are laden with 100,000+ books, CDs, DVDs, magazines, greeting cards, steep discounts, and Starbucks Coffee cafés, independent bookstores base their success on serving neighborhoods and knowing their customers. Karen Beem, co-owner of Newtown Bookshop (Newtown, PA) from 2000 to 2006, shares her insights in a local newspaper article (*Time Off Bucks County*, 7/28/06–8/6/06 issue), "We hire a knowledgeable staff, people who know books and who stay with us for years. They get to know the stock, they're people who read. We get to know everybody who comes in and what they like to read, so we can make recommendations." To co-exist, side-by-side, with the chains, independent bookstores offer their customers a varied array of the following incentives:

* Cozy and inviting children's book area

* Money-saving "frequent buyer" programs

* Low-priced remainders

* Older eclectic reading material

* Book clubs for adults and children

* Author events and signings

* Help desk

* Expanded inventory—stationary, magazine, and gift items

* In-store café

Some independent bookstore owners, such as Ellen Mager of Booktenders' Secret Garden (Doylestown, PA), work closely with community schools and education groups to coordinate visiting author programs and reading lists for children.

The American Booksellers Association

American Booksellers Association (ABA, www.ambook.org) is the largest and most prestigious trade association of independent booksellers. A strategic marketing campaign, Book Sense, has been successfully implemented to unify "the knowledge and diversity" of independent booksellers in combating the foreboding base of mega-book chains. Its motto is, "Independent Bookstores for Independent Minds." The Web site, www.booksense.com, sells Book Sense gift cards that are redeemable at independent bookstores throughout the U.S. The well-promoted Children's Book Bestsellers List, generated by independent bookstore sales figures, is currently running in more than a dozen newspapers—as well as monthly in *U.S. News & World Report* and on C-Span. The *Children's Book Sense Picks*, a seasonal publication of recommended children's picture books, is based on nominations by many independent booksellers. It is distributed, free of charge, at independent bookstores throughout the country.

The Scoop!

To increase chances of being considered for the Children's Book Bestsellers List and *Book Sense Picks*, traditional and self-publishers are encouraged to mail FREE advance reading copies to 25–50 independent booksellers—through the popular Book Sense Advance Access program.

If you are interested in participating in the Advance Access program, specific guidelines are available through www.bookweb.org/booksense/publisher/3311.html. As a member of SPAN or PMA, the Advance Access program fee is $50—versus the standard $100. Mail your Book Sense Advance Access check to:

American Booksellers Association
828 S. Broadway
Tarrytown, NY 10591

For convenience, you may pay by credit card; call 914-591-2665, ext. 273. State your affiliation with SPAN or PMA to receive your $50 discount.

The Association of Booksellers for Children

The Association of Booksellers for Children, ABC, is a national association of approximately 200 members, and includes:

* Independent bookstores engaged in the retail sale of books for children

* Publishers of children's literature

* Publishers' representatives

* Librarians

* Wholesalers

* Literary agents

* Prospective booksellers

A $50 annual fee entitles the author/self-publisher to the following:

* Complimentary set of membership mailing labels for book promotion purposes

* Workshops/networking opportunities at regional meetings and BookExpo America

* ABC Newsletter

* *ABC Best Books for Children* Annual Holiday Catalog

According to Kristen McClean, executive director of ABC, "Self-published children's book authors benefit greatly from networking with booksellers at industry events. If booksellers believe that you have a quality children's book to offer ... and get to know you, they are more likely to stand behind your title."

Through June of each calendar year, ABC accepts submissions for *ABC Best Books for Children* from traditional and self-publishers with adequate book quantities, established distribution channels, and a moderate advertising budget. For consideration, send a sample of your children's picture book, activity kit, and media kit—complete with favorable articles/reviews to:

ABC National Office
62 Wenham Street
Jamaica Plain, MA 02130

Visit ABC's Web site, www.ABFC.com, and/or call 617-390-7759 for further information.

Regional Booksellers Associations

Independent bookstores are actively engaged in strong, cohesive regional associations that work closely with the American Booksellers Association. For a comprehensive listing of regional booksellers associations, including president/executive director contact information, visit www.bookweb.org. Highlight "Organizations & Events" on the upper left menu, followed by "Regional Booksellers Associations." Regional booksellers associations include:

* Chesapeake Regional Area Booksellers

* Great Lakes Booksellers Association

* Midwest Booksellers Association

* Mountains & Plains Independent Booksellers Association

* New Atlantic Independent Booksellers Association

* New England Booksellers Association

* New Orleans-Gulf South Booksellers Association

* Northern California Independent Booksellers Association

* Oklahoma Independent Booksellers Association

* Pacific Northwest Booksellers Association

* Southern California Booksellers Association

* Southern Independent Booksellers Alliance

These powerful associations coordinate effective marketing/advertising vehicles including:

* Professional newsletters

* Author events

* Brainstorming activities

* Holiday catalogs

* Trade shows

To generate that infamous word of mouth "buzz" among independent booksellers, consider exhibiting your new children's book at one or more association trade shows. Fees are reasonable, and vary according to the region and size of your exhibit.

Spotlighting the Independents

High-profile regional holiday catalogs are produced by several regional booksellers associations including:

* Midwest Booksellers Association (MBA)

* New Atlantic Independent Booksellers Association (NAIBA)

* Southern California Booksellers Association (SCBA)

* Great Lakes Booksellers Association (GLBA)

* Mountains & Plains Independent Booksellers Association (MPBA)

* New England Booksellers Association (NEBA)

* Northern California Independent Booksellers Association (NCIBA)

* Pacific Northwest Booksellers Association (PNBA)

* Southern Independent Booksellers Alliance (SIBA)

Contact regional booksellers associations directly regarding children's holiday catalog advertising opportunities. Some regional catalogs are more popular than others. Research your options carefully. Visit www.bookweb.org; highlight "Organizations & Events" on the upper left menu, then "Regional Booksellers Associations." Holiday catalogs are distributed after Thanksgiving—free of charge—through:

* Local media insertions

* Direct mail

* Independent bookstore point of purchase

Advertisement placement within the regional holiday catalog determines your fee schedule. If you purchase front cover placement—costing $2,000–$4,000 depending upon circulation— regional independent booksellers will commit to actively promoting your title during the holiday season. Though this commitment does not guarantee book sales, it does increase the odds! Any unsold books will be returned to your vendor of record at the start of the new year. Holiday catalog advertising, though expensive, is likely to be beneficial. Determine your independent bookstore advertising budget prior to investing large sums of capital in multiple holiday catalogs. A wise first step is to target your local region—where your foundation is strongest!

> ## The Scoop!
>
> It is exhilarating to see your picture book on the front cover of a popular regional bookseller association holiday catalog! To maximize sales efforts, ensure that your book distribution channels are firmly in place—and that adequate title quantities are available for sale at targeted booksellers.

Bonkers for the Bookshelf

Several regional booksellers association holiday catalogs are closely affiliated with *BookPage*—a monthly book review publication distributed by more than 3,000 independent bookstores and libraries throughout the U.S. (circulation: 1.8 million). An advertisement in the *BookPage Holiday Catalog* ensures that your children's book is "guaranteed for stock" in Books-A-Million chain stores during the holiday season; visit BookPage.com for details. Though Books-A-Million shelf space for your title is highly advantageous, sales are not guaranteed. Unsold copies of your title will be returned to your wholesaler/distributor at the start of the new year.

PMA (www.pma-online.org) offers a cooperative catalog (circulation: 3,500) that features your book cover image and 100-word description for a fee of $230. Atlantic Publishing offers a targeted bookstore mailing of 30,000 ($.07 per piece), four times per year, through its cooperative marketing program; call 352-622-1825 for details. Inexpensive advertising is available through *Independent Bookstore*, a quarterly newsletter distributed to approximately 4,000 independent bookstores. For pricing information and/or a newsletter sample, contact Ed Davis via phone at 866-443-7987—or via e-mail at edavis@marionstreetpress.com.

Spend your advertising dollars wisely, and proceed cautiously. Bookstore competition is fierce. The reality is that bookstores are among the most challenging outlets for selling your children's picture book!

THE SCOOP!

Without grand scale national media attention—and sustained advertising budget to compete with the majors—isolated and sporadic bookstore promotion is unlikely to result in a significant sales increase of your picture book.

As a self-publisher with limited funds, it is best to saturate one region at a time with publicity and promotion—beginning with your own! Consider targeting independent bookstores in your region via a direct mail campaign. Member store mailing lists are available for purchase through your regional independent booksellers association.

THE SCOOP!

To obtain a listing of independent booksellers by city/state and specialty i.e. children's independent booksellers, visit the American Booksellers Association Web site at www.bookweb.org. Scroll down to: "Find Independent Booksellers in Your Area." Click "Advance Search" or "Browse Bookseller Directory." You may rent a current mailing list of independent bookstores (fee: $375/members, $475/non-members) by contacting American Booksellers Association at 800-637-0037 or 914-591-2665, ext. 6636.

Wooing Your Local Booksellers

The strength of your author base lies within your own community. Independent booksellers are acutely aware that popular local authors provide the ultimate sense of community at a community bookstore. Local authors can successfully generate a "buzz" through:

* Strong local media

* Word of mouth

* In-store promotional events—bolstered, if necessary, by personal invitation to friends and family

If you do not have a distributor to actively hand-sell your title into independent bookstores, you must do the footwork yourself. Encourage store managers to display several copies of your signed book to coordinate with your upcoming local publicity and scheduled book events.

The Scoop!

Some independent booksellers prefer the use of a wholesaler/distributor to purchase—and potentially return—copies of your title. Others may bypass standard distribution channels altogether in favor of working with you directly on a consignment basis.

Making Contact

Ensure that your title is available at as many local independent bookstores as possible. Contact the buyers/managers of independently owned and operated bookstores within a 25–50 mile radius of your home. Search online, check the *Yellow Pages*, or rent a current independent bookstore mailing list from your regional booksellers association or the American Booksellers Association (800-637-0037 or 914-591-2665, ext. 6636). Depending on bookstore proximity and convenience, mail or hand-deliver your "local author" promotional package including:

* Review copy of your picture book with "Local Author Review Copy" sticker—including contact information—on outside front cover. Insert loose "pub" sheet just inside front cover.

   (Option: Attach reduced-size "pub" sheet to inside front cover via double-sided tape—or use adhesive-backed label imprinted with same information.)

* Media kit—including thematic book launching device

* One-page marketing plan

* Brief description of your proposed in-store children's book event—including a personal hand-written note on a "post-it," for example, "I'm a local author … and look forward to creating a special children's event at your store!"

Mailing this package to multiple regional independent bookstores is an expensive endeavor. Refer to "Adventures in Shipping" on p. 107 for cost effective delivery options. As your time permits, visit as many local independent bookstores as possible to introduce yourself—and your title. Be persistent, and follow up! Your personal touch can truly impact the sales of your title!

Cooperative Marketing ... Maybe!

Larger publishers provide independent booksellers with cooperative marketing funding (co-op) to coordinate local newspaper ads and in-store displays—on behalf of their new titles. Penguin, for example, recently paid a local independent bookstore $100, in co-op, to feature its twelve-book "dump" (a disposable cardboard book display) for a two-week period. With limited retail space and the desire to earn extra revenue, independent bookstores readily support publishing houses that grant co-op.

Proceed cautiously if you decide to grant co-op funding, on behalf of your children's picture book, to an independent bookstore. As a result of a Federal Trade Commission ruling, a publisher must extend the same co-op privileges to all like-business entities.

The good news is that many independent bookstores enthusiastically promote their local authors—even when there is little to no co-op funding available. In some cases, independent booksellers may be willing to share the cost of local newspaper advertising with a valued community author. Discuss book marketing opportunities with the publicity coordinators of several independent bookstores in your area.

Independent Bookstores Depend on You

Your local independent bookseller depends on YOU to "move" your picture book—via successful publicity and in-store events. Promotional event flyers and display posters may be provided by the hosting bookstore. If you discover that this is not the case, offer to create your own!

Be cognizant of children's nap times when scheduling your appearance. If you have neither the time nor the means to generate your own audience, consider the bookstore's pre-slotted story hour as an event vehicle. You'll enjoy presenting your picture book to a "built-in" audience of enthusiastic toddlers, parents, and nannies. In either case, utilize your talents to make your event shine! During several of my local independent bookstore events, featuring *The Zebra-Striped Whale with the Polka-Dot Tail*, I unveiled a huge sheet cake iced with an edible, full color photographic image of my picture book cover. Bookstore customers enjoyed reading my book—and eating it too!

Independent booksellers, like their mega-book chain cousins, respond to the bottom line—earning money from the sales of your title. Since you are your own publisher, you are responsible for bringing extra copies of your picture book to events. This safeguard surely beats the alternative of lost sales.

As independent bookstore personnel and/or customers praise your title, invite them to fill out a Testimonial Permission Form. (Refer to p. 181 for a sample Testimonial Permission Form.) Utilize their heartfelt endorsements as Web site and media kit testimonials.

When signing copies of your picture book, verify the proper spelling of each recipient's name. Take time to inscribe a brief, meaningful message. The customer is always appreciative of the added personal touch.

The Scoop!

Bring a camera from home, and pose for a photograph with staff and/or audience participants. Send the independent bookstore manager a copy of the photograph—along with a note of appreciation for hosting the event.

Being Your Own Publicity Agent

Though independent bookstore event coordinators are likely to be enthusiastic about your in-store event, you must be the driving force! According to Krisy Paredes, Publicity/ Ad/Co-op Director for Doylestown Bookshop (Doylestown, PA), "The harder you work to promote your in-store event, the better the outcome. A successful event that generates an ample audience is the result of effective communication with the public via sufficient media coverage, free community announcements, paid local ads, and promotional in-store flyers and posters. Focus hard at first on providing local book events at your neighborhood bookstores, libraries, and schools—then build on your success by expanding into neighboring areas."

The local media is always looking for community news of interest to share with their audiences. Build a timely children's event that attracts the media. John Kremmer's title, *1001 Ways to Market Your Book*, offers a host of innovative book marketing ideas.

Consider tying your event to a worthy cause! For example, during the holiday season, inform the media that you will be donating 50% of the proceeds from books sold during your event to the "Toys for Tots" foundation. Invite local journalists to the event for a photo opportunity.

Take full advantage of the numerous FREE community announcement services offered by your local newspapers, radio/cable stations, and online billboards. Community announcement contact information can be obtained via a Google search. Only free-to-the-public events are accepted for community announcements. At least 3–4 weeks prior to your children's event, e-mail or fax event specifications—including time, date, location, and contact information— to your targeted list of community announcement providers. These popular public service announcements are usually listed on a "first come–first serve" basis.

Making the Most of In-Store Book Signing Events

Bookstores are among the most competitive environments for selling books—even during book-signing events. Stephanie Chandler, owner of Book Lovers Bookstore in Sacramento, CA (and author of *The Business Startup Checklist and Planning Guide* as well as *From Entrepreneur to Infopreneur: Make Money with Books, E-books and Information Products*), states in the May 2006 PMA *Independent* newsletter, "Book-signing events bring other benefits. Think of them as tools for  publicity (getting your name out there) and for networking opportunities. You never know who is going to show up and what alliances will be formed. Set your expectations realistically, and try to learn something from every event. If you sell a lot of books, first pat yourself on the back, and then figure out how to repeat the success at other venues." A helpful list of Stephanie Chandler's "Dos and Don'ts of Book Signing Events" follows.

DOs:

- ✔ Seek media coverage prior to the event by contacting local editors, reporters, columnists, and radio show producers. A story in the newspaper or on the radio can boost attendance dramatically.

- ✔ Send posters and bookmarks to the store at least two weeks before the event.

- ✔ Ask whether the store will hand out bag-stuffers/small flyers that promote the event. If so, get some printed and drop them off at least two weeks in advance so they can be distributed with everything purchased at the store.

- ✔ Find out what kind of promotion the store will do (probably not much). If necessary, take it upon yourself to get your event listed in community calendars in the local papers and on www.craigslist.org.

- ✔ Tell everyone you know about your event and encourage them to attend and invite their friends. If you have a lot of people around you in the store, others will come to find out what the fuss is about.

- ✔ Use props or gimmicks—anything you can bring to capture the attention of passers-by. Even a bowl of candy can draw people to you.

- ✔ Offer to give a talk or a presentation instead of just sitting there and signing books.

- ✔ Set up an eye-catching sign. It could feature a picture of your book, other relevant artwork, a quiz or interesting pertinent statistics … anything to capture interest.

- ✔ Smile! This is basic, but easily forgotten, especially if you're nervous. Sometimes a friendly smile and "Hello" is all it takes to start a conversation with a shy person that then leads to a purchase.

- ✔ Be ready to talk about your book. Prepare short presentations on five to ten key selling points to share when people inquire.

- ✔ Get up from your chair. You are not chained to that table! If you're sitting there all alone, get up and walk around. Make friendly conversation with the bookstore staff and customers.

- ✔ Keep a sign-up sheet at your table or bring along a jar to collect business cards. Later, you can add the contact information to your database and follow up by sending your newsletter, your e-zine, or a personal message of thanks for attending your event. You can even offer a prize drawing for business cards, with the prize being an autographed copy of your book or special report.

- ✔ Stand out from the crowd by sending the store manager or owner a thank you note after your event.

DON'Ts:

✔ Don't just sit there like a bump on a log. Be engaging and friendly.

✔ Don't wait for customers to come to you. You can go to them, or simply smile and welcome them as they come into the store.

✔ Don't disrespect the store staff. These people will have a hand in selling your books—or burying them on low-lying shelves after you leave.

✔ Don't use a hard sell. Nobody likes the message, "Buy this, or feel guilty." If someone says your genre doesn't appeal, point out that such-and-such a holiday is approaching and the book makes a great holiday gift. Ask, "Do you have a relative or friend who might like a copy?"

✔ Don't expect the store to rally an audience for you. Some stores may list events in their newsletters and/or in community calendars, but they aren't going to be your personal publicity agents. Do the legwork, and don't be too disappointed if you don't have a crowd.

Word of Mouth "Buzz"

According to Sheila Kowalsky, the former book buying manager for Koen-Levy (no longer in operation), "Word of mouth is the critical factor in selling books." As a children's picture book author, word of mouth enthusiasm for your title can indeed be contagious, spreading from you to the bookseller … from the bookseller to the customer … from the customer to the customer's friends and relatives … from the customer's friends and relatives to the friends and relatives of the customer's friends and relatives … and on and on, from region to region to region, throughout the country—and beyond!

THE SCOOP!

In Howard Schultz's book, *Pour Your Heart Into It*, he shares with his readers, "In this ever-changing society, the most powerful and enduring brands are built from the heart. ...Their foundations are stronger because they are built with the strength of the human spirit, not an ad campaign."

Case in point: An advertised children's book event at Doylestown Bookshop (Doylestown, PA)—featuring Rob Scotten, the talented author of *Russell the Sheep*—attracted a small audience. (Even a major publisher, such as HarperCollins, cannot guarantee audience size!) Despite the disappointing turn-out, *Russell the Sheep* has become an absolute favorite among Doylestown Bookshop staff. Within several weeks following the event, store customers purchased over 50 copies of *Russell the Sheep*, due to the staff's genuine enthusiasm for the picture book—and the author! Hand-selling by bookstore staff is one of the most effective tools utilized to establish a strong market presence. As HarperCollins' alternative to the highly successful *Olivia* series, *Russell the Sheep* is a fun, beautifully illustrated children's picture book that has been building this sort of momentum across the country.

THE SCOOP!

Word of mouth "buzz," fueled by the passionate hand-selling of bookstore personnel, has enabled several children's titles—including *Old Turtle*, *Quiltmaker's Gift*, and *Stranger in the Woods*—to reach the pinnacle of "bestseller" status!

The "Blitz" Maneuver

The publishing game is not for the faint of heart—and requires abundant footwork, stamina, and shameless self-promotion. Hand-selling, in conjunction with creative niche channel marketing, is an exceptional tool for small publishers. Donald A. Tubesing, principal of Pfeifer-Hamilton—publisher of two American Booksellers "Book of the Year" award winners, *Old Turtle* and *Quiltmaker's Gift*—recommends that you first "blitz" your own city to "get the buzz going." According to Tubesing, "Concentrate either on concentric circles moving from the center regionally, or saturate one channel at a time so that you have great stories to tell the other markets later. Do not go lightly anywhere—ever!" As a result of powerful hand-selling, Tubesing was able to prove strong, verifiable bookstore sales in his own region prior to "conquering" adjacent cities. With confidence, he stated, "Look what we did in Minnesota—we can do the same in your region!"

Sales of books increase when they can be sold through non-traditional outlets, as well as the standard bookstore arena. Uncovering an existing sales channel, in addition to bookstores, minimizes book competition while further promoting title enthusiasm. Tubesing experimented with *Quiltmaker's Gift* at quilting stores. Quilting group members adored *Quiltmaker's Gift*, and eagerly spread the word. In less than three years, 600,000 copies were purchased! Tubesing ultimately sold the *Quiltmaker's Gift*, and its companion quilting instructional manual, to Scholastic at a sizable profit. Tubesing shares his words of wisdom, "Find a different angle—one that sparks interest and gets attention. Plan a marketing sequence of events and products in support of the book that continues to build momentum over five years minimum."

Community Matters

To extend your community word of mouth buzz, consider promoting your children's picture book to the owner/manager of local drug stores, gift shops (remember hotel, museum, and hospital gift shops too!), grocery stores, cafés, children's clothing stores, etc. Courageously walk in and introduce yourself. Warmly state that you are a local author, and share your willingness to leave several of your autographed books on consignment. If the manager/owner consents (and hopefully he/she will!), leave a handful of autographed picture books—each with an "Autographed Copy" sticker on the cover to emphasize the added selling feature!

The Scoop!

Promotional stickers can improve book sales! "Autographed Copy," "Great Gift Idea," and "Local Author" stickers may be purchased from SPAN, in packages of two hundred, for $10. Call 719-395-4790 with credit card information—or send your check payable to:

SPAN stickers
P.O. Box 1306
Buena Vista, CO 81211

Encourage the owner/manager to sign your company letterhead designating the quantity left on consignment, as well as an agreed-upon discount (usually 20% to 50%). Leave your business card. Follow up by phone, e-mail, and/or in-person—within two weeks—to stay abreast of book sales. Restock as necessary. In the event that the retailer is unable to accept your children's picture book on the spot, he/she may refer you to another staff member—or perhaps the distributor that you must contact for product approval. In either case, request a business card.

The Scoop!

Write "reminder" notes on the back side of the store's business card upon leaving each location. Unless there is absolutely no interest in carrying your title, follow up ... follow up ... follow up!

Viable "Non-Returns" Venues

Due to aggressive bookstore returns, many self-publishers pursue a variety of non-returns, direct sales venues such as:

* Book signing parties

* Flea markets

* Craft expos

* Book festivals

* Religious/non-secular organization fundraising events

* Community fairs

* Industry-specific seminars

* Airport/mall kiosk sales

Be certain to sign copies of your picture book for recipients. Autographed picture books are greatly appreciated by customers—and significantly reduce the potential for returns. Ensure that a friend, relative, or colleague is present to actively hand-sell your title—if you feel awkward doing so on your own.

The Scoop!

Aggressive overselling can be just as detrimental to sales as passive underselling and customer avoidance. Be sensitive to the cues of others!

During a busy outdoor community fair in my quaint hometown of New Hope, PA, a local "Main Street" shopkeeper invited me to display my children's picture books outside of her storefront. (I insisted on paying her $50 for the privilege.) Tourists and community residents alike respond especially favorably to the autographed books of local authors. I enjoyed spending that sunny Sunday afternoon—with my husband and children by my side—autographing copy after copy of my children's picture books to enthusiastic passers-by. My husband is a great asset to my publishing endeavor (thankfully!)—especially because he is so undeniably comfortable sharing his overt enthusiasm for my titles with anyone ... anywhere ... anytime!

Fabulous Festivals

If you enjoy travel, consider participating in children's book festivals at destinations of interest. Combining book business with pleasure enables you to benefit from a partial business-related "write-off." Speak to your accountant regarding specifics. Children's book festivals, featuring prominent children's authors and illustrators, are frequently held at colleges and universities across the country. The Connecticut Children's Book Fair, for example, is held at the University of Connecticut. Event proceeds are donated to the Northeast Children's Literature Collection (Archives & Special Collections) at the Thomas J. Dodd Research Center, University of Connecticut Libraries.

According to Patricia Fry, president of SPAWN (Small Publishers, Artists and Writers Network) in the January 2006 PMA *Independent* newsletter, "A key to selling books at a festival is connecting with potential buyers. ...Be observant; learn to read body language; know how to talk about your book; practice your sales pitch. ...Ask everyone who visits your booth for their contact information. Have them sign up for a contest or a drawing for a prize at the end of the event. Put their names on your mailing list and send promotional packages to them periodically."

If revenue earned at a particular festival proves to be disappointing, chalk the event up to invaluable marketing exposure! For a listing of U.S. book festivals, visit www.loc.gov/loc/cfbook/bookfair.html or www.lights.com/publisher/bookfairs.html. Search the Web utilizing key words, "book festivals" or "book fairs." (The use of quotations in a Google search guarantees more precise output.) SPAWN designated booths/tables are available to members at several popular book festivals. Visit www.spawn.org for details.

Presentation Is Everything

When displaying your title(s) at an event, focus on presentation. Ensure that your exhibit is inviting. Utilize attention-grabbing balloons, an attractive table covering, and easy-to-read signage/banners. Feature effective promotional pieces reflecting the tone and appearance of your title(s)—such as high impact posters, postcards, bookmarks, flyers, brochures, activity kit, and imprinted give-away items i.e. stickers, pins, balloons. Incorporate a thematic approach whenever possible. For example, if your children's picture book is about a cuddly cow, place a plush battery-operated cow on your exhibit table to "moo-ve" around—and capture the attention of passers-by.

THE SCOOP!

Place a bowl of wrapped candy, such as Hershey's Kisses, on your exhibit table to attract picture book buyers ... with a sweet-tooth!

Package several of your favorite picture book illustrations—using neutral mat-framing and acetate wrapping—to sell on the spot. Place a small sign on your display table that reads, "Autographed Copies." Encourage booth visitors to leave their business cards as a means of registering for a free raffle to win an autographed picture book. Compile the list of contacts for future use. Bring business cards, order forms, pens, bags, colorful tissue paper, scissors, tape, bookstands, chairs (if necessary), plenty of change, cash box, and credit card machine (optional). Consider accepting personal checks to maximize your sales potential.

CHAPTER

11

Navigating
Niches

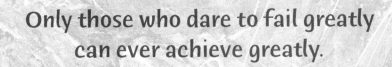

Only those who dare to fail greatly
can ever achieve greatly.

–Robert F. Kennedy

Natural Niches versus Mass Market Mania

Traditional bookstore and library markets account for less than 60% of all books sold. Well financed, multi-title publishers are suited to high volume book sales through mass merchandisers, including:

* Discount stores

* Warehouse clubs

* Grocery chains

* Drug chains

THE SCOOP!

Mass merchandisers purchase their book inventory directly from publishers—or through powerful middlemen, such as Anderson Merchandisers, Charles Levy, and Advanced Marketing Services.

According to Karen Carson, Advanced Marketing Services Representative, wholesale club sales of general children's picture books have been flatter than interactive, "lift-the-flap" titles such as *Dragonology* and *Wizardology*. Experienced corporate buyers select product for prime shelf space that targets at least 75% of the customer base. Even if a self-publisher produces a picture book that is appropriate for the mass merchandiser market, the relationship is difficult to endure as a result of the following:

* Fierce inventory requirements of 10,000–1,000,000 copies

* 100% fully guaranteed sales policy

The vast majority of self-publishers simply cannot risk the potential loss from extensive product returns. Whereas large, powerful publishing houses work effectively with mass merchandisers —such as Toys "R" Us, Wal-Mart, Target, Sam's Club, and B.J.'s—self-publishers benefit from concentrating on local markets and niche channels.

Naming Your Niche

Never underestimate the magnificent marketing power of niches! Whereas a general title is forced to bear scrutiny in an ultra-competitive bookstore environment, a niche title is a unique commodity that naturally ties into the avid interests of a targeted group. Sales soar when niche markets can be readily established and pursued. According to Kate Bandos, president of KSB Promotions, "Children's titles are best sold through means other than the mass retail shelf." Traditional publishing terms—such as front list (to describe a hot, new title) and back list (to describe an older title that continues to be promoted by the pub-

lisher)—have little bearing in the world of self-published niche titles for children. Some children's picture books are more conducive to powerful niche marketing than others.

The more general your children's picture book, the more challenging it is to determine viable sales angles. Find your audience; target promotion is key. Examples of niche channels include:

* Aquariums—for a children's book relating to tropical fish

* Art museums or galleries—for a children's book relating to Picasso

* Jewish museums or Judaica gift stores—for a children's book relating to the Holocaust

* Zoos—for a children's book relating to a hibernating bear

* Airports—for a children's book relating to flying lessons

* Hospitals—for a children's book relating to an exciting overnight hospital stay

* Dental offices—for a children's book relating to proper brushing

* Chiropractic offices—for a children's book relating to a chiropractic adjustment

* Gyms/athletic clubs—for a children's picture book relating to aerobic exercise

* Soccer stores—for a children's book relating to scoring a soccer goal

* Bakeries—for a children's book relating to cupcake decorating

* Hotel gift shops—for a children's book relating to a child's first hotel stay

THE SCOOP!

It is beneficial to review the *Encyclopedia of Associations*—available in database and print formats—a listing of more than 100,000 membership organizations by category, such as museums, pets, education, religion, sports, etc.

When you select your most promising non-bookstore channel(s), it is advantageous to become affiliated with established niche distributors. For consideration, submit the following materials to niche distributors of interest:

* Review copy of your picture book (with review copy sticker and "pub" sheet)

* Media kit—complete with reviews and articles as available

* One-page marketing plan geared to the specified non-bookstore channel

* Samples of promotional items to be used as customer "giveaways"

Follow up, and be politely persistent! If you decide to work with your niche channel on a direct basis, target your optimal contacts. Purchase industry-specific mailing lists, as necessary. (Refer to Appendix D for mailing list providers.) Mail channel-specific promotional postcards or flyers—with testimonials—to stimulate interest in your picture book. Do not waste your time sending general material. Relate specifically to the needs of your intended niche audience!

Holiday & Seasonal Titles: The Renewal Factor

Children's holiday and seasonal picture books are effective niche titles—due to the renewal factor associated with the onset of a particular holiday or season. *The Polar Express* (1986 Caldecott Medal winner), by Chris Van Allsburg, is a prime example of a children's holiday picture book that has evolved into a Christmas classic! (Did you know that Chris Van Allsburg nonchalantly entered the field of children's picture books as a diversion from his tedious work as a sculptor?) Once a holiday-related title takes hold, word of mouth builds sales momentum —year in and year out. In my picture book, *Celebrate Hanukkah with Me*, a young Jewish girl shares her celebration of Hanukkah with her best friend, who is Christian. This diversity title has found its way into public, private, and religious schools—encouraging children of all faiths to embrace each other's differences. Though I published the title back in 1998, I am pleased to rediscover its renewal factor with each approaching Hanukkah/Christmas. This past holiday season, I was pleasantly surprised to see my title featured in a widely disseminated *Chanukah Wonderland* brochure produced by the regional Lubavitch organization of Bucks County, PA. This coverage caught the attention of a local journalist—who in turn interviewed me for a lengthy feature article in *The Advance*, a local newspaper in Bucks County, PA. One nice event can surely lead to another!

Military Maneuvers

The military market can be an effective sales vehicle for self-published authors of children's military niche titles. Over the past few years, my publishing company has received several submissions about courageous parents—who must sadly leave their young children for active military duty in the Middle East. This type of picture book is likely to appeal to military families living on U.S. military bases throughout the country and abroad—in addition to school, library, and traditional bookstore markets.

The Scoop!

The military rules! The marketplace of the armed services is composed of 1.4 million active duty personnel, more than 700,000 Department of Defense personnel, and almost 2,000,000 retired service personnel—in addition to their families. There are more than 2,000 libraries in the federal government library system under the Department of Defense. The Defense Department Child Development Program, serving children from infancy through twelve years of age, is the largest employer-sponsored child-care program in the country. The Department of Defense Education Activity (DoDEA), stationed in the U.S., Europe, and the Pacific, serves the 100,000+ children of those serving in the military.

Exchanges that provide merchandise and services on behalf of the Army & Air Force, U.S. Coast Guard, Navy, and Marine Corps are the largest buyers of all types of books for the military market. The majority of books and publications are supplied to exchanges by local distributors—on a guaranteed sales basis. Distributors are required to provide in-store service and accept returns of poorly selling and/or out-of-date publications. Google each of the exchange Web sites for vendor information, and an approved distributor list. If you feel that you have an appropriate niche title for the military audience, contact approved local distributors for title consideration. Coordinate a promotional book event/signing at a military exchange within your region. For military base contact information, visit www.armytimes.com/story.php?s+0-292258-locator.php. To post a message on the military bulletin board regarding your children's picture book, visit www.militarycity.com/forums.

Warning: Do Not Leave Your Day Job

Do not leave your day job to become a successful children's picture book author. Your current profession actually benefits you in your exciting new publishing role! A natural niche emanating from your career can provide you with a viable market channel to optimize sales of your niche-related children's picture book. The enthusiastic community is likely to spread word of your wonderful achievement. As impressive feature articles regarding your authorship appear in industry-specific newsletters, journals, magazines, and newspapers—clip, frame, and proudly hang them in your office or public space. Take advantage of the exposure and niche selling opportunities that your profession offers. Your notoriety as a local author is surely good for business!

"Natural" Career-Related Niche Opportunities

A children's title that is a teaching tool for young children—written by a local expert or professional—fills a natural niche, and increases the likelihood for sales success. For example, a self-published juvenile book, entitled *When I Grow Up I'm Going to Be a Millionaire (A Children's Guide to Mutual Funds)*—written by Ted Lea and illustrated by his wife, Lora Lea—not only teaches personal finance to children, but also serves as a resource for financial practitioners to share with their clients (a multiple revenue stream!).

Your community-based profession is pivotal to the success of your new title! Regardless of your occupation, you have the phenomenal opportunity to promote your self-published children's picture book during the course of interfacing with the public. Your children's picture book is likely to sell as a by-product of your likability within your community.

* As an office-based community professional, such as a pediatrician, child psychologist, nutritionist, chiropractor, dentist, optometrist, etc., you'll find that the public will eagerly peruse your featured children's picture book and displayed feature articles while sitting patiently in your waiting room. What a great way to promote … and sell … your book!

* As a teacher, watch your enthusiastic students spread word about your picture book to their parents, friends, and friends' parents. Word of mouth sells books! Your invaluable teaching techniques will also enable you to engage a young audience while fulfilling your role as a highly paid visiting school author!

* As a firefighter whose self-published picture book is about little Timmy who practices the techniques of "Stop, Drop and Roll," enjoy promoting your title during the "Fire Prevention Week" assemblies at local elementary schools. Word of mouth—potent FREE advertising—is likely to spur sales of your picture book … before, during, and after your popular community events!

The Scoop!

If you have excellent public speaking skills, consider selling your title during speaking engagements, workshops, and/or seminars—in your area of expertise—at churches/synagogues, community centers, hotels, or even your place of employment.

Court a Catalog ... Or Two

If you have published a niche-oriented children's picture book in certain categories—such as oral hygiene, chiropractic, finance, motorcycles, military, horses, etc.—you can cater directly to your valued niche audience via industry-specific trade shows, advertising journals, and catalogs. Search the Web and/or contact industry professionals for further information. Some very successful small to mid-sized publishers have veered away from general book trade consignment altogether to focus on the more lucrative "non-returns," catalog-driven markets. Niche catalogs, comprised of complementary product lines, offer title exposure to potentially hundreds—even thousands—of buyers interested in the specified category of your title. Author Brian Jud states in his book, entitled *Beyond the Bookstore*, "Look at your product not as a book, but as an accessory to a particular industry." General book-only catalogs, like their bookstore counterparts, tend to be highly competitive for small publishers due to the singular product line offering. A vast list of catalogs can be obtained through *The Directory of Mail Order Catalogs*—in addition to a variety of Web sites including:

* ✳ www.catalogs.google.com

* ✳ www.catalogocity.com

* ✳ www.cataloglink.com

* ✳ www.buyersindex.com

Selecting Your Niche Catalog(s) of Interest

When you determine your catalog(s) of interest, order a copy of each to verify that it is indeed a fit for your niche children's picture book title. Once you have made your final selection, contact each catalog company for submission guidelines and forms. Forward a sample of your title (whether or not one is requested) with your media kit, and any additional requested information i.e. product shipping weight. Don't be insulted if you do not receive an immediate call back. Politely follow up by phone—within 1–2 weeks. Submit early for particular catalogs of interest. Product decisions may be determined 6–12 months prior to the actual catalog shoot.

The design of your picture book cover is critical to its viability as a successful catalog candidate. When reduced to a 1″ x 1″ square, it must maintain its readability and eye-catching appeal. If your title is in fact accepted for catalog inclusion, you are required to have sufficient inventory to fulfill potential orders at a guaranteed price—typically a 50%–80% discount (based on size of catalog distribution). Catalogs rarely require an exclusive arrangement and usually pay within 30 days. Best of all, sales are usually non-returnable. Over the past several years, I have worked with a handful of catalog-based Judaica book resellers for children—including Chai Kids. My Passover book, entitled *My Favorite Family Haggadah*, continues to be ordered by a loyal base of catalog customers—year in and year out—long after its third and final printing, back in 1998.

The Scoop!

Regardless of "age," a solid niche children's title that virtually advertises itself—through catalog presence and enthusiastic word of mouth—is a self-publisher's dream!

Embracing Early Childhood Education

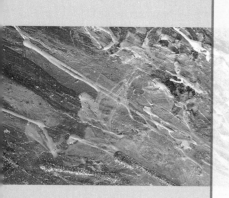
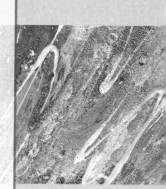

The great man
is he who does not lose
his child's heart.

—Mencius

Becoming a Visiting School Author

It is common knowledge that connecting students with enthusiastic children's book authors inspires lifelong readers and writers. What a win-win for both authors and students! School author visits are funded by:

* PTA

* Adopt-a-School Sponsors

* Friends of the Library

* Title I or VII

* SIP

* LAAMP

* Goals 2000

* Grants

* Gifts from grandparents

Public and private elementary school visits are exceptionally lucrative for traditional and self-published children's picture book authors—on a local and national basis. Word of mouth among teaching staff can generate much enthusiasm for a particular visiting author—from school district to school district—across the country. Schools pay hundreds—even thousands—of dollars for this highly regarded service. Author visit programs result in selling books, and can provide added credibility to a children's picture book author! *The SCBWI Publications Guide to Writing & Illustrating for Children* offers useful information regarding national and international school author visits, as well as a school speaking engagement sample contract.

Practice Makes Perfect

Your children's picture book is certain to soar when you perfect your skills as a visiting school author. First, make an effort to observe the presentations of established visiting authors at conferences or elementary schools in your region. Learn by example. Once you are comfortable with the general author visit process, develop a presentation that is 30–45 minutes in duration. Practice in front of friends and family, and/or at local bookstores and libraries.

Gain awareness of your strengths and weaknesses by video taping your session. Join your community Toastmasters Club (www.toastmasters.org) to obtain the feedback of a warm, inviting audience. Continually improve upon your public speaking skills. Make your presentation style your own!

Plan a successful event based on the following variables:

* ✳ Grade level

* ✳ Audience size

* ✳ Equipment needs

* ✳ Maximum daily sessions (typically 3–4)

Determine the guidelines that work best for you! Patiently answer questions at the end of each presentation, as time permits. It is entirely possible that your engaging presentation will spark the creative writing talents of at least a handful of exuberant students. Thanks to you, some young listeners may emerge as famous authors one day! Follow up with a note of appreciation to your key elementary school contact(s).

The Scoop!

For assistance with tailoring your presentation to your young school audience, read *Terrific Connections with Authors, Illustrators, and Storytellers*, by Toni Buzzeo and Jane Kurtz. For a few laughs about all that can go wrong as a visiting author, enjoy the picture book, *Author's Day*, by Daniel Pinkwater.

Building a Lucrative Part-Time Career

Your knowledge and creativity will enable you to build a lucrative part-time career as a visiting school author. At the onset, charge a daily fee of $500+ for your services. Payment is due to you on the day of the event. In addition to your presentation fee, earn extra revenue by selling autographed picture books to the school librarian, classroom teachers—and an adorable group of enthusiastic students. Consider offering a book promotion such as:

* 10% buyer discount

* Percentage of sales to be used as a school fund-raiser

* One free copy per specified quantity sold

Florrie Binford Kichler, publisher of the *Young Patriots* series, states in the April 2006 PMA *Independent* newsletter, "For our school visits, we create a flyer in advance for teachers to send home with their students (always with permission, of course). In the flyer, we generally provide a discount to the buyer and offer to donate one book to the school's library for every ten books sold—added value in terms of an incentive without much added cost."

The Scoop!

Whether you are a non-fiction or fiction children's book author, students will be certain to benefit from your talents, expertise, and ability to enhance the curriculum.

Children's book awards—honoring titles in the categories of science and social studies—expand a winning title's academic reach. Betty Tatham, author of several non-fiction titles for children, including the award-winning *Penguin Chicks* (HarperCollins), utilizes her title as an invaluable curriculum supplement during her school author visits—both nationally and internationally. Author/illustrator Jehan Clements not only reads his books, *Alfred the Ant* and *The Banana that Ate New York*, but uses his musical/storytelling skills and costume to humorously "perform" them. Accentuate your unique skill sets!

* If you are the illustrator, as well as author of your children's picture book, draw a sample illustration right before the children's eyes.

* If you play the guitar or keyboard, dazzle the children with your musical talents.

* If you are a magician, create a magic show.

* If you are a puppeteer, present a puppet show—incorporating the characters from your children's picture book.

Consider including a creative writing exercise for some added zest. Share special insider secrets. Inform the children that with focus, passion, persistence, and drive, anything in life is possible—including authoring and/or illustrating a children's picture book! Encourage laughter, participation, and interaction. Most importantly, be yourself.

Engaging Your Young Audience

During your author visit day, it is likely that you will address 3–4 different age groups. Ensure that each of your presentations is age appropriate. Whether you are a non-fiction or fiction children's book author, your ability to engage the elementary school students will determine your success as a visiting author. When I feature *The Zebra-Striped Whale with the Polka-Dot Tail* as a visiting

author, I present a plentiful array of fun-to-feel elements that I utilized in my dimensional collage illustrations—foil, wire, yarn, cellophane, glitter, clay, mesh, raffia, squeeze paint, paper, cotton, costume jewelry, dollar bills, and even candy—and compare them to the pages of my book. (The illustrated pages with the dollar bill and candy always evoke the widest grins!) Because the text in my picture book is relatively sophisticated for the very young, I invite the children to respond with two hand claps and two foot stamps at the turn of each page—to promote interactivity. Following the reading of *The Zebra-Striped Whale with the Polka-Dot Tail*, the children participate in a creative, hands-on collage art project. When finished, each child is presented with a colorful zebra-striped whale sticker and activity kit to take home—along with his/her one-of-a-kind collage masterpiece!

The Scoop!

Kids love collage! Collage is an enticing, magical medium—because it is virtually impossible to make a mistake. Any materials from home can easily be transformed into a prized art piece with just a bit of glue ... and imagination!

At day's end, I enjoy working with students of the after-school program on the thematic Polka-Dot Bowl of Love project. Using colorful paint pens, the children decorate tiny, circular glass discs—that I hot-glue to a heavy glass bowl in a polka-dot pattern formation. Within approximately 30 minutes, the once plain vessel is transformed into a magnificent gallery-quality art piece. The appreciative students are absolutely amazed by their own creation! The Polka-Dot Bowl of Love is proudly displayed in the main lobby—and then sold, via auction, as a popular school fund-raiser.

Creating a Network of Alliances

To promote yourself as a visiting author, you must continually build a network of contacts and alliances. Attend teacher conferences—and distribute your school-visit related flyers and brochures to everyone you meet. In addition to a review copy of your picture book, forward a media kit—including cover letter (with reference to your Web site), press release, bio, testimonial sheet, reviews/recent articles, activity kit, school visit brochure/calendar, and premium promotional material (especially bookmarks and stickers!)—to a targeted group of elementary school decision makers and influencers, such as:

* Principals

* School librarians

* PTO presidents

Follow up by phone. If you don't receive a response, call again. Be politely persistent! Feel free to meet with local school librarians who may exhibit some "pull" regarding author selection. Consider participating in virtual classroom author visits—including online chats and publishing projects—as posted on school Web sites.

THE SCOOP!

Introduce yourself to powerful, independent children's book-sellers in your region, and share your interest in becoming a visiting school author. Build strategic alliances. Independent booksellers frequently fulfill book orders on behalf of visiting school authors, and profit from the transaction. Book sales emanating from in-school visits can translate to added income—for both you and the bookseller!

Booksellers—in the business to sell books—sponsor in-store programs to unite local authors with community teachers. Authors provide mock presentations to teachers with the hopes of being hired for profitable school events. The names and contact information of visiting school authors and illustrators are frequently posted on independent bookseller Web sites. Several other beneficial Web sites include:

* Society of Children's Book Writers and Illustrators
  www.scbwi.org

* Children's Book Council
  www.cbc.org

* The Best Book Bin
  www.thebestbookbin.com

* Author Illustrator Source
  www.author-illust-source.com

* Children's Authors Network! (CAN!)
  www.childrensauthorsnetwork.com

The Scoop!

Consider registering for state arts commission—or education department—grant-based sponsorships that assist participating schools in compensating writers and illustrators for educational programming. You will be notified, via e-mail, as school programs are requested.

Enhancing Curriculum

Award-winning, non-fiction children's books—in the areas of science and social studies—offer the greatest ease of entry into the academic marketplace. Educators respond favorably to recognizable, series-based books that comply with standards of learning and performance. For information on national and state standards, visit www.educationworld.com/standards. School boards and districts are likely to follow state adoption schedules based on subject areas and grade levels. Though school boards publish local approval lists annually, state adoptions are typically based on 3–7 year selling cycles.

Follett Educational Services is a leading distributor of books to the elementary school market. Visit www.fes.follett.com—or call 800-621-4272—for distribution guidelines. Educational products are also available for sale through the following channels:

* School supply stores

* Educational dealers

* Catalogs

For a list of catalogs to promote your title to the educational market, research *The Directory of Mail Order Catalogs*—and/or visit:

* www.catalogs.google.com

* www.catalogocity.com

* www.cataloglink.com

* www.buyersindex.com

THE SCOOP!

The early childhood market is composed of over 50,000 public elementary schools, 14,000 private elementary schools, and 100,000 preschools/child care centers throughout the U.S. In addition, more than two million children are home schooled.

Targeting Educational Customers

Determine the preferred customer base for your children's picture book, such as:

* Teachers

* Reading specialists

* Parents of home schooled children

Early childhood educators are responsive to:

* Peer input

* Book reviews and awards

* Industry journals

* Direct mail

* Catalogs

* Web site promotions

* Telemarketing

* Trade show exhibits

* Association newsletters

* Workshops

* Association meeting presentations

Visit www.ed.gov/about/contacts/gen/othersites/associations.html for a comprehensive directory of associations. Invite relevant educators and experts to review your title. Specify student grade level and academic ability i.e. average, gifted, special needs. Seek endorsements. Request classroom and home schooling trials.

The Scoop!

A Web site, rich in content with plentiful links, enables you to build a strong and loyal customer base in the educational marketplace. Include a lesson plan, teaching guide, bibliographies, student workbook, activity kit, school visit calendar, educational market testimonials, etc.—that are geared toward your targeted audience.

According to Mary Ellen Lepionka—author, speaker, and textbook development consultant—in the April 2006 *SPAN Connection* newsletter, "Consider sharing the costs of direct mail with colleagues whose carefully chosen high quality products are for the same market as yours. Networking is important in educational publishing, and four flyers in an envelope might attract more attention and have more credibility than one, in addition to reducing costs." Educational mailing lists may be rented from:

* Quality Education Data (QED)—a wholly owned subsidiary of Scholastic Inc. www.qeddata.com

* Market Data Retrieval (MDR) www.schooldata.com

Proceed cautiously prior to committing your advertising budget. Journal advertising tends to be expensive, but may be useful if you have the funds to saturate a particular market. Read publications of interest to verify that subscribers are the intended decision makers for your title. To obtain a listing of early education journals, visit www.google.com/Top/Reference/Education/Journals.

Lovin' Lexiles

Teachers, reading specialists, librarians, and parents are turning to Lexiles to match children's reading comprehension with text level in states such as MS, GA, OR, CA, NC, and TX. Lexiles are based on word frequency and sentence strength—not subject matter or content. The Lexile Framework for Reading is an innovative approach to text comprehension—enabling educators to confidently select books to improve their students' reading skills. The same Lexile scale reflects text difficulty and reading comprehension, ranging from 200L for a beginning reader to 1700L for an advanced reader. Major standardized reading tests report their results in Lexiles. Approximately twenty-five million students will receive Lexile measures during 2007–08. Lexile workshops and reading conferences support assessment measures to differentiate instruction, and enhance student achievement.

To meet the growing demand for tracking reading progress, publishers are opting to Lexile their titles for a fee of $100 per ISBN. If you are considering a Lexile Analysis to support your children's book in the educational market, visit www.Lexile.com—or call the Lexile Text Measurement Department at 800-LEXILES or 919-547-3426.

The Scoop!

The Lexile measure—based on word frequency and sentence length—enables writers to confirm that their manuscripts are age-appropriate. Visit www.Lexile.com for a free Lexile analysis of your manuscript.

Title Comprehension Quiz Assessment

Accelerated Reader by Renaissance Learning produces and sells student comprehension quiz software for selected children's books in the academic market. Children's books having the Accelerated Reader "seal of approval" tend to be popular among school librarians and K–12 teachers on a nationwide basis—and are widely supported by library wholesalers. To submit your title for Accelerated Reader comprehension quiz consideration, forward two review copies of your finished children's book, a letter of intent, "pub" sheet, and media kit to:

Content Development
Renaissance Learning, Inc.
2911 Peach Street
Wisconsin Rapids, WI 54494.

Include all favorable and unfavorable reviews as well as awards.

According to Christina Sering, Publisher Account Representative for Accelerated Reader, any book review is considered to be a "good" review. Both favorable and unfavorable reviews result in the same Accelerated Reader "Reviewed Title" status that stimulates the interest of school librarians and teachers alike.

If your title is accepted by Accelerated Reader—typically the result of a school librarian/teacher recommendation—a reading comprehension quiz is immediately generated for school use, at no charge to you. As a marketing tool, you may include the phrase, "This book has an Accelerated Reader quiz available," in your school-related promotional material. If your title is refused during the standard selection process, but meets specific criteria, you may purchase a minimum of 150 Accelerated Reader quizzes at $1.50 each—for a total fee of $225. Any quizzes that are utilized by school librarians and/or teachers within a designated time frame will be credited to your account. For further information, contact Christina Sering at 715-424-3636, ext. 4052—or visit the Accelerated Reader Web site, www.renlearn.com. Scholastic offers its own school-based, quiz-generating reading comprehension program—called Scholastic Reading Counts. Visit www.scholastic.com for further information.

School Book Fairs

Major children's book publishers coordinate book fairs at elementary schools throughout the country—and sell large quantities of books to teachers, students, and their families during these events. Contact elementary schools in your area, and offer to sign copies of your title at upcoming school book fairs on a consignment basis. Proudly donate 50% of the proceeds to the hosting school. Both students and teachers alike are enthusiastic about local authors—especially if the local author is the mom or dad of one of the students!

Consider submitting your title to Books Are Fun, Ltd—a Reader's Digest Company. This company is the leading national book fair display marketer of premium hardcover books and educational gifts—at over 70,000 schools, 15,000 early learning centers, and other venues such as hospitals and corporations. Its mission is to provide premium books and gift products that educate, inspire, and enrich educators, parents, and students alike. To submit your children's picture book to Books Are Fun, send a review copy of your title, letter of intent, "pub" sheet, and media kit—including your activity kit and thematic book launching device—to:

Submissions
Books Are Fun
1680 Highway 1 North
Fairfield, IA 52556

Visit www.booksarefun.com for further information.

Harvesting the Home Schooling Segment

A plethora of active, predominantly Christian organizations promote home schooling as a viable alternative to the public and private school sectors. Based on estimates provided by the Home School Legal Defense Association (HSLDA), home schooling is a growing segment that increases by 7–15% per year. The U.S. home schooling market—currently composed of more than two million children—can offer vast opportunities to self-published children's picture book authors.

According to the National Center for Education Statistics (NCES), $600 per year is spent on educational resources by the average home school family.

Home schooled children and their parents learn about new children's books through a variety of sources:

* Web site communities

* Home school associations

*   Book fairs/expos/trade shows

*   Catalogs

*   Direct mail

*   Journals such as *Home Schooling Today* and *Practical Home Schooling*

*   Excursions to destinations of interest—museums, theatres, landmarks, historical sites, etc.

*   Word of mouth

In addition to curriculum-building titles, a faith-based picture book featuring the adventures of a home schooled child is likely to fare well in this sector.

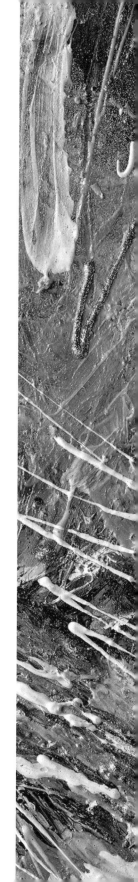

CHAPTER

Children's
Picture Book
Promotion

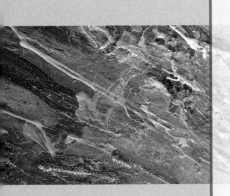

Reach high,
for stars
lie hidden in your soul.
Dream deep,
for every dream
precedes the goal.

—Pamela Vaull Starr

Boost Your Book with Free Local Publicity

You are likely to receive your strongest media boost as an "up and coming" picture book author in your own local arena. Local media outlets—eager to impart timely, relevant information to their community/regional audiences—benefit greatly by dispersing news of your picture book's release. Customer demand for your children's picture book is initially generated by the local media—and further propelled by word of mouth.

The Scoop!

Media coverage is considered to be seven times more effective than paid advertising. Unlike an ad that promotes your title as you pay for the privilege, a book review, newspaper/magazine feature, or television/radio interview is construed as more genuine and sincere.

Take advantage of this powerful FREE exposure! Informing the public of your picture book through free media coverage is certain to result in spiked sales—IF your sales channels are firmly established.

Media Exposure Generates Public Interest

To fully optimize your local publicity campaign, ensure that your picture book is available to the public through a variety of sales vehicles. Otherwise, you run the risk of alienating the public—motivated by the media—to purchase your title. Congratulations are in order if you have succeeded in making your title available via the Web (Amazon.com, Barnesandnoble.com, and your own Web site), independent/chain bookstores, at least one non-book channel, and even a toll-free number. Bookstores, both independent and chain, respond quickly to customer requests, and will reorder your title as much—or as little—as demand dictates.

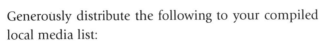

THE SCOOP!

Media exposure generates public interest. Public interest generates sales activity. Sales activity generates profits.

Publicity begets more publicity. Be certain to coordinate your free publicity with the planned introduction of your children's picture book at viable sales outlets.

Monopolize Your Local Media Contacts

First saturate your local/regional market where your foundation is strongest. Obtaining free local media coverage is a statistics game; the more media contacts you generate, the greater your likelihood of success! First prepare a thorough and comprehensive local media list. Visit the news section of your local drug store or supermarket, and jot down the names of all local newspapers/magazines in your area. Contact information for local newspapers, magazines, radio, and network/cable TV may be accessed via the Web.

Generously distribute the following to your compiled local media list:

1. Review copy of your picture book

    *   Place a "Local Author Review Copy" sticker—with your complete contact information—on the outside front cover.

    *   Insert a loose "pub" slip just inside the front cover.

        (Option: Consider attaching a reduced-size "pub" sheet to your inside front cover via double-sided tape—or use an adhesive-backed label imprinted with the same information.)

2. Media kit—including your thematic book launching device and reviews

Refer to "Adventures in Shipping" on p. 107 for cost effective media kit delivery options. If permissible to particular media outlets, e-mail the digitized contents of your media kit—and save on time and postage. Follow up with your local media contacts by phone, fax, or e-mail within a week to ten days. Be politely persistent!

The Scoop!

The local media outlet is likely to contact you to schedule a personal interview and private photo shoot. If the writing staff is short on time, a feature article may be taken, verbatim, from your press release—with your media kit head shot utilized as the accompanying photograph.

Media repetition, initially at a local/regional level, is key to your publishing success. As feature articles and favorable reviews emerge in the local media, add copies to your media kit—and compile your own personal scrapbook! Acknowledge all local media coverage with a personal note of appreciation to the radio/TV host and/or journalist. For print media, your photo-copied article—with a brief hand-written message—can serve as an effective "thank you."

Lights ... Camera ... Action!

If you enjoy being interviewed—even if you get a little nervous—you'll love the "lights ... camera ... action" of a live television broadcast! Consider hiring a media training professional to polish your on-air presence. (Refer to Appendix D for a listing of media trainers and coaches.) Upon introducing *The Zebra-Striped Whale with the Polka-Dot Tail*, I appeared on the Philadelphia NBC Morning Show with host, Steve Levy. What a memorable experience! I high-ly recommend that you send a review copy of your picture book and media kit to your local television morning show—a fabulous venue for spreading the word about your new children's picture book. Refer to "Mastering Your Media Kit" on p. 178 to ensure that you have submitted all of the proper components (including your thematic book launching device and recent articles/reviews). Local broadcast media sources benefit from you as much as you benefit from them. That's a "WIN-WIN" for all! In fact, don't be surprised to receive a phone call from a television or radio producer—who has ironically searched for you! When I first introduced *Philly's Favorites Recipe Collection,* I was astonished to hear from a local cable television station that I had never before contacted. The producer was following up on a newspaper article that featured my recipe book—and enthusiastically invited me to be a guest on his show!

The Scoop!

Inform local/regional bookstores, via fax, e-mail, and/ or phone, about your scheduled television or radio publicity well in advance. Verify sufficient stock of your title. A coordinated author appearance at a local bookstore— immediately following your media event—is a phenomenal way to draw a significant audience and maximize book sales!

National Press Coverage: A Life of Its Own

According to publicist, Paul J. Krupin, "Getting publicity to attract attention and get the word out ... is crucial to jumpstarting any marketing or promotion effort." His Web site, www.directcontactpr.com, offers free, informative media-related articles including:

* "The Hot Button Theory: Maximizing Media Response to Your News Releases"

* "Following Up with Media—Calling Will Get You More Publicity"

* "Ten Tips for Using E-Mail to Get More News Coverage and Publicity"

Your media coverage is likely to translate into increased book sales—if your title is readily available for consumers to purchase. National publicity efforts can be futile without adequate supply of your children's picture book in targeted retail locations. Alert the children's department managers of bookstores—via phone, fax, or e-mail—regarding probable media-related demand surges for your title.

Read Susan Raab's book, *An Author's Guide to Children's Book Promotion*, for viable information regarding children's book marketing and author promotion; visit www.raabassociates.com. (Refer to Appendix D for a listing of publicity resources.)

When calling your national media contacts, be prepared and know your angle! The media can immediately detect a novice. Refrain from stating that you are calling to verify receipt of your press release. Be politely persistent, and follow up! For optimal results, consult with a public relations specialist. (Refer to Appendix D for a listing of marketing and public relations specialists.)

The Scoop!

The U.S. media is composed of more than 1,700 daily newspapers, 6,900 weekly newspapers, 12,000 magazines, 8,500 radio talk shows, and 10,000 TV anchors. Popular media resources, such as Bacon's Media Directories (www.bacons.com) and The Gale Database of Publications and Broadcast Media (www.gale.com), may be reviewed in library reference rooms (though not always current)—or purchased directly from the publishers.

Children's Book Media Reviews

Children's picture books are not reviewed by every media outlet. Just eighteen editors from daily newspapers—and two from national news syndicates—actually use the title, "children's book editor." The *SCBWI Publications Guide to Writing & Illustrating for Children* features an annually updated list of freelance children's picture book reviewers. Don't overlook the importance of acquiring online in addition to traditional reviews. At www.childrenslit.com, for example, more than 4,000 books are critically reviewed annually to assist teachers, librarians, child-care providers, and parents in their literary choices; 150 titles are recognized per year via the Children's Literary Choice List. (Refer to Appendix C for a listing of online and traditional children's picture book reviewers.) It is essential to adhere to the submission guidelines of each media outlet that you are targeting. Online reviewers typically accept an electronic version of your media kit contents with a PDF of your cover image—and a simple link to request a review copy.

It is wise to contact traditional children's picture book reviewers by phone or e-mail—prior to submitting your review copy and media kit—as follows:

* Share a brief sound bite about your picture book with the reviewer, and offer to send your media package.

* Verify the reviewer's contact information including address, phone, e-mail, and fax … as well as the proper spelling of his/her name.

Refer to "Mastering Your Media Kit" on p. 178 to ensure that your media package contains all of the proper components. Remember to include your thematic book launching device and recent articles/reviews. Forward your media package, without delay, via UPS, FedEx, or U.S. Priority Mail. Follow up—by phone, fax, or e-mail—within a week to ten days of submitting your materials. As always, be politely persistent! If the reviewer requests additional information, respond quickly.

The Scoop!

To help promote your title to the media, PMA offers a cooperative mailing of 3,500 catalogs to daily metro and weekly newspaper book reviewers for a fee of $210. Catalogs feature the front cover of each title with a 100-word description. Visit www.pma-online.org for program details.

Nurturing Niche Publicity

You can readily obtain publicity for a solid niche children's picture book outside of your local region. Prepare a thorough and comprehensive niche media list—including print, radio, and television. Use the Internet to research niche-related media outlets that complement your children's picture book, such as:

* Equine publications—for children's farm-related titles

* Christian-related newspapers and radio/television networks—for children's Christmas and Easter titles

* Judaism-related newspapers and radio/television programs—for children's Passover and Hanukkah titles

* New Age publications—for children's yoga and meditation titles

* Non-profit organization newsletters—for children's fund-raising titles

Verify that your niche media contact information is current and accurate.

The Scoop!

For some niche children's titles, it is wise to target the segment editor of a newspaper—such as the sports editor for a baseball title or the travel editor for an airplane adventure title. He/she receives far fewer books, and is likely to write a more comprehensive article. Submitting your picture book for general book review may not be your most effective route to press coverage.

Generously distribute the following to your compiled niche media list:

1. Review copy of your picture book

* Place a "Review Copy" sticker—with your complete contact information—on the outside front cover.

* Insert a loose "pub" slip just inside the front cover.

(Option: Attach a reduced-size "pub" sheet to your inside front cover via double-sided tape—or make use of an adhesive-backed label that has been printed with the same information.)

2. Comprehensive media kit—including your thematic book launching device as well as copies of recent articles and reviews

Refer to "Adventures in Shipping" on p. 107 for cost effective media package delivery options. The shipping of review copies can be an expensive endeavor. In lieu of submitting a review copy with every niche-related media package, consider enclosing a stamped, pre-addressed Review Copy Request Card as described on p. 192. If permitted by particular media groups, e-mail the digitized contents of your media kit—to save time and postage. Follow up with your niche media contacts by phone, fax, or e-mail, within a week to ten days. Be politely persistent. Determine the time frame in which your article is likely to appear—usually not more than a few weeks for newspapers, 3–4 months for magazines. Media-driven niche channel publicity stimulates word of mouth enthusiasm—and ultimately niche customer demand for your title. In addition to targeted online and traditional bookstores, coordinate your children's picture book introduction at viable niche-oriented outlets, such as:

* Aquariums

* Craft stores

* Knitting stores

* Judaica gift shops

* Christian gift shops

* Bakeries

* Airports

* Eating establishments

Deem Yourself an Expert

Unless you are already famous with a following of fans—or the author of a solid niche title—your authorship status of a general children's picture book is not likely to draw immediate attention beyond your local region. National publicity may be at your fingertips, however, if you deem yourself an expert—and provide beneficial, newsworthy material to the media featuring your area of expertise.

THE SCOOP!

Expertise is the winning combination of knowledge and hard-earned credentials in a particular field of interest. A children's picture book that can be tied to author expertise is more likely to be the recipient of national media attention.

The media is eager to disperse fresh, timely information by an author who is also a designated expert. For children's picture book authors, the "soft sell" approach can indeed be effective—as exemplified by the fictitious story that follows.

Everyone Loves an Expert!

Dr. Flossie White, a pediatric dentist, is the author of a new children's picture book, entitled *The 10-Foot Long, Wiggly Toothbrush*. In a two-page article that appears in *Tooth or Consequences Magazine*, Dr. White reveals, "Ten Easy Ways to Reduce Children's Cavities by 50%." In return for her fascinating interview, Dr. White receives a complimentary written byline about the release of her new children's picture book—including Web site referral and essential book ordering information. Though *The 10-Foot Long, Wiggly Toothbrush* is not the article's featured topic, increased sales of her title are likely to be the indirect result of her sheer expertise.

According to publicity guru Dan Smith, "No talk show producer—or newspaper reporter—wants to hear you talk endlessly about your book. If you want to sell directly, buy an ad, but if you want to get hours of free time ... give the media a compelling topic, and become adept at pitching your book without really trying."

To further gain invaluable marketing exposure, write original articles that relate to your area of expertise. Submit your articles to the media as well as to popular online article banks such as www.ArticleCity.com, www.GoArticles.com, and www.AssociatedContent.com. Your online article bank submission should consist of the following five key elements:

1. Attention-grabbing headline

2. Compelling one-sentence article description

3. Core article text—written in short paragraph format

4. Topic-related keyword subtitles—to maximize search engine ranking

5. Resource box—to promote your expertise, and drive traffic to your Web site i.e. "To learn more, please visit ..."

According to Melissa A. Rosati, author of *The Top 60 Article Banks*, in the December 2006 issue of the *SPAN Connection* newsletter, "Placing an article in an article bank is like dropping a pebble in a pond. The energy expands the rings of influence."

THE SCOOP!

To track the flow of your content over the eight billion pages that exist on the Web, set up a "Google Alert" account through www.Google.com. You will receive an e-mail link every time your information-packed article is posted to a Web site by a third party.

Advertising Advantage

Do not underestimate the exposure benefits that your picture book has already derived from the following vehicles:

* Media publicity

* Online reviews

* Word of mouth recommendations

* Retail store visibility

* Web promotion

* Non-traditional market stimulation

Consider investing in advertising once you have leveraged all of your free publicity. Paid advertising, if used wisely, functions as yet another exposure vehicle to stimulate sales of your children's picture book. Proceed cautiously. Advertising can be risky—and does not guarantee sales. Determine your budget objectives carefully prior to committing to specific forms of advertising.

One-title publishers, essentially with all of their eggs in one basket, tend to be more vulnerable than multi-title publishers. The return on advertisement investment may not fully justify costs when promoting just one title.

According to Elmer C. Meider Jr., president of *Highlights for Children*, "The more products you bring to market, the more options you have when the market changes."

For large multi-title publishers, extensive financial outlays for slick national advertising campaigns are effectively amortized over multiple titles. If one title is a flop, there are others in the mix to drive advertising-based sales. The reality is that the advertising budget of most one-title publishers simply cannot compete on this basis.

THE SCOOP!

Per Inquiry (PI) is a unique form of advertising that does not require financial investment. Several smaller television/radio stations, newspapers, magazines, and newsletters generate additional income by running free ads—in return for 35%–50% of the revenue from attributed product sales. Once incoming customer orders are processed by the participating media, the PI advertising client is mailed his/her share of the earnings. Contact media advertising departments directly for information regarding potential PI ad opportunities.

Repetition ... Repetition ... Repetition

Repetitive advertising with a clear, concise message is an effective strategy—IF ad-responsive consumers can purchase your title, on impulse, through multiple sales channels such as:

* Independent and chain bookstores

* Online bookstores

✳   Toll-free phone ordering services

✳   Specialty stores

✳   Non-traditional category channels

Studies have shown that at least 7–12 marketing exposures are required for a product/service to capture consumer awareness—and impact buying behavior. Repetition is vital to the success of any promotional campaign. As cited in the *Sales Management Report* (2006 Sample Issue), Thomas Smith, an astute nineteenth century London businessman, imparted advertising advice in the year 1885 that remains relevant today.

Thomas Smith's Words of Advertising Wisdom:

✔ The first time people look at any given ad, they don't see it.

✔ The second time, they don't notice it.

✔ The third time, they are aware that it is there.

✔ The fourth time, they have a fleeting sense that they've seen it somewhere before.

✔ The fifth time, they actually read the ad.

✔ The sixth time, they thumb their nose at it.

✔ The seventh time, they start to get a little irritated with it.

✔ The eighth time, they start to think, "Here's that confounded ad again."

✔ The ninth time, they start to wonder if they may be missing out on something.

✔ The tenth time, they ask their friends and neighbors if they've tried it.

✔ The eleventh time, they wonder how the company is paying for all these ads.

✔ The twelfth time, they start to think that it must be a good product.

✔ The thirteenth time, they start to feel the product has value.

✔ The fourteenth time, they start to remember wanting a product exactly like this for a long time.

✔ The fifteenth time, they start to yearn for it because they can't afford to buy it.

✔ The sixteenth time, they accept the fact that they will buy it sometime in the future.

✔ The seventeenth time, they make a note to buy the product.

✔ The eighteenth time, they curse their poverty for not allowing them to buy this terrific product.

✔ The nineteenth time, they count their money very carefully.

✔ The twentieth time prospects see the ad, they buy what it is offering.

Focusing on Non-Traditional Niche Markets

Don Tubesing of Pfeifer-Hamilton Publishers advises, "Don't trick yourself into trying to do everything. Make forced choices ... do not go lightly anywhere—ever!" Do not attempt to cover the entire country lightly with sparse advertising. Spending your advertising budget on isolated ads is highly ineffective. It is wiser to select the category or categories—outside of the national mass book trade—that would most likely benefit from your advertising dollars i.e. non-traditional niche markets. If you spread your advertising dollars too thinly, you cannot build sufficient momentum to achieve success.

The Scoop!

To attract optimal attention in space ads, your message should be conveyed in seven words or less. As numerous memory experiments have revealed over the past 100 years, the human short-term memory is capable of retaining no more than seven items at one time.

Partnering Is the Name of the Game

Think in terms of partnering opportunities with like-minded publishers and/or complementary businesses. Combining promotional efforts can strengthen overall market presence while amortizing the hefty costs of advertising and promotion. To achieve optimal results, synergistic partners must be unified under a single marketing umbrella. Consider sharing ad space in popular publications—such as *Publishers Weekly* (announcement issue) or the *New York Times* (holiday book review). Other marketing opportunities include cooperative print promotions —such as brochures, catalogs, flyers, and postcards—targeting acquisition librarians, bookstore buyers, non-traditional channels, and the media.

Doing It Your Way

Customize your own cooperative marketing program with partners of your choice. To meet fellow publishers who are interested in coordinating and implementing a shared advertising program:

* Attend industry trade shows/expos and writer's conferences.

* Participate in Internet-based industry chat rooms.

* Place a classified ad in a popular industry newsletter (such as SCBWI, PMA, SPAN, or SPAWN).

Partnering programs provide an added tier of cost-effective marketing/advertising exposure; the fewer the participants, the more attention each participant is likely to receive. For example, two picture book self-publishers can effectively partner on a postcard mailing by placing an image of each picture book—with brief title summaries—on the front side, and contact information on the back side. Consider the use of one common toll-free phone number to direct all incoming calls.

The Scoop!

Make your cooperative postcard stand out from the crowd by featuring a postcard header such as, "Season's Greetings from ...," and mailing it as a holiday greeting card to your targeted list of book buyers.

Hassle-Free Cooperative Marketing Programs

If your have neither the time nor inclination to develop your own cooperative marketing strategy, participate in a hassle-free publisher partnering program that does the footwork for you. PMA (www.pma-online.org) offers children's picture book authors and self-publishers shared advertising opportunities i.e. *Publishers Weekly* children's announcement issues—as well as an array of flyer/catalog partnering programs, such as:

1. K–12 library mailings—3,500 flyers supplied by participating publisher (mailed 3rd class bulk), for a fee of $215

2. Cooperative catalogs featuring book cover image and 100-word description of each represented title

   * 3,500 catalogs to daily metro and weekly newspaper book reviewers, for a fee of $210

   * 3,500 catalogs to independent bookstore and chain buyers throughout the U.S., for a fee of $230

   * 10,900 catalogs to target markets, for a fee of $350 (catalog distribution: 3,500 children/young adult reviewers, 3,500 children/young adult book buyers, and 3,900 children/young adult acquisition librarians)

Atlantic Publishing forwards a targeted mailing of 25,000 catalogs ($.07 per piece) to libraries and/or bookstores four times per year through its cooperative marketing program; call 352-622-1825 for further information.

Showing Your Wares

Trade shows, expos, association conferences, and industry book fairs serve as additional vehicles for title promotion and networking opportunities. Thousands of new titles are introduced at industry trade shows—both large and small—each year. Though having your own exhibit booth is truly an exhilarating experience, it does not supersede the need for:

* Local media publicity

* Book promotions

* Non-traditional channel stimulation

* Paid advertising

* Overall shameless self-promotion

The opportunity to show your wares does not exist in a vacuum. Wise, well-funded publishers and distributors utilize a hefty portion of their budgets on the following:

* Pre-event mailers and/or publication ads that invite buyers to their exhibit booths

* Post-event national trade promotion—including advertising campaigns, media publicity, and aggressive co-op reimbursement programs

Exhibiting to the Masses

BookExpo America (BEA, www.bookexpoamerica.com) is the largest publishing trade show for the U.S. retail book buying community. (For information on BookExpo Canada, visit www.bookexpo.ca.) BEA features over 2,000 exhibits, attracting an array of attendees including:

* Bookstore buyers

* Gift store buyers

* Librarians

* Catalogers

* Internet retailers

* Foreign rights licensing agents

The American Library Association (ALA, www.ala.org) Annual Conference Exhibition is the largest national trade show for the public/school library market—featuring over 1,600 exhibits, and attracting over 20,000 librarians. The ALA Midwinter Conference attracts approximately 10,000 librarians.

The Scoop!

National publishing conferences, such as BEA and ALA, create comfortable, energized environments for like participants to share ideas, network, attend workshops, and stay abreast of the publishing industry's "latest and greatest."

Among the smaller industry shows is the Independent and Small Press Book Fair, hosted by The Small Press Center in New York City each December. Approximately 150 independent publishers exhibit their titles on display tables. Admission is free to the public. Though there is little focus on children's picture books, you will enjoy the opportunity to network with other independent publishers and attend a handful of informative workshops; call 212-764-7021 for further details. Visit the *Publishers Weekly* Web site, www.publishersweekly.com, for an updated list of conferences and dates.

The Latest & Greatest for Children

Consider attending the National Association for the Education of Young Children (NAEYC) Annual Conference and Expo—one of the largest, best attended early childhood education conferences in the world. The event targets:

* Teachers

* Program administrators

* Researchers

* Trainers

* College/university students

* Instructors

* Consultants who work with children from birth through age eight

Trade show exhibit space is costly. Many NAEYC affiliate groups host their own state or promotional conferences to promote high-quality education for young children. Consider exhibiting your children's picture book through your local NAEYC affiliate group, if one is available in your region. As your budget permits, national advertising programs are available through NAEYC's bi-monthly publication, *Young Children* (circulation 100,000), in conjunction with a special online link to select audiences. For exhibit, sponsorship, and advertising opportunities—as well as regional affiliate information—visit webmaster@naeyc.org.

Trade Show Triumph

At both BEA (www.bookexpoamerica.com) and ALA (www.ala.org), book competition is fierce and exhibit space is costly. Endless rows of book exhibits presented by hundreds of publishers—both large and small—flank the floors. Small, relatively unknown publishers find themselves awash in a sea of publishing giants. The expensive, extravagant, eye-catching booths of the larger publishers and distributors feature an enticing array of well publicized, "hot off the press" titles—successfully reinforcing their undying prowess in a mature, saturated, book-bulging market.

There is power in numbers in the publishing industry; the greater the quantity of titles, the stronger the publisher/distributor. Through vast multiple title catalogs, large publishing houses and distributors lure book buyers to their exhibit booths to make purchases during pre-scheduled show appointments. Show specials, such as free shipping and percentage discounts, reinforce on-site trade show purchases.

The Scoop!

If your self-published children's picture book is the recipient of highly respected industry awards, consider a high-visibility exhibit booth at BEA and/or ALA. Upon winning PMA's Ben Franklin Award for their first children's book, *Stranger in the Woods*, talented husband and wife photography/self-publishing team Carl Sams II and Jean Stoick invested in an exciting, eye-catching BEA exhibit booth. This highly acclaimed nature title has since sold more than one million copies—and has led to a variety of spin-off products including teacher's guide, calendars, note cards, tote bags, DVD documentaries, plush toys, and other award-winning children's photographic books.

Tackling Trade Shows

If you are interested in exhibiting at BookExpo America, visit the BEA web site at www.bookexpoamerica.com. If you are interested in exhibiting at the American Library Association annual or mid-winter conference, visit www.ala.org. You may also consider the option of renting a full or shared BEA or ALA exhibit booth at the large Publishers Marketing Association complex—located centrally on the main floor of BEA/ALA. Each exhibiting self-publisher is provided with a complimentary trade show attendance badge. Visit the PMA Web site at www.pma-online.org for exhibiting details. When joining forces with PMA at BEA or ALA, the following fee structure applies.

Joining Forces with PMA!

BookExpo America:

* $3,300—for a full exhibit booth (10′ x 10′)
* $1,650—for a shared exhibit booth (5′ x 10′)

American Library Association:

* $2,200—for a full exhibit booth (10′ x 10′)
* $1,100—for a shared exhibit booth (5′ x 10′)

Making your booth emerge from the crowd at BEA or ALA is not an inexpensive endeavor. In addition to booth rental charges—as determined by square footage—you must invest in:

* Carpeting

* Electricity

* Lighting

* Chairs

* Tables

* Table coverings

* Posters

* Easels

* Shelving

* Balloons

* Special effects

* Transportation costs (booth set-up and breakdown)

Be aware that less expensive exhibit tables may be rented in the small press section of major trade shows. Self-publishers, however, are often frustrated by their lack of proximity to the main exhibit floor. Regardless of your location, consider offering show specials i.e. free shipping and/or percentage/quantity discounts to compete with other exhibiting publishers. Utilize promotional materials, such as flyers, brochures, bookmarks, postcards, gimmicky items, etc., to promote trade show sales of your children's picture book.

According to the *Wall Street Journal*, 75% of the marketing material distributed to trade show visitors is discarded prior to exiting the trade show site. To combat this disturbing trend, many exhibitors mail brochures and promotional kits directly to the offices of their guests—in envelopes that are hand-addressed and marked, "PERSONAL." Today, a portable, lightweight attendee badge scanner—located in the exhibit booth—simplifies the process of collecting relevant contact information to support a viable customer database.

Grasping the Enormity of the Publishing Universe

Exhibiting your children's picture book at BEA and/or ALA provides you with an insider's glimpse of the publishing industry in all of its glory. There is no guarantee that your children's picture book sales will dramatically increase as a result of your trade show presence. At New York City's BEA several years ago, the Barnes & Noble children's book buyer stepped into my exhibit booth, pleasantly introduced herself, and presented me with a conservative purchase order

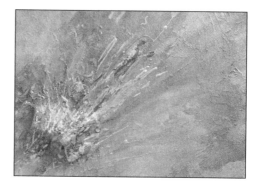

for a newly introduced title. Though the interaction was truly exciting, book sales at trade shows rarely meet exhibiting costs for self-publishers. The decision to exhibit at BEA or ALA is contingent upon your financial position. Trade shows are a legitimate business expense— and can always be rationalized as invaluable marketing exposure!

The Scoop!

I highly recommend the awe-filled experience of exhibiting at BEA or ALA—not because of the likelihood of a multi-million dollar contract with a distinguished book buyer, mega-publisher, or distributor walking the floors (long shots at best in such a competitive environment) ... but to grasp the enormity of the publishing universe of which you are now part!

Trade Show "To Dos"

1. Be engaging—in and out of your exhibit booth. Chat with EVERYONE in your path. You never know who you'll meet!

2. Collect business cards. Jot down your post-conversation notes on the back side of compiled business cards, and follow up via e-mail immediately after the trade show.

3. Invite a friend, family member, or colleague to relieve you temporarily from your in-booth duties so that you can walk the trade show. Review the exhibitor directory for publishers' booths of interest—in order of location—so that you don't wander aimlessly. There is too much to see to waste precious time!

4. Study trade show patterns. Visit exhibit booths that generate the biggest "buzz" and attract the most visitors.

5. Observe exhibit booth details and nuances. Learn how other picture book publishers promote similar titles. "Borrow" ideas for future trade shows.

6. Distribute your promotional material EVERYWHERE—in bathrooms, lobbies, restaurants, and even taxicabs!

Cooperative Exhibits: Sharing the Showcase

Cooperative book exhibits enable publishers of all sizes to inexpensively promote their titles to bookseller/librarian conference attendees—especially when lacking sufficient manpower and/or funding to exhibit on their own. If purchasing your own exhibit space is cost-prohibitive, consider displaying your title—face out—in a cooperative book display. Companies, such as Combined Book Exhibit, PMA, and EBSCO Sample Issue & Book Program, offer traditional and self-publishers reasonably priced title exposure at popular trade shows and conferences.

The Scoop!

Though it is impossible to track actual book sales as a result of this added exposure, combined exhibiting programs are much like vitamins—good they can do you ... and bad they can't!

Determining Your Budget

Promoting your title via cooperative book displays is just one segment of your entire marketing strategy. With the usual budget constraints, publishers must invest their advertising/promotional dollars wisely to optimize exposure. Because it is critical to spend a large proportion of your budget on other forms of marketing, you must determine the amount that realistically remains for national and regional cooperative book display programs. Even nominally priced cooperative exhibits grow costly over time. If you have ample funds available, consider working simultaneously with Combined Book Exhibit, PMA, and EBSCO Sample Issue & Book Program—to maximize title exposure at venues of interest. Target booksellers and librarians in your region, as well as popular industry shows including:

* BookExpo America (BEA)

* American Library Association (ALA)

* Public Library Association (PLA)

   ✽ American Association of School Librarians (AASL)

   ✽ Regional Booksellers Associations

If you are feeling motivated, you may create your own traveling cooperative book exhibit. Have fun promoting your own title—in addition to titles from fellow publishers—on a fee for service basis!

THE SCOOP!

Cooperative book exhibits—in conjunction with local media publicity, author-driven children's book events, promotional mailings, paid advertisement, journal reviews, awards, individual trade show exhibits, catalogs, and non-traditional channel stimulation—work in harmony to generate powerful word of mouth enthusiasm for a title.

The Combined Book Exhibit (CBE) Option

Combined Book Exhibit (CBE) presents "The New Title Showcase" in a high-traffic exhibit area of the BEA conference lobby. In addition to showcase visibility, you will receive a title listing in the Showcase Catalog (circulation: 10,000) to be distributed to BEA attendees. The fee is $250 per title—reduced to $195 per title if you rent your own BEA booth. CBE also features displays at:

   ✽ American Library Association

   ✽ Public Library Association—division of ALA; meets every other year

   ✽ American Association of School Librarians—division of ALA; meets every other year

   ✽ Popular annual state/regional library association shows—TX, NJ, CT, OH, FL, NY, NE, CA, PA

   ✽ International shows in Frankfurt, London, and Beijing—targeting reprinting, translation, and distribution rights

Exhibit fees are as follows:

* $79 per title for state/regional shows

* $95 per title for national shows

* $125 per title for international shows

Your title and contact information will be included in CBE's exhibit-specific catalog and online database for one year. Annual membership fee is $125. Visit www.combinedbook.com for further information.

The Publishers Marketing Association (PMA) Option

Publishers Marketing Association (www.pma-online.org) offers cooperative book marketing opportunities for publishers at:

* BEA ($85 per title)

* American Library Association Annual Conference ($85 per title)

* Public Library Association—division of ALA; meets every other year ($80 per title)

* Frankfurt Book Fair—targets reprinting, translation, and distribution rights ($95 per title)

* Regional Booksellers Association Shows ($275 per title for 6 shows)
    * Mountain & Plains Booksellers Association [MPBA]
    * Southeastern Booksellers Association [SEBA]
    * New England Booksellers Association [NEBA]
    * Northern California Independent Booksellers Association [NCIBA]
    * Pacific Northwest Booksellers Association [PNBA]
    * Upper Midwest Booksellers Association [UMBA])

Participation in PMA's cooperative book display programs entitles you to:

* Face-out title display

* Inclusion in the PMA catalog to be distributed during event

* Assigned working time in booth (optional)

* One-year listing of your title on PMA's Web site

* Discounted attendance badges for BEA, ALA, and PLA

The Scoop!

Your active participation in the PMA combined book exhibit at BEA will provide you with a rewarding show experience—and heavily discounted entry badge fee too! Through the PMA discount, your standard entry badge fee is reduced from $150 to $55—a $95 savings. ($80 of your $95 savings can pay for the PMA combined book exhibit fee ... with $15 remaining to purchase a pizza slice and soda!) While your title is being displayed at the PMA booth—just waiting to be "discovered"—you'll enjoy walking the BEA floor, studying the exhibit booths of fellow publishers, and networking with individuals who love the world of children's picture books just as much as you and I do!

The EBSCO Sample Issue & Book Program Option

In addition to the CBE and PMA combined book display programs, the EBSCO Sample Issue & Book Program (www.ebsco.com/sibp/publisher) is yet another cooperative book marketing program that includes print/Web advertising options. SPAN members benefit from a 15% conference title display discount. Conferences include:

* Public Library Association

* American Association of School Librarians

* Texas Library Association

* Annual and Midwinter American Library Association

EBSCO Sample Issue & Book Program offers a variety of promotional packages. The basic package, the Ultimate Conference Special, costs $325 and features:

* Conference book display

* Cover shot beside description in the *Title Guide*

* Color descriptive listing in the *Title Guide*

* Three-month Web title listing

CHAPTER

14

Dare to be Different...
& Succeed

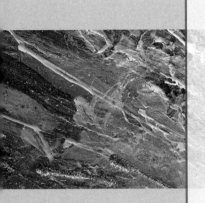

The minute
you begin to do
what you really want to do,
it's really a different
kind of life.

–*Buckminster Fuller*

Thinking Outside the Box

A Self-Publishing Fable: Once upon a time, a teeny-tiny one-title publisher was so frustrated by the boxes of unsold books collecting dust in his garage that he opted to open his own one-title bookstore in a quaint nearby village. The villagers laughed and laughed at the spectacle of the teeny-tiny publisher stocking shelf … upon shelf … upon shelf with nothing other than copies of his one and only title! The teeny-tiny publisher simply sighed—and hand-delivered his attention-grabbing press release to the local media. News of the teeny-tiny publisher's one-title bookstore spread throughout the land. Enraptured tourists from near and far traveled by foot—from every direction—to purchase autographed copies of the teeny-tiny publisher's infamous, one-of-a-kind title. The teeny-tiny publisher, completely unaware that he was practicing innovative "guerilla" marketing tactics, laughed and laughed as his newest problem unfolded—the dire need for a second print run!

THE SCOOP!

Whereas mega-publishing houses adhere strictly to self-prescribed standards that bolster their unparalleled strength in the publishing arena, self-publishers must rely on their innate skill sets and sheer tenacity to make their titles soar. Stay abreast of new and unique avenues to generate enthusiasm for your title(s) within your community. Be creative. Think outside the box! Dare to be different! Find your unique path to success.

Did You Say ... Gourmet Ice Cream & Coffee Café?

I wrote and illustrated my children's picture book, *The Zebra-Striped Whale with the Polka-Dot Tail*, to honor the memory of my dad, Leon Leigh Faden. The depth of heartfelt inspiration that emanated from the loss of my father, a man whom I cherished, has somehow trans-formed me into "writer," "artist," "publisher"—and now, "entrepreneur." My journey continues to enlighten me with the message that anything in life can be yours—if you deem it possible!

Based on the whimsical concept of *The Zebra-Striped Whale with the Polka-Dot Tail*, a unique franchise prototype was born: the Zebra-Striped Whale Ice Cream & Coffee Café (ZSW, www.zebrastripedwhale.com)—located in the Philadelphia suburb of Newtown, Bucks County. Hand-made, one-of-a-kind artisan furnishings and menu boards—designed and built by our oldest daughter, Maxx, with the help of her friend, Chris—accentuate the palate-pleasing, candy-laden cornucopia of edible delights, attracting the young and old alike. Logo aprons, tee shirts, sweatshirts, tote bags, and baseball caps—as well as autographed copies of *The Zebra-Striped Whale with the Polka-Dot Tail* (of course!)—are favorites among ZSW's loyal and enthusiastic clientele. ZSW-catered ice cream socials, both on and off premise, are popular for celebratory events ranging from birthday extravaganzas … for all ages … to corporate employee-recognition days! Children's "Make Your Own Sundae" parties include festive zebra-striped whale balloons, thematic games such as "Pin the Polka-Dot Tail on the Zebra-Striped Whale," and a complimentary activity booklet—"borrowed" from the same media kit that introduced my hardcover title to children's book buyers … several years earlier.

A Winning Strategy

Within nine months following our opening date of December 3, 2004, ZSW received two highly coveted awards:

✱ "Best of Philly"—awarded by *Philadelphia Magazine*

✱ "One of Bucks County's Finest"—awarded by the *Bucks County Courier*

As a result of the "Best of Philly" honor, ZSW was featured in the September 2006 issue of *Home & Garden Magazine*. This media publicity, in turn, caught the attention of the producer of the CBS "Eyewitness News" morning show. With the Eyewitness News van parked outside of our café—and camera rolling—the reporter began her television interview. My husband and I responded candidly to questions regarding our fondness for Newtown, our enticing "Whirlwind" ice cream creations, and ZSW's inspiration—my children's picture book—*The Zebra-Striped Whale with the Polka-Dot Tail*. The two-minute vignette that aired in October 2006 begins with a full-screen image of my picture book cover—and ends with a close-up of a Golden Retriever happily licking a cone of vanilla ice cream. For a peek at this fun, televised segment, visit www.zebrastripedwhale.com.

The symbiotic link between "author" and "entrepreneur" has created a natural angle—resulting in generous publicity for both. Shortly after the opeing of our café, Sherry Elfman, editor for a local newspaper, *The Trend*, wrote a glowing, full-page article (February 2, 2005) featuring the headline: "Creating A Sweet Success … Shari Faden Donahue turned a rave review into a dream come true." The unique tie-in from picture book to café—and vice versa—continues to capture the attention of the local media. The press release for the Zebra-Striped Whale Ice Cream & Coffee Café follows.

12 South State Street
Newtown, PA 18940

Telephone: 215-860-4122
Fax: 215-860-4177
E-Mail: tomdonahue@zebrastripedwhale.com

News

FOR IMMEDIATE RELEASE   CONTACT: Public Relations Mgr., Thomas W. Donahue
LOCAL AUTHOR OPENS NEWTOWN BOROUGH STORE: *ZEBRA-STRIPED WHALE*

Local Author's
Zebra-Striped Whale
Ice Cream & Gourmet Coffee Cafe
Makes a Splash
in Newtown Borough

Newtown, PA - Zebra Striped Whale (ZSW) is making a huge splash in Newtown! Situated at 12 South State Street directly across from the Temperance House, in the heart of Newtown Borough, this new ice cream and gourmet coffee dessert haven is attracting an excited stream of locals and visitors alike. This *sweetery of an eatery* features a mouth-watering array of dairy-fresh ice cream, coffee and espresso freshly roasted by *Small World Coffee Roasters*, signature steamed hot chocolate beverages (with or without a scoop of ice cream!), and desserts prepared daily by Bucks County's top local bakers. As if that's not enough to stimulate the senses, a four-foot granite cold stone surface enables ice cream lovers to add their favorite candy, nut, and/or fruit to their ice cream selection for a delicious "create-your-own," one-of-a-kind dessert sensation known as the *Whirlwind*. The ZSW *Create-Your-Own-Whirlwind Contest* features the winning innovative *Whirlwind of the Month*.

Creativity and uniqueness are the cornerstones of *Zebra-Striped Whale*. The name/concept of this happily heavenly hot (and cold) spot is inspired by the popular hardcover children's picture book, *The Zebra-Striped Whale with the Polka-Dot Tail* (first and second printings: 12,500 copies, 2001), written and illustrated by local author Shari Faden Donahue, of Upper Makefield. To complement her multi-level passages of poetic food-for-thought, Donahue utilized actual candy elements in her dramatic multi-dimensional collage picture book illustrations. Yearning to bring her vividly colored canvasses to life, Donahue and her family have created a visually appealing, palate-pleasing, candy-laden cornucopia for the young ... and young-at-heart ... to savor.

Donahue has written and published several other books including *Philly's Favorites Recipe Collection I* (1992), *My Favorite Family Haggadah* (first printing, 1994; second printing, 1996; third printing, 1998), and *Celebrate Hanukkah with Me* (1998) through Arimax, Inc., her own publishing company. The initial idea for the store was sparked by a 2001 review of *The Zebra-Striped Whale with the Polka-Dot Tail* in the acclaimed *Bloomsbury Review*: "...A story for both children and parents, a tasty morsel to chew and stew over, evening after evening. Donahue is making a strong statement in her ice-cream sundae world, a place where *...Air is pure for all to breathe/A baby never cries/The young need not grow old/Nothing living dies. ...*Swim through questions of philosophy that would surely keep any coffee shop buzzing until wee hours in the morning." A resident of Bucks County since 1993, Donahue was compelled by the reviewer's commentary to envision a stylish, "kick-your-heels-up" coffee shop-like setting for locals and visitors to relax, converse and celebrate the creative spirit.

The journey from book cover to café seat cover is indeed a most unusual transition in the world of children's book authors. Family-owned and operated, Donahue's oldest daughter, Maxx (a 2002 graduate of Council Rock High School and junior majoring in education at University of AZ) and her friend, Chris (a junior majoring in Engineering at University of AZ), seized the hands-on "work-study" opportunity to develop and implement the *Zebra-Striped Whale* operational business plan and renovate the premise. The young college students emerged with an unexpected set of skills designing and constructing a unique and innovative line of artisan furnishings, wall-hangings and menu boards. The twosome accented their distinctive wood pieces in richly colored hues of metallic paint to provide the franchise prototype with an edgy, creative flair that is at once elegant, whimsical and fun. Made-to-order customized furnishings, manufactured in their New Hope workshop/studio, are on display at *Zebra-Striped Whale* and available for purchase.

A comfortable, spacious stone-embellished sitting area for patrons, complete with cathedral ceiling, provides the perfect setting for works of other talented artists and photographers to be showcased monthly. Live jazz, performed by talented local musicians, is featured every Thursday evening. Donahue is currently spearheading the *Zebra-Striped Whale* picture book foundation that publishes original titles by first-time authors and illustrators, to raise money for charitable causes.

Donahue's publishing company, Arimax, Inc., receives hundreds of children's picture book manuscripts each year from aspiring children's picture book authors. The industry standard is that less than 2% of manuscripts submitted to traditional publishers are ever published. In an effort to improve the odds, Donahue is currently writing her newest book, *Children's Picture Books: How to Self-Publish Your Way to Success!*

Zebra-Striped Whale is open from 11AM – 10PM, Sunday through Thursday, and from 11AM – 11PM, Friday and Saturday, and offers free "Wireless/Wi-Fi Hot Spot" Internet to computer users. Children's literature is enthusiastically promoted at *Zebra-Striped Whale*. Picture books as well as manuals related to the field of children's book publishing are on hand for patrons to peruse. Personalized autographed copies of Donahue's books are available for purchase. Events including children's author book signings and the *Reading Is Sweet* story time for toddlers are scheduled to begin this spring.

###

Zebra-Striped Whale

12 South State Street   Telephone: 215-860-4122
Newtown, PA 18940   Fax: 215-860-4177
E-Mail: tomdonahue@zebrastripedwhale.com

www.zebrastripedwhale.com

The Best Gift of All: Giving to Others

A favorite quote by an unknown author is, "One of the deep secrets of life is that all that is really worth the doing is what we do for others." Use your self-publishing endeavor—big or small—to make a difference in the lives of others. My passion for children's picture books—in conjunction with a strong, entrepreneurial spirit on behalf of the Zebra-Striped Whale Ice Cream & Coffee Café—has enabled me to spearhead the non-profit Zebra-Striped Whale Foundation (ZSWF, www.zebrastripedwhale.org). ZSWF is a charitable organization whose mission is to raise funds for those in need through the publishing of original children's picture books by first-time authors and illustrators. The first ZSWF project is a full color picture book—entitled *Cop Buddy*—in memory of recently slain Police Officer Brian S. Gregg. One hundred percent of the proceeds from this book will be donated to the Brian S. Gregg Fund, established at The First National Bank and Trust Company of Newtown.

Cop Buddy is based on a touching, true story written by a local resident, Jennifer Beagle Hannon, and illustrated by talented local illustrator Barbara Dove Kinnon. The title also features fifteen mosaic murals—composed of several hundred tiles—hand-decorated by community school children and seniors. The mosaic murals were proudly exhibited at the Zebra-Striped Whale Ice Cream & Coffee Café prior to auction. A headline in a recent issue of the *Bucks County Courier Times* reads, "Mosaics to be made into children's book. … Newtown business owner and children's book author, Shari Donahue, hopes to preserve the murals in the pages of a new book."

The ability to utilize my publishing expertise—with the objective of giving back to community—continues to be the highlight of my publishing career. The following non-profit organizations are recipients of proceeds derived from the sale of my self-published titles:

* ✳ Project H.O.M.E.—to house the homeless

* ✳ MAZON—to feed the hungry

* ✳ City of Hope—to research and treat life-threatening diseases

Self-Publish Your Way to Success

At its inception, your exciting new venture is likely to be a challenging, flexible part-time sideline. Before you begin, determine the approximate sum that you are willing to expend on fulfilling your self-publishing endeavors. Your financial decisions will undoubtedly impact the quantity of books that you produce—as well as the printing process that you utilize to do so. In all probability, you and/or your significant other must maintain a job, at least initially, to fund your project. It is also entirely feasible that family members or friends, enthralled by your sheer tenacity to succeed as a children's picture book author, may choose to invest in you—and your title!

Achieving Your Dream

I wish you the best of luck in your self-publishing adventure. Luck is created when opportunity meets preparation and hard work, according to an old adage. Whether you sell five or five thousand copies of your title—or donate the proceeds from your children's picture book to charity—the true reward emanates from your ability to touch others. "Signing" a book to an enthusiastic "fan" is priceless. The smile that emerges from such a simple gesture is among the most joyful experiences that I have known throughout my publishing career.

A self-publishing company may not turn you into a millionaire overnight—or perhaps ever. The gold that you discover at the end of the rainbow may take the form of self-actualization and sense of achievement, rather than fame and fortune. If you think practically, and comprehend the nature of niche promotion, your self-published children's picture book is likely to provide you with an added stream of income that grows over time. Prove a successful sales history—and a traditional publisher may opt to negotiate the rights to your title. (You may surprisingly choose to refuse the offer!)

Regardless of your current occupation, I encourage you to seize the opportunity to learn and grow from the energizing, multi-tiered self-publishing process. Your passion, fervor, and single-minded determination are certain to transform your picture book dreams into a magnificent reality!

Appendix A

A

AA The abbreviation for author's alterations. Changes dictated by and charged to the author during the book development/printing process.

acquire The process by which a publisher selects and contracts a manuscript for publication (acquisition).

acquisitions editor The individual at a publishing company who is responsible for the initial selection and contracting of a manuscript for publication—and may or may not be responsible for its development into a book.

adhesive case A hardcover book in which the signatures are glued in place.

advance The money paid to an author or illustrator, by the publisher, in anticipation of future sales. The advance must earn out in actual sales of the title before royalties are paid.

agent An individual who helps to get a work published through his/her connections with the right publishers. He/she receives a percentage of author earnings—usually 10% or 15%—and is likely to be involved in contract negotiations, career guidance, and minor manuscript editing/recommendations. This professional may also be called author's representative.

attachment The process of sending a document, in the form of an electronic file attached to an e-mail, via the Internet.

audience The specific segment or age level for whom the author of a book is writing.

author's representative See agent.

B

backlist Previously published books that are promoted by the publisher as a continuing source of revenue.

back matter Optional supplementary material located at the back of the book i.e. glossary, index, reading lists, donation information, after-word, etc.

backorder A book order that is scheduled to be filled as soon as the new supply of books becomes available.

binding The material by which the pages of a book are held together.

bleed When the color is printed to the edge of the page.

blues or bluelines A printing proof used as a final check for correctness. Changes, though expensive, may be made prior to the actual print run of a book.

board books Extremely durable, simple first books for infants and toddlers.

boiler plate Standard contract language.

book plus A book packaged in conjunction with another item, such as a toy.

C

CIP The abbreviation for cataloging-in-publication—typically used by commercial publishers, representing at least three authors.

C1S The abbreviation for coated one side. The printing term refers to a sheet of paper.

CMYK   The four colors—Cyan, Magenta, Yellow, and Black—used to create the appearance of full color in traditional four-color printing.

caliper   The thickness of a sheet of paper i.e. 10 point or 12 point (common in paperbacks); 12 point is slightly thicker than 10 point.

case   The cover of a hardcover book—typically a board that is wrapped/glued with material, such as printed paper (casewrap), Kivar, or cloth.

chains   Powerful companies—such as Barnes & Noble and Borders—comprised of multiple superstores.

chapter books   Books for older children—with substantial text to tell a story; illustrations are optional.

clips   Writing sample.

colophon   Front matter designation of a book's particular specifications, such as typeface, paper type, artist's materials, etc.

commission   The fee paid by the hiring publisher for a work in lieu of a royalty payment.

concept book   A picture book that features a particular concept i.e. colors, shapes—with or without a storyline.

conglomerate   A large division-based company—quite typical in the children's book industry.

consolidation   The process of joining companies, shutting down divisions, and laying off employees to maximize business operations and revenue.

co-op   Money that is reimbursed to the bookseller by the publisher on behalf of promoting featured books.

copy editor   The individual who is responsible for ensuring that a manuscript is error-free—in areas such as style, grammar, spelling, and punctuation.

copyright   The right of an individual to copy and distribute his/her original work. In copyright law, the copyright exists from the moment a work is created.

cover letter   The letter of introduction that accompanies a manuscript.

critique   The evaluation of a manuscript—written or verbal—with regard to tonality, structure, characterization, style, etc.

D

development editor   The professional who is responsible for ensuring that the book is cohesive and structurally sound.

draft   One version of a manuscript.

dummy   The mock-up of a manuscript in book format—complete with positioning for roughly sketched illustrations.

E

EAN bar code   The abbreviation for European Article Number bar code—a title's unique scanner-readable formatted fingerprint—used for standard order processing.

early/easy readers   Children's books having age appropriate vocabulary for beginning readers.

earn out   The process of incoming royalty earnings meeting the advance that has already been paid to the author.

e-book   A paperless book in electronic format—on a personal computer or handheld reader.

endpaper   A folded sheet of plain or printed paper (typically 80# offset) in which one half is glued to the inside front/back case and the other half to the first/last page of the book. Endpaper stock is usually thicker than the interior pages, with the exception of self-ended books in which the end sheets are actually part of the first and last signatures of the book.

exclusive submission   A manuscript that is forwarded to one publisher at a time for consideration.

F

FOB   The abbreviation for free on board. A freight term designating that freight is not included in the cost of the print job.

fairytale   A bigger-than-life story brimming with literary elements for children.

fantasy   A fictitious story characterized by fanciful elements and supernatural tendencies i.e. If You Could Talk to the Animals

fiction   Writing based on imagination, fable, or tale.

finishing   Post printing add-ons—such as film lamination, shrink wrap, or inserts.

flat back   The spine of a hardcover binding that is constructed with board to appear flat, common in standard 32-page children's picture books.

flat fee   A compensatory payment made to the author or illustrator for his/her work in lieu of an advance against royalty arrangement.

folktale   A story that has been passed down orally though the generations, and often appeals to children and parents.

freelance   A non-salaried worker hired on a per project basis.

front matter   The material that precedes the body of a work i.e. title page, copyright page, foreword, introduction, acknowledgements.

frontlist   Publisher's new release of books—usually each spring and fall

G

galley   Lengthy pages of non-book formatted typeset text—rarely used today.

glossary   A listing of book-related terms and definitions.

H

halftone   A special effect in the black and white, or color, reproduction of printed artwork—having values between 1 and 100%. Today, with the use of digitally scanned images, the more proper term would be screened DPI (dots per inch).

hard copy   A tangible, rather than virtual, record of computer output i.e. laser copy.

hardcover   A book that is bound with stiff cardboard covers that are wrapped with treated paper, cloth, vinyl, or the like.

I

ISBN   The acronym for International Standard Book Number—the numeric identifier of a book.

imprint   A distinctly identified entity of a conglomerate—having its own company name and staff.

independents   Independently owned and operated bookstores—unaffiliated with major chains.

index   A key word list, accompanied by page numbers, located at the back of a book.

inkjet A type of high speed computer guided printing process that breaks up jets of ink into electrostatically charged droplets; typically used to print mailing labels.

institutional The school and library markets for children's books.

inventory Publisher's stock of books that is available for sale.

invoice A bill accompanying a book order.

J

jacket The removable cover on a hardcover book that is used for protection as well as to capture consumer attention with marketing information. Also termed dust jacket since it prevents dust from forming on books.

journal Bound blank pages that enable you to jot down ideas, sketches, and events to stimulate the creative thinking process.

K

kill fee The final payment received by an author or illustrator at project cancellation.

Kivar The least expensive cloth-like material used to cover the boards of a hardcover book. Though it gives the appearance of leather, it is actually paper that can be easily foil stamped.

L

lamination The protective coating on cover, casewraps, and jackets. Several types are available: (1) varnish/aqueous (the least expensive, but also the least durable—not recommended), (2) UV coating (a cost-effective option for print runs, usually 25,000+, depending upon the printer), (3) gloss or matte film lamination (the best choice!).

large publisher A publishing entity that produces 52+ books per year, approximately 4+ books per month; also known as major publisher.

layflat lamination A highly recommended type of film lamination that is intended to lay flat under all weather conditions and reduce potential cover curl.

layout The arrangement of elements throughout a book.

line-up The books produced by a publisher as designated by its catalog.

literary agent See agent.

M

major publisher A publishing entity that produces 52+ books per year, approximately 4+ books per month; also known as large publisher.

manuscript A writer's work prior to getting published.

marketing plan A publisher's designated promotional/advertising plan for selling books.

mass market Popular consumer-responsive books sold through the channel of low cost, general retail outlets i.e. warehouse discount stores, drug stores, groceries, newsstands.

N

niche publisher A publisher that produces books with a specified category of interest—and incorporates targeted avenues to promote sales.

non-fiction An informative book that is written with the objective of conveying knowledge, concepts, or ideas; also known as informational book.

novelty book A book that offers saleable, consumer-responsive features—beyond simple text—such as lift-the-flaps, pop-ups, and sound chips.

O

OP The abbreviation for out of print. A term used to designate that the publisher has no more copies of a book to sell, and has no intentions of reprinting in the future.

OSI The abbreviation for out of stock indefinitely. A term used to designate that the publisher has no more copies of a book to sell, but may have the intention of reprinting in the future.

offset A type of printing process used in web and sheetfed presses. Utilizes an intermediate cylinder (known as blanket) to transfer images from the image carrier (known as plate) to the paper. Offset may also be a reference to uncoated paper utilized in the printing process.

on spec On speculation work that is done without a signed contract in hand—for which the author/illustrator may not receive remuneration.

P

PDF The abbreviation for electronic portable document format files.

POD The abbreviation for print on demand; a form of digital printing that offers swift turn around time, in quantities as low as one copy.

PP&B The term used for paper, printing & binding costs to produce a finished book.

PPI The abbreviation for pages per inch—a term that refers to paper thickness. The PPI determines the bulk of a book. Book pages can have the same weight, but a different PPI based on the amount of air added during the paper manufacturing process. For example, the same 50# offset paper can vary from 600 PPI to 400 PPI. This represents the difference between 5/8″ and 7/16″ on a 256-page book. Because the consumer pays for a book based on perceived value, paper bulk plays a significant role in buying behavior.

pallet A low-to-the-ground warehouse storage /transportation platform, usually made of wood.

packager A company or individual that is paid to develop or produce a book—according to publisher specs—on behalf of the publisher.

paper Usually half the cost of manufacturing a book (choose wisely!). Paper characteristics include brightness (the amount of light reflected by the sheet), opacity (the amount of light that passes through the sheet), and finish (surface of the paper—shiny or dull, smooth or vellum/textured).

paperback A softcover cover book. See perfect bound, Wire-O, and spiral.

paper grade Ranges from highest quality (grade 1) to lowest quality (grade 5). Grade 1 is used primarily in the preparation of annual reports.

paper weight Designated in "pounds" with the # symbol. In the U.S., the poundage of offset paper used in books is determined by the weight of five hundred sheets, (termed "basis" size). For example, five hundred 25″ x 38″ sheets of 50# offset paper weighs 50 pounds; five hundred 25″ x 38″ sheets of 60# offset paper weighs 60 pounds. Bond paper, used primarily in copy shops, is calculated using a different "basis" size: 17″ x 22″. As a result, five hundred sheets of 20# bond is comparable to 50# offset, and five hundred sheets of 24# bond is comparable to 60# offset.

pedantic A term used to describe a story in which the plot is infiltrated with the author's heavy-handed moral or message.

perfect binding A popular type of paperback binding in which the book's signatures are glued together at the spine—providing prime space for book title, author/illustrator names, and publisher insignia.

permissions The legal right of a publisher to reproduce another's work.

picture book The category of illustrated books for young children—usually up to eight years old—that depicts a story through expressive pictures in addition to text.

polybag A loose transparent bag used to wrap a book for protection in packing.

press kit See media kit.

pre-press The necessary preparation of electronic files on disk prior to the actual printing of a book.

pre-writing The development/outline of story ideas prior to the actual writing of a manuscript.

printed casewrap See casewrap. In children's picture books, the image on the printed casewrap and dust jacket are the same.

process Colors used in the printing process including: cyan, magenta, yellow, and black, known in the industry as CMYK. In offset printing, the combination of CMYK inks, in dot format, creates the appearance of full color. In most digital printing presses, CMYK toners versus inks are utilized to create the appearance of full color—without the use of dots.

proof The formatted pages of a book produced by the printer for accuracy verification prior to the actual press run.

proofreader The individual who analyzes a proof for errors prior to the actual press run.

publication (pub) date The date, selected by the publisher, that determines a book's availability in the marketplace.

public domain Non-copyrighted material that may be used without permission.

publicist An author's public relations representative.

publishing committee Known as the editorial board of a publishing company, individuals in this group share the responsibility for book acquisition. Today, book acquisition is rarely the role of just one editor.

Q

query letter The letter that you send to a publisher to stimulate interest in your manuscript.

R

RFQ The abbreviation for request for quotation. A term used in the obtaining of book manufacturing bids.

reading fees Payment to a professional to evaluate the viability of your manuscript. Beware of non-legitimate agents who request reading fees to peruse your manuscript for the purpose of representation.

regional publisher A publishing house with specialized titles featuring a particular geographic location of the country—and primarily utilizes that region to distribute its books.

rejection letter A letter refusing a submission. Some rejection letters offer insights and recommendations for manuscript improvement.

remainders The publisher's steeply discounted surplus books with the objective of entirely or partially reducing its stock.

response time The period of time for a publisher to respond to a manuscript submission —usually at least several months.

reprint A printing term that generally describes an additional printing of the same book.

returns Surplus and damaged stock sent back to the publisher—usually for a full refund—up to two full years beyond the date that a book is considered out of print. Unlike other industries, books in reality are sold to retailers on a consignment basis.

revise To make changes to a manuscript for the purpose of improvement.

royalties The dollar amount remitted to the author or illustrator by the publisher. May be a percentage of list price, publisher's wholesaler net (usually 50–55% discount), or some other agreed upon formula.

S

SASE The abbreviation for self-addressed stamped envelope forwarded with manuscript submission or query to improve the likelihood of publisher response.

saddle stitch A type of softcover binding process utilizing two metal stitches that resemble staples. The term emanates from the actual binding equipment in which pages are laid over a piece of metal that looks like the saddle on a horse.

sales representative (rep) The selling arm of a publisher responsible for optimizing book sell-through at the retail level.

search engine The most effective process for uncovering Internet resources.

self-publisher The individual who pays to print his/her own book for sale or distribution.

series Multiple books that are connected by commonalities such as characters, theme, or purpose—and often share an umbrella title.

sheetfed press The offset printing process that utilizes sheets of paper as opposed to rolls of paper—printing usually one side at a time. See offset.

short run A small book manufacturing print run of less than 3000 copies.

shrink wrap The process of wrapping books in heat shrunk/sealed plastic for protection.

side sewn A sturdy hardcover binding in which all signatures are sewn together approximately 3/8″ from the spine—prior to being glued into the cover.

signature A sheet of paper—printed on both sides and folded to trim size format—to form a section of a book.

simultaneous submission The same manuscript that is submitted to more than one publisher at a time.

slush pile Incoming unsolicited manuscripts received by a publisher.

small publisher A publisher that produces fewer than 12 books per year, approximately 1 book per month.

Smythe sewn Each printed signature is sewn down the center, in sections, prior to being glued into the hardcover case. Smythe sewing is a costly, sturdy binding that enables a book to flatten fully when open.

softcover A book bound with light, flexible front/back cardboard covers. Also termed paperback.

special sales Books sold as premiums as well as through non-traditional outlets.

spine The panel that connects the front and back covers of a book—and often designates title, author/illustrator, and publisher insignia.

spiral binding A type of softcover binding in which a spiral-like wire—sometimes covered in colored coated plastic—is thread through tiny holes across the binding edge.

spot illustration A small, non-bleed page illustration.

spread The two facing pages of a flat, opened book.

stamping A book cover impression produced by a die that may or may not use colored foil. A stamp that simply leaves an impression, without the use of colored foil, is called a blind stamp.

stock A printing term that refers to paper.

structural editing Early stage manuscript revision that improves upon content and composition.

submissions Manuscripts forwarded to publishers by authors or agents. May be exclusive, multiple, or simultaneous.

subsidiary rights The multiple avenues for a published book to be licensed—such as book club, movie, theme park, clothing, etc.

subsidy publisher A company that is paid by the author to publish a book in his/her behalf.

superstore A chain bookstore, such as Barnes & Noble and Borders, that stocks 100,000+ books—and offers an upscale coffee shop, gift items, and other amenities.

T

text A printing term that refers to all of the pages in a book—including blank pages—with the exception of the cover.

thread seal A type of sewn reinforcement in which each printed signature is sewn down the center with heat-sealed, plastic-coated thread. Signatures are not sewn together prior to being glued into the cover.

thumbnails An artist's roughly drawn mini-sketches prior to full blown illustrations.

trade books High quality books—typically casewrap/dustjacket and perfect bound softcover—available through bookstores and libraries.

transparencies Transparent slide-like material used in the reproduction of photographs or illustrations.

trim size The horizontal and vertical measurements of the pages of a book—not the hardcover case.

U

uncoated paper Smooth or vellum (textured) finish. See paper.

unsolicited manuscript An author-submitted manuscript that has not been requested by the publisher.

V

vanity publisher A book producer that is paid by the author to publish his/her book. The term, vanity, implies that the author's vanity is the motivating factor behind paying large sums of money to see his/her own words in print. This term is interchangeable with subsidy publisher.

W

web press A type of offset printing that utilizes rolls of paper as opposed to sheets of paper. Prints both sides at a time, and folds in one operation. Typically used for larger print runs—depending upon the printer.

wholesaler A company such as Ingram Book Company or Baker & Taylor that buys inventory on consignment from a publisher to sell to bookstores, libraries, and other outlets.

Wire-O binding A type of paperback binding in which a double series of wire loops—usually plastic-coated—are thread through punched slots across the binding side of the book.

word of mouth An informal passing of information from one individual to another.

work-for-hire Fee-based To Specification work — created on behalf of publishers who are likely to retain the copyright.

Y

young adult (YA) In use since the 1960s, this term designates the upper age category of children's books—typically 12+ years of age.

Appendix B

Organizations

American Booksellers Association (ABA)
828 South Broadway
Tarrytown, NY 10591
www.ambook.org
800-637-0037

American Library Association (ALA)
50 East Huron Street
Chicago, IL 60611
www.ala.org
800-545-2433

Association of Authors' Representatives (AAR)
676A Ninth Avenue #312
New York, NY 10036
www.aar-online.org
212-840-5777

The Association of Booksellers for Children (ABC)
National Office
62 Wenham Street
Jamaica Plain, MA 02130
www.abfc.com
617-390-7759

The Author's Guild
31 East 28th Street 10th Floor
New York, NY 10016
www.authorsguild.org
212-563-5904

Canadian Society of Children's Authors, Illustrators, and Performers (CANSCAIP)
35 Spadina Road
Toronto, Ontario
Canada M5R 2S9
www.canscaip.org/
416-515-1559

The Children's Book Council (CBC)
12 West 37th Street, 2nd Floor
New York, NY 10018
www.cbcboooks.org
212-966-1990

Children's Literature Association
P.O. Box 138
Battle Creek, MI 49016
http://ebbs.english.vt.edu/chla
616-965-8180

Graphic Artists Guild
90 John Street, Suite 403
New York, NY 10038
www.gag.org
212-791-3400

The Institute of Children's Literature
93 Long Ridge
West Redding, CT 06896
www.institutechildrenslit.com
203-792-8600

International Reading Association (IRA)
Headquarters Office
800 Barksdale Road
P.O. Box 8137
Newark, DE 19714
www.reading.org
302-731-1600

National Association of Women Writers
24165 IH-10 W, Ste. 217-637
San Antonio, TX 78257
www.naww.org
866-821-5829

National Center for Children's Illustrated Literature
102 Cedar
Abilene, TX 79601
www.nccil.org
325-673-4586

National Writers Union
National Office East
113 University Place, 6th Floor
New York, NY 10003
www.nwu.org
212-254-0279

National Office West
337 17th Street, #101
Oakland, CA 94612
www.nwu.org
510-839-0110

Publishers Marketing Association (PMA)
627 Aviation Way
Manhattan Beach, California 90266
www.pma-online.org
310-372-2732

Small Publishers, Artists & Writers Network
(SPAWN)
PMB 123
323 E. Matilija St., Suite 110
Ojai, CA 93023
www.spawn.org
818-886-4281

Small Publishers Association of North America
(SPAN)
1618 West Colorado Avenue
Colorado Springs, CO 80904
www.SPANnet.org
719-475-1726

Society of Children's Book Writers and Illustrators
(SCBWI)
8271 Beverly Boulevard
Los Angeles, CA 90048
www.scbwi.org
323-782-1010

Society of Illustrators
Museum of American Illustration
128 East 63rd Street
New York, NY 10021
www.societyillustrators.org
212-838-2560

Web Sites

About Books, Inc.
www.about-books.com

America Writes for Kids
http://usawrites4kids.drury.edu

Authors and Illustrators for Children Webring
www.geocities.com/aicwebring

Author Illustrator Source
www.author-illust-source.com

Authorlink!
www.authorlink.com

The Best Book Bin
www.thebestbookbin.com

Best Children's Books
www.best-childrens-books.com

Big Universe
www.biguniverse.com

Booklist
www.ala.org/booklist

Bookweb
www.bookweb.org

Bookwire
www.bookwire.com

Theresa Brandon, Illustrator
http://members.aol.com/thebrandon

Cachibachis Blog
http://cachibachis.blogspot.com

Children's Authors Network! (CAN!)
www.childrensauthorsnetwork.com

Children's Book Committee at Bank Street College
www.bnkst.edu/bookcom

Children's Book Council
www.cbcbooks.org

Children's Book Insider
www.write4kids.com

Children's Literature Guide
www.nypl.org/research/chss/grd/intguides/
children.html

The Children's Literature Web Guide
www.ucalgary.ca/~dkbrown

Children's Picture Books
www.justselfpublish.com

Children's Writer
www.childrenswriter.com

The Children's Writing Supersite
www.write4kids.com

Colossal Directory of Children's Publishers
www.signaleader.com/childrens-writers/index.html

Direct Contact P. R.
www.directcontactpr.com

The Drawing Board
www.members.aol.com/thedrawing

Fairrosa Cyber Library
www.dalton.org/libraries/fairrosa

The Horn Book, Inc.
www.hbook.com

Illustrating Children's Books—A Student's Guide
www.mindspring.com/~amoss/teaching/1intro.html

Illustration for Children's Publishing
www.phylliscahill.com

Inkspot
www.inkspot.com

Institute of Children's Literature
www.institutechildrenslit.com

Internet Public Library Youth Reading Zone
www.ipl.org/div/kidspace/browse/rzn0000

Literary Market Place
www.literarymarketplace.com

Midwest Book Review
www.midwestbookreview.com

New York Public Library—On-Lion for Kids
www.nypl.org/home/branch/kids

Open Horizons
www.bookmarket.com

PRWeb Press Release Newswire
www.prwebdirect.com

Picturebook Sourcebook
www.picture-book.com

Dan Poynter's Self-Publishing Resources
www.parapublishing.com

Publishers' Catalogues Home Page
www.lights.com/publisher

Publishers Weekly
www.publishersweekly.com

Purple Crayon
www.underdown.org

RJ Communications
www.selfpublishing.com

School Library Journal
www.slj.com

Self-Publishing Resources
www.selfpublishingresources.com

Cynthia Leitich Smith
www.cynthialeitichsmith.com

Society of Book Writers & Illustrators (SCBWI)
www.scbwi.org

Vandergrift's Children's Literature Page
www.scils.rutgers.edu/special/kay/childlit.html

Dr. Joe Vitale
www.mrfire.com

Writer's Digest
www.writersdigest.com

Writersinkville
www.writersinkville.com

Writers Write
www.writerswrite.com

Writing World
www.writing-world.com

Conferences/Workshops

PMA Publishing University
www.pma-online.org

SCBWI Conferences & Workshops
www.scbwi.org

SPAN Marketing Conference & Tradeshow
www.SPANnet.org

SPAWN Member Events
www.spawn.org

Shari Faden Donahue
www.justselfpublish.com

Brian Jud
www.bookmarketingworks.com

Dan Poynter
www.parapublishing.com

Susan Raab
www.raabassociates.com

Fern Reiss
www.publishinggame.com

Tom & Marilyn Ross
www.about-books.com

Joe Vitale
www.mrfire.com

Appendix C

Pre-Publication Journals

Booklist
America Library Association
50 E. Huron Street
Chicago, IL 60611
www.ala.org
800-545-2433

BookPage
2143 Belcourt Avenue
Nashville, TN 37212
www.bookpage.com
615-292-8926

ForeWord Magazine
1291/2 E. Front Street
Traverse City, MI
www.forewordmagazine.com
231-933-3699

Horn Book Guide
56 Roland Street, Suite 200
Boston, MA 02129
www.hbook.com
800-325-1170

Horn Book Magazine
56 Roland Street, Suite 200
Boston, MA 02129
www.hbook.com
800-325-1170

Kirkus Reviews
VNU US Literary Group
770 Broadway
New York, NY 10003
www.kirkusreviews.com
646-654-5500

Publishers Weekly
360 Park Avenue South
New York, NY 10011
www.publishersweekly.com
646-746-6781

School Library Journal
360 Park Avenue South
New York, NY 10011
www.schoollibraryjournal.com
646-746-6763

Post-Publication Journals

The Bloomsbury Review
1553 Platte Street, # 206
Denver, CO 80202
www.bloomsburyreview.com
303-455-3123

The Bulletin of the Center for Children's Books
501 East Daniel Street
Champaign, IL 61820
http://bccb.lis.uiuc.edu
217-244-0324

Midwest Book Review
278 Orchard Drive
Oregon, WI 53575
www.midwestbookreview.com
608-835-7937

Bibliographic Source (K-8)

Book Links
American Library Association
50 East Huron
Chicago, IL 60611
www.ala.org
800-545-2433

"In the News" Book Reviews

Los Angeles Times Book Review
202 W. First Street
Los Angeles, CA 90012
213-237-2651

New York Times Book Review
229 W. 43rd Street
New York, NY 10036
212-556-7267

Freelance Reviewers

The following reviewers are members of SCBWI. To increase your likelihood of a favorable response, be certain to mention your membership affiliation with SCBWI, PMA, and other publishing-related organizations.

Vicki Arkoff
varkoff@yahoo.com
The Midwest Book Review, The Book Review Index, Smartwriter.com, Amazon.com, BarnesandNoble.com, The Booklist, Children's literature

Nancy Garhan Attebury
garbury@eoni.com
Children's Literature Comprehensive Database, Bethesda

Dori Butler
dhbutler@kidswriter.com
The Cedar Rapids Gazette

Angelica Carpenter
angelica@csufresno.edu
The Baum Bugle, The Lewis Carroll Review, The Fresno Bee

Bobbie Combs
bcombs@twolives.com
Philadelphia Parents Express

Michele Corriel
mcorriel@imt.net
Montana Parent and other parenting magazines throughout the country

Tracey Cox
traceycox@yahoo.com
Tifton Gazette & Ocilla Star

Sue Bradford Edwards
suebe@brick.net
The St. Louis Post-Dispatch

Lucy Fuchs
labefuchs@aol.com
The Small Press Review

Mary Rodd Furbee
Mary.furbee@mail.wvu.edu
Washington Post, Gannett News Service, Charleston Gazette, Progressive Magazine, Stars & Stripes, Cleveland Plain Dealer

Linda Johns
lindajohns@mindspring.com
Authorlink.com

Angela Leeper
Angela.leeper@earthlink.net
Kirkus Reviews, MultiCultural Review, The Bark, ForeWord

Margo Lemieux
mlemieux@lasell.edu
Sun Chronicle

Sharon Levin
sharonlevin@mindspring.com
*Childrenslit.com and numerous California
school newsletters*

Lynda Dale Maclean
rosebeewillow@comcast.net
TheCelebrityCafe.com

Peter Mandel
pmandel@worldet.att.net
The Providence Journal-Bulletin

Parvati Markus
parvatim@aol.com
Transitions Radio Magazine

Judith Nasse
nasse@kitcarson.net
And Baby Magazine

J. L. Parker
Parker9793@sbcglobal.net
Children's Museum of Northern Nevada

Pamela C. Patterson
grammarcop@smartypants.net
January Magazine Web site

Phyllis J. Perry
dpperry@att.net
Above & Beyond, Think & Discover

Lynne Marie Pisano
UnderCoveReader@aol.dom
Midwest Book Review, SCBWI Bulletin

Meribeth C. Shank
meribeths@earthlink.net
South Florida Sun Sentinel

Terry Miller Shannon
Terryms2001@yahoo.com
KidsRead.com and other parenting newsletters

Lu Ann Brobst Staheli
luannstaheli@prodigy.net
*Read All about It (Spanish Fork Press),
Utah Children's Writers Listserv,
The ALAN Review*

Debbie Stewart
dstewart@grpl.org
School Library Journal

Whitney Stewart
kunzedolma@aol.com
*The Times-Picayune Newspaper, Blueear.com,
online journals*

Diana Thompson
diana@momsbookthing.com
MomsBookThing.com

Julie Yates Walton
jywalton@eathlink.net
*Child Magazine, Publishers Weekly,
New York Times Book Review*

Katie McCallaster Weaver
kidlitkt@aol.com
Fish Eggs for the Soul, BookPage

Laurie Whitman
jlwhitman@hotmail.com
BookReview.com

Mark L. Williams
scribe@dangerboy.com
Studio City Sun Kids' Shelf Column

Lisa A. Wroble
lwroble@lisawroble.com
Wonder Years/Partnership for Learning

Online Book Reviews

Haemi Balgassi
www.haemibalgassi.com

Wendy Bett's Notes from the Windowsill
www.armory.com/~web/notes.html

Bookpage
www.bookpage.com

Children's Bookwatch
www.midwestbookreview.com

Children's Literature
www.childrenslit.com

Carol Otis Hurst
www.carolhurst.com

Independent Publisher Online
www.independentpublisher.com

The Scoop
www.friend.ly.net/scoop

Through the Looking Glass
www.lookingglassreview.com

Appendix D

Advertising Specialty

AZ Advertising Specialties, Inc.
www.azadvertising.com
800-572-7641

Advertising Specialties, Inc.
www.adspecialtiesinc.com
887-274-6684

Blueberry Ink
www.blueberryink.com
800-837-0337

Superior Promos
www.superiorpromos.com
888-577-6667

Book Distribution Services

BWI
www.bwibooks.com

Biblio Distribution—NBN's sister company
www.bibliodistribution.com

Book Clearing House
www.bookch.com

BookMasters, Inc.
www.bookmasters.com

BookWorld Services, Inc.
www.bookworld.com

Bound To Stay Bound Books, Inc.
www.btsb.com

Brodart
www.brodart.com

Follett
www.follett.com,

Greenleaf Book Group
www.greenleafbookgroup.com

Independent Publishers Group (IPG)
www.ipgbook.com

Midpoint Trade Books Inc.
www.midpointtrade.com

National Book Network (NBN)
www.nbnbooks.com

Perma-Bound
www.perma-bound.com

Perseus Distribution
www.cdsbooks.com

SCB Distributors
www.scbdistributors.com

Book Fair Exhibiting Services

Combined Book Exhibit
www.combinedbookexhibit.com
800-462-7687

EBSCO Sample Issue & Book Program
www.ebsco.com/sip/sippub
888-306-9492

Publishers Marketing Association
www.pma-online.org
310-372-2732

Book Designers

Abacus Graphics
www.abacusgraphics.com
760-724-7750

Budget Book Design
www.budgetbookdesign.com
800-621-2556

Desktop Miracles
www.desktopmiracles.com
802-253-7900

Eisler Design
www.eislerdesign.com
215-750-9513

George Foster
www.fostercovers.com
800-472-3953

Opus 1 Design
www.opus1design.com
800-590-7778

Pneuma Books
www.pneumabooks.com
410-996-8900

Rosa+Wesley
e-mail: rw@rosawesley.com
630-588-9801

Karen Ross
www.karenross.com
310-397-3408

Shooting Star Graphics
Kimle58@montana.com
406-273-0206

Book Stickers

SPAN ("Autographed Copy," "Great Gift Idea,"
"Local Author")
www.SPANnet.org
719-475-1726

Bookstores (Chains)

For information on additional chains, review *The American Book Trade Directory*, available at your public library.

Barnes & Noble, Inc.
122 5th Avenue, 4th floor
New York, NY
www.bn.com
212-633-3300

Books-A-Million, Inc.
402 Industrial Lane
Birmingham, AL 35211
www.booksamillion.com
800-201-3550

Borders Group, Inc.
100 Phoenix Drive
Ann Arbor, MI 48108
www.borders.com
800-770-7811

Bookstores (Online)

Amazon.com
www.amazon.com

Barnesandnoble.com
www.bn.com

Books-A-Million, Inc.
www.booksamillion.com

Compliance

ISBN

R. R. Bowker
121 Chanlon Road
New Providence, NJ 07904
www.isbn.org
877-310-7333

EAN Bar Code

For a comprehensive listing of EAN bar code suppliers, visit www.isbn.org/standards/home/isbn/us/barcode.asp.

Bar Code Graphics
875 North Michigan Avenue, #2640
Chicago, IL 60611
www.barcode-us.com
312-664-0700

R. R. Bowker
121 Chanlon Road
New Providence, NJ 07904
www.bowkerbarcode.com
877-310-7333

Film Masters
11680 Hawke Road
Columbia Station, OH 44028
www.filmmasters.com
800-541-5102

Fotel
1125 E. St. Charles Road, #100
Lombard, IL 60148
www.fotel.com
800-834-4920

General Graphics
PO Box 3192
Arnold, PA 15068
www.ggbarcode.com
800-887-5894

Infinity Graphics
2277 Science Parkway
Okemos, MI 48864
www.infinitygraphics.com
800-292-2633

Library of Congress Control Number

Library of Congress
101 Independence Avenue, S.E.
Washington, D.C. 20540-4320
http://pcn.loc.gov/pcn
202-707-5000

Credit Card Processing

Electronic Transfer, Inc. (ETI)
www.electronictransfer.com
800-757-5453, ext. 201

Displays

City Diecutting, Inc.
www.bookdisplays.com
973-736-1224, ext. 11

Display International
www.universaldisplays.com
800-600-1919

Meridian Display
www.meridiandisplay.com
800-786-2501

Siegel Display Products
www.siegeldisplay.com
800-626-0322

Editors/Manuscript Doctors

Carol Barkin
e-mail: cbarkin@optonline.net
914-478-0612

Olga Cosso
e-mail: odonolga39@cs.com
831-475-0207

Sandy Ferguson Fuller
e-mail: sffuller@alparts.com
303-582-5189

Esther Hershenhorn
e-mail: esthersh@aol.com
773-880-1988

Eileen Heyes
e-mail: heyeswaters@mindspring.com
919-848-3858

Jacqueline Horsfall
e-mail: jack@stny.rr.com
607-962-3552

Marya Jansen-Gruber
e-mail: lookingglasscritique@direcway.com
804-440-0031

Susan Korman
e-mail: susanjkorman@comcast.net
215-295-7503

Judi Miller
e-mail: judimiller28@aol.com
215-741-0198

Judy Carey Nevin
e-mail: careycritiques@hotmail.com
540-456-7198

Lisa Rojany-Buccieri
e-mail: esola@adelphia.net
818-707-1042

Julie J. Roth
e-mail: jersildroth@earthlink.net
612-928-0204

Carol Fisher Saller
e-mail: bookhelp@sbcglobal.net
773-363-317

Peggy Spence
e-mail: peggyspence1@msn.com
928-537-2897

Melissa Stewart
e-mail: hbeeprod@msn.com
978-263-7279

Writer's Ink
Stephanie Jacob Gordon & Judith Ross Enderle
e-mail: judink@aol.com
805-644-3354

Linda Zuckerman, The Friday Group
e-mail: lindaz@teleport.com
503-590-6947

Illustration Directories

American Showcase
800-894-7469

Picture Book
888-490-0100

Stock Illustration Sourcebook
800-4-IMAGES

Illustration Web Sites

www.corbis.com (stock illustrations)

www.creativemoonlighter.com

www.illustrationweb.com

www.illustrators.net

www.istockphoto.com (stock illustrations)

www.picturebookartists.org

www.picturebk.com

www.societyillustrators.com

Mailing Lists

Hugo Dunhill Mailing Lists, Inc.
www.hdml.com

InfoUSA
www.listbazaar.com

Mailings Clearing House
www.mailings.com

Market Data Retrieval (educational)
www.schooldata.com

Quality Education Data (educational)
www.qeddata.com

Marketing & Publicity

Kate Bandos
www.ksbpromotions.com
616-676-0758

Book Flash
www.bookflash.com
520-798-2356

Brian Jud
www.bookmarketingworks.com
800-562-4357

John Kremer
www.bookmarket.com
505-751-3398

Paul J. Krupin
www.directcontactpr.com
800-457-8746

Marketability
www.marketability.com
303-279-4349

PeopleSpeak
www.pitchperfectmarketing.com
949-581-6190

Power Promotions
www.powerontheweb.com
830-755-4728

The Publicity Hound
www.publicityhound.com
262-284-7451

Susan Salzman Raab
www.raabassociates.com
914-241-2117

Fern Reiss
www.publishinggame.com
617-630-0945

Rocks-DeHart Public Relations
www.rdpr.com
412-784-8811

Send2Press
www.send2press.com
866-473-5924

Smith Publicity
www.smithpublicity.com
856-489-8654, ext. 111

Joe Vitale
www.mrfire.com
512-847-3414

Media Trainers & Coaches

Kare Anderson
www.sayitbetter.com
800-488-KARE (5273)

Susan Harrow
www.prsecrets.com
888-839-4190

Natalie H. Rogers
www.talkpower.com
800-525-3718

Success in Media
www.successinmedia.com
631-431-8251

Picture Book Manufacturers/Brokers

360 Digital Books
www.360digitalbooks.com
866-379-8767

Bang Printing
www.bangprinting.com
800-328-0450

Four Colour Imports
www.fourcolour.com
502-896-9644

Lightning Source
www.lightningsource.com
615-213-5815

Palace Press
www.palacepress.com
212-462-2622

Publisher Graphics
www.pubgraphics.com
888-404-3769

RJ Communications
www.selfpublishing.com
800-621-2556

Taylor Specialty Books
www.taylorspecialtybooks.com
800-331-8163

Worzalla Printing
www.worzalla.com
715-344-9600

Print On Demand (POD) Publishing Service Providers

AuthorHouse
www.authorhouse.com
888-519-5121

BookSurge
www.booksurge.com
843-579-0000

Lulu
www.lulu.com
(919) 459-5858

Trafford Publishing
www.trafford.com
888-232-4444

Wordclay
www.wordclay.com
877.655.1720

Xlibris
www.xlibris.com
888-795-4274

Promotional Printing

Growl.com
www.growl.com
877-678-6537

ModernPostcard
www.modernpostcard.com
800-959-8365, ext.2500

PostcardMania
www.postcardmania.com
800-628-1804

Simply Postcards
www.simplycatalogs.com
800-770-4102

Tu-Vets Corporation
www.tu-vets.com
800-894-8977

Twig
www.twigonestop.com
561-740-9901

Promotional Writing

Susan Kendrick Writing Team
e-mail: Kendrick@cheqnet.net
715-634-4120

Joe Vitale
e-mail: quotes@mrfire.com
512-847-3414

Publicity Resources

All-in-One Media Directory
www.gebbiepress.com

Bacon's Media Directories
www.bacons.com

Book Marketing Update Subscription Newsletter
www.bookmarket.com

Bulldog Reporter
www.bulldogreporter.com

The Gale Database of Publications and Broadcast Media
www.gale.com

Gordon's Radio List
www.radiopublicity.com

Harrison's Guide to the Top National TV Talk and Interview Shows
www.freepublicity.com

Media Directory—Local, Daily and Weekly Newspapers
www.bizmove.com

PartyLine
www.expertclick.com

The Publicity Hound
www.publicityhound.com

Radio Station Directory
www.radio-directory.com

Joe Sabah's Radio List
www.sabahradioshows.com

Publishing Attorneys

Darla R. Anderson
e-mail: darla@darlalaw.com
805-690-1044

Jaffe, Raitt, Heuer, & Weiss, P.C.
e-mail: ljordan@jaffelaw.com
734-222-4776

Law Offices of Lloyd J. Jassin
e-mail: jasssin@copylaw.com
212-354-4442

Law Office of Lloyd Rich
e-mail: info@publaw.com
303-388-0291

Rich Schell
e-mail: richschellcareer@hotmail.com
847-759-9833

Publishing Consultants

Shari Faden Donahue
www.justselfpublish.com
215-205-2227

Bob Erdmann
www.bob-erdmann.com.com
209-586-1566

Margaret Klee Lichtenberg Coaching
www.coachingcollective,com
505-986-8807

Help-U-Publish.com
www.help-u-publish.com
310-722-1957

John Kremer
www.bookmarket.com
505-751-3398

Dan Poynter
www.parapublishing.com
800-PARAPUB

Ellen Reid's Book Shepherding
www.bookshep.com
866-406-4352

Fern Reiss
www.publishinggame.com
617-630-0945

Tom & Marilyn Ross
www.about-books.com
719-395-2459

Radio Interviews

Bradley Communications Radio-TV
Interview Report
www.rtir.com
800-553-8002, ext. 558

Broadcast Interview Source
www.expertradio.com
202-333-5000

Remainder Dealers

Half Price Books
mitchell@halfpricebooks.com
214-678-6680

Strictly by the Book
erezb@strictlybythebook.com
508-675-5287

Taylor Marketing
vtaylor@taylromarketing.com
281-213-8658

School Visit Network

Author Illustrator Source
www.author-illust-source.com

The Best Book Bin
www.thebestbookbin.com

Children's Authors Network! (CAN!)
www.childrensauthorsnetwork.com

Children's Book Council
www.cbc.org

Society of Children's Book Writers and Illustrators
www.scbwi.org

Shipping

AES Logistics
www.aeslogistics.com
877-890-2295

CGL PrintShippers Network
e-mail: jmendes@cglship.com
916-564-3292

Freight Management Systems (FMS)
e-mail: barbsmith@tds.net
866-922-7491

PartnerShip
www.partnership.com
800-599-2902

Web Design

Abacus
www.abacusgraphics.com
760-724-7750

American Author
www.americanauthor.com
877-700-2519

Better E. Marketing Online
www.konsultco.com
480-614-1020

Blue Sky
www.bswsolutions.com
360-527-9111

Eisler Design
www.eislerdesign.com
215-750-9513

Lightbourne
www.lightbourne.com
800-697-9833

Raab Associates
www.raabassociates.com
914-241-2117

Wholesalers (National)

Baker & Taylor
www.btol.com
908-541-7425

Ingram Book Company
www.ingrambook.com
615-213-7308

Wholesalers (Regional)

Bookazine
www.bookazine.com
201-339-7777

The Distributors
www.thedistributors.com
574-232-8500

Partners Book Distributing
www.partnersbook.com
517-694-3205

Southern Book Service
E-mail: bfranzen@southernbook.com
305-681-3424

Sunbelt Publications
www.sunbelt.com
619-258-4911, ext. 110

Appendix E

Reference Books

1001 Ways to Market Your Books by John Kremer

An Author's Guide to Children's Book Promotion by Susan Salzman Raab

Author's Day by Daniel Pinkwater

A Basic Guide to Writing, Selling, and Promoting Children's Books: Plus Information about Self-Publishing by Betsy B. Lee

Beyond the Bookstore by Brian Jud

Book Markets for Children's Writers 2006, Institute of Children's Literature

The Business of Writing for Children: An Award-Winning Author's Tips on How to Write, Sell, and Promote Your Children's Books by Aaron Shepard

The Chicago Manual of Style (University of Chicago Press)

Children's Books: Awards and Prizes (Children's Book Council Staff)

Children's Books and Their Creators by Anita Silvey

Children's Books in Print/Subject Guide to Children's Books in Print (R. R. Bowker, annual)

Children's Writer's & Illustrator's Market by Alice Pope

Children's Writer Guide, edited by Susan M. Tierney

The Complete Guide to Self-Publishing by Tom & Marilyn Ross

The Complete Idiot's Guide to Publishing Children's Books by Harold D. Underdown and Lynne Rominger

The Complete Idiot's Guide to Self-Publishing by Jennifer Basye Sander

Could You, Should You Self-Publish a Picture Book by Anne Emerick (eBook only, www.write4kids.com)

The Giblin Guide to Writing Children's Books by James Cross Giblin

Graphic Artists Guild Handbook: Pricing and Ethical Guide (Graphic Artists Guild)

The History of Children's Literature: A Syllabus with Selected Bibliographies by Margaret Hodges

How to Publish Your Children's Book by Liza N. Burby

How to Write a Children's Book and Get It Published by Barbara Seuling

How to Write and Illustrate Children's Picture Books by Jean E. Karl

It's a Bunny-Eat-Bunny World by Olga Litowinsky

How to Get Happily Published by Judith Applebaum

Origins of Story: On Writing for Children by Barbara Harrison and Gregory Maguire

Publishing Basics for Children's Books: A Guide for the Small Press and Self-Publisher by Iwana Ritabooke and Ima Bookeprinta

The Publishing Game Series by Fern Reiss

Publishing Gems, Insider Information for the Self-Publishing Writer by Brent Sampson

The Self-Publishing Manual: How to Write, Print & Sell Your Own Book by Dan Poynter

A Sense of Wonder: On Reading and Writing Books for Children by Katherine Paterson

Ten Steps to Publishing Children's Books: How to Develop, Revise & Sell All Kinds of Books for Children by Berthe Amoss and Eric Suben

Terrific Connections with Authors, Illustrators, and Storytellers: Real Space and Virtual Links by Toni Buzzeo and Jane Kurtz

Trash-Proof News Releases: The Surefire Way to Get Publicity by Paul J. Krupin

The Way to Write for Children by Joan Aiken

Word Magic for Writers by Cindy Rogers

Writer's and Illustrator's Guide to Children's Book Publishers and Agents by Ellen R. Shapiro

Writing Books for Young People by James Cross Giblin

Writing a Children's Book: How to Write for Children and Get Published by Pamela Cleaver

Writing Children's Books for Dummies by Lisa Rojany Buccieri and Peter Economy

Writing for Children by Catherine Woolley

Writing Hannah: On Writing for Children by Libby Gleeson

The Writer's Idea Book by Jack Heffron

Writing with Pictures: How to Write and Illustrate Children's Books by Uri Shulevitz

You Can Write Children's Books by Tracey E. Dils

Young at Heart: The Step-by-Step Way of Writing Children's Stories by Violet Ramos

Newsletters

Children's Book Insider
www.write4kids.com

Children's Bookshelf
www.publishersweekly.com

Children's Writer
www.childrenswriter.com

Index

S

X

Y

Z

Notes

Notes

_____

_____

_____

_____

_____

_____

_____

_____

_____

_____

_____

_____

_____

_____

_____

_____

_____

Notes

Popular Titles by Shari Faden Donahue

www.arimaxbooks.com

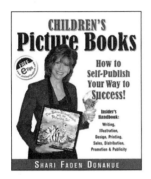

Check out this title by the
Zebra-Striped Whale Foundation too!

www.zebrastripedwhale.org

Shari Faden Donahue is the Executive Director of the Zebra-Striped Whale Foundation—a charitable, non-profit organization whose mission is to raise funds for those in need through the publishing of original children's picture books by first-time authors and illustrators.